THE TRAP

THE
TRAP

◆ SELLING OUT
TO STAY AFLOAT IN
WINNER-TAKE-ALL
AMERICA

DANIEL BROOK

TIMES BOOKS

HENRY HOLT AND COMPANY ◆ NEW YORK

Times Books
Henry Holt and Company, LLC
Publishers since 1866
175 Fifth Avenue
New York, New York 10010
www.henryholt.com

Library of Congress Cataloging-in-Publication Data

Brook, Daniel.
    The trap : selling out to stay afloat in winner-take-all America /
Daniel Brook.—1st ed.
        p. cm.
    ISBN-13: 978-0-8050-8065-0
    ISBN-10: 0-8050-8065-1
    1. Professions—United States.   2. Income distribution—United
States.   3. Cost and standard of living—United States.   I. Title.

HF5382.5.U5B735   2007
339.2'20973—dc22   2006051439

First Edition 2007

Designed by Victoria Hartman

Printed in the United States of America
10 9 8 7 6 5 4 3 2 1

In memory of Grandpa—

"Sov gott."

CONTENTS

The research for this book included personal interviews with dozens of people. Some individuals interviewed appear in the book under their real names; others have been given first-name-only pseudonyms. At times, certain other identifying details have also been eliminated to preserve privacy or in response to a specific request.

THE PAM PERD GENERATION

Waiting on the drink line at a wedding reception, I explained the premise of this book to my ex-girlfriend's new boyfriend. From the social circumstances alone, I was not expecting a sympathetic hearing. Having been tipped off by the groom that the new boyfriend worked on Wall Street for Lehman Brothers, and seeing his advantage in height and weight, I hoped he wasn't a belligerent drunk. To my relief, he greeted my ideas with enthusiasm (and sobriety). " 'Sellout' is harsh," he said, "but it's not too strong a word." A leftist with a liberal arts degree, he had gone to Wall Street after years stuck in unpaid internship limbo convinced him to give up on his dream of a career as a muckraking journalist. "That's how hegemony works," he offered, referencing a key concept of Antonio Gramsci, the Italian Marxist theorist. "The system can contain all of the dissenters."

This seemingly surprising exchange no longer surprised me. During my months of interviewing young professionals, I often felt as if I was hearing the same joke over and over—the one about the anticorporate corporate lawyer; or the anticonsumerist adman; or the Lehman Brothers leftist. Each time, the joke got a little less funny. And in the end, I still enjoyed its first telling the most.

My first interview had been with Pam Perd, who served as national director of public relations for Billionaires for Bush, the tongue-in-cheek "pro-Bush" activist group, during the last presidential campaign. To lampoon administration policies that exacerbate economic inequality, the Billionaires, who go by clever noms de guerre, protest in tuxedos and evening gowns, smoking cigars and wielding wads of fake cash. Pam Perd came late to the group; her favorite name, Lucinda Regulations, was already taken.

While serving as national PR director often meant putting in upward of forty hours a week, the work was all pro bono. Pam already had a full-time salaried position: doing PR for mere millionaires for Bush. In her day job, Pam handled public relations for Fortune 500 companies at one of the largest public relations firms in the world.

"I was very, very happy to hear that my main client did not give money to the Bush campaign. That made me smile. But overall I know a lot of our clients at my firm absolutely did give to the Bush campaign and that makes me uncomfortable," the jean jacket–clad thirty-one-year-old confessed in her local coffee shop, on the edge of Tompkins Square Park in Manhattan's East Village. "It makes me question what I'm doing and why, but at the same time I also know I need to survive. I need to feed myself and house myself. So you have to do what you have to do. That's why you end up having two lives."

Despite her day job helping giant corporations push product, Pam eschews consumerism in her own life, living simply in a fifth-floor walk-up studio apartment. Her income gives her financial security, not a ritzy lifestyle. "I'm going to want to have a family and I have to prepare for that," Pam says, referring to rising college tuition costs. Her two lives, she admits, are a compromise: "I would much prefer to work in the nonprofit world where I'd be able to work on issues that I feel very passionately about, but at the same time, the nonprofit world is not going to pay me what I need to make to feel comfortable and have a sense of security."

I met Pam on one of the handful of perfect spring days allotted to New York City each year. I had last been to Tompkins Square Park the previous fall, having happened upon a reading of Allen Ginsberg's poetry, part of the annual Howl Festival of East Village Arts. I took my seat on a park bench as a young poet howled the eponymous poem, mourning the destruction of "the best minds of my generation," by a system Ginsberg dubbed "Moloch," after the fiery-eyed Babylonian idol lit from within by the smoldering flesh of sacrificed children. "Moloch whose mind is pure machinery! Moloch whose blood is running money!" the poet raged. "Moloch whose soul is electricity and banks!" The reading was sponsored by the Discover Card.

From the introductory bios it became clear that none of the readers at the festival lived in the East Village. Instead, they hailed from places like Brooklyn, Philadelphia, even Poughkeepsie— the very places young poets fled to the East Village *from* in the beatnik era. In today's East Village, where a sign on a nearly completed condominium informed passersby that units were available "from $3.2 million to over $12 million," there are no poets, only millionaires and people like Pam.

◆

Claire, a twenty-seven-year-old activist, can't afford to live in the East Village. In fact, she can barely afford to be an activist. "I'm pretty anxious about it and often have the sense that I can't hold out much longer, that I just have to find a position that may compromise some of my political views," she told me. With a public policy degree and a Fulbright under her belt, Claire now works at a nonprofit in Jackson Heights, Queens, that combats the trafficking of sex workers around the globe. "This job's been a dream come true in that it's within my value system to work alongside the people that you ultimately advocate for," she explained, her mild face radiating concern not just for her clients but for herself as well. On paper, her $35,000-a-year salary puts her squarely within the middle class. But a middle-class salary can't buy a middle-class life in a major American city these days. To make ends meet, Claire works fourteen hours each weekend taking reservations at Café des Artistes, a long-established French restaurant on the Upper West Side, where the only *artistes* to be found are on the waitstaff.

"It's a confusing time. I'm not sure how I got into this position," she told me over dosas at an inexpensive South Indian restaurant near her office. "I always thought in grad school and with a Fulbright that I would end up having a pretty different lifestyle now." Claire had gotten a full ride for graduate school and her Fulbright grant covered living expenses while she conducted research on trafficking in Chile, but years of just covering costs meant that her undergrad debt never got paid off. Today, Claire works seven days a week to share an apartment in Long Island City with an editorial assistant at Random House.

Claire knows she could earn more—considerably more—if she sold out, abandoning her human rights work for a corporate job. But that would mean abandoning work on a problem she has spent years preparing herself to combat. She could also leave New York for cheaper pastures, but that would mean abandoning the potential for global impact that comes with having the United Nations a few subway stops from the office. With her skills, talents, and passion, Claire has found her calling. Yet she doesn't know how much longer she can afford to follow it.

◆

Despite their divergent careers and incomes, Pam and Claire have a lot in common. They were both born middle class—Pam to a pair of financial planners on Long Island; Claire to a high school teacher and a professor in New Mexico. They both attended selective private colleges. They are both politically progressive, well educated, and drawn to big-city life. And they both faced the same hard choice but made different decisions. Pam earns a comfortable living but pays the psychological price of doing a job she doesn't believe in; Claire finds her work fulfilling but pays the economic price of just getting by.

A generation ago, these two women would have earned similar incomes and would have likely lived in the same neighborhood—say, the Upper West Side. These days, in a more class-stratified city and nation, they can't. If they came together socially, it would likely be at the kind of event that brings together people from similar educational backgrounds but divergent income brackets—the drink line at a wedding, for example. And as with my run-in with my ex's new Wall Street beau, after moving beyond simple introductions of "I work in PR," "I work at a nonprofit," they might find out they had more in common than they assumed.

Or maybe they wouldn't. Maybe Pam would dismiss Claire as sanctimonious. Maybe Claire would dismiss Pam as a hypocrite. The "gotcha game" of deciding who's a bigger sellout has become the leading parlor game of recent liberal arts college graduates, and they might be tempted to play a round. But the game misses the point. Just as women balancing work and family waste energy relentlessly attacking each other for the choices they've made rather than questioning why the United States does not offer free universal child care until age five, so educated young people waste energy criticizing one another's decisions rather than questioning a system that imposes such wrenching choices. Whatever one thinks of Pam's or Claire's decisions, the choice educated, idealistic young people now face—to be a sellout or a saint—has no place in a prosperous modern democracy.

◆

While the pressure to sell out has grown in recent years, the phenomenon is not new. Starting in the 1980s, the media began to note that more and more of the best and the brightest were going to work for corporate America. Reagan was in power, greed was good, and young people acted accordingly, the thinking went. But when these trends didn't change in the 1990s, new explanations arose—and they sounded like rationalizations.

In their 1995 book, *The Winner-Take-All Society,* economists Robert Frank and Philip Cook probed their students at Cornell and Duke looking for answers. They concluded that their students were being lured into lucrative fields like management consulting and away from vital but less remunerative work like teaching middle school because of new reward structures in corporate America that were pushing executive pay through the roof. Being economists, Frank and Cook viewed their students as little more than profit-maximizing calculators who saw a high-stakes lottery and naturally wanted a ticket. Their analysis focused on the proverbial carrot, never considering the stick.

In the real world that exists outside of economics department models, some bright young people are determined to get rich, but many just don't want to be poor. And as America has been transformed into a nation with literally millions of millionaires, a concentration of wealth not seen since the Gatsby era, the prices of the finite goods desired by the now-numerous wealthy have been bid up wildly, far exceeding inflation. That would be fine if all that those "millionaires next door" wanted were Impressionist paintings and similar luxuries. But America is a nation where what are considered human rights in the rest of the developed world are sold to the highest bidder. Today's young people have to make far more money than their parents' generation needed simply to attain a home, health care, and college educations for their children—no yachts, no Van Goghs. Is it any surprise that those with the opportunity to make enough to stay afloat—even those, like Pam Perd, who disdain corporate America—generally take it?

Yet conservative apologists for rising inequality claim it doesn't matter if the rich get richer as long as everyone else isn't getting poorer. Apologist-in-chief Mickey Kaus explains in *The End of Equality* that though he agrees with George Orwell's observation from 1930s Spain that "a fat man eating quails while children are begging for bread is a disgusting sight," he isn't upset by "a fat man eating quails while children are eating Bob's Big Boy hamburgers"—a rough approximation of the situation in contemporary America. What Kaus fails to see is how a rise in the concentration of wealth reshapes markets, inflating the prices of goods whose supply is fixed, like homes within a reasonable commuting distance of a major city or degrees from top colleges. In postwar America, when income tax rates went up to 91 percent, there was an effective limit on the incomes of the corporate elite and, in turn, on the prices of the commodities they desired. But since Reagan and his tax cuts, the rich have proliferated and gotten richer—and the prices of these commodities have gone up for everyone.

Reaganomics transformed the face of metropolitan America. A 2006 Brookings Institution report found that in a dozen metro areas studied, the proportion of middle-class central-city neighborhoods was cut in half between 1970 and 2000; the number of poor and rich neighborhoods grew. Most metropolitan neighborhoods were middle class in 1970; only 41 percent were by 2000. In the most cosmopolitan and influential parts of the country, the middle-class family has become an endangered species, hunted almost to extinction. By 2000, the New York area had the smallest share of middle-class families of any major metropolitan area. In the Los Angeles area, which had been majority middle class in 1970, by 2000 only 28 percent of its neighborhoods were middle class. As joining the ever-shrinking metropolitan middle class has become less and less of an option for the rising generation, those young people with the educational credentials to have some say over whether they end up rich or poor are more and more likely to exercise the option to become rich, making the necessary career choices. And public service and intellectual fulfillment rarely make the cut. The new economic realities are shaping people's lives, closing off certain career and lifestyle options. They are reducing freedom.

Bright young people have gotten the message. A biomedical researcher with a recently minted PhD colloquially explained the phenomenon: "$250,000 is the new $100,000." This sounds like an incredibly obnoxious statement, but when you learn that nearly half of children from six-figure-earning families are now going into debt just to go to college, you realize his observation is, sadly, right on target. And the post-Reagan decline in social mobility puts even more pressure on parents to ensure they can send their child to a top college, giving them their ticket to the right side of the ever-growing class divide. Under these circumstances, what an earlier generation took for granted and those in the rest of the developed world still do, has become a hefty six-figure proposition. The European stereotype is that Americans are greedy; older Americans stereotype younger ones as a mercenary generation out to get rich quick. What neither the Europeans nor the senior citizens understand is that young Americans *want* more money because they *need* more money. Even if they don't covet mansions and luxury cars, they need big bucks for housing, health care, and education. In the 1980s, young people sold out to enjoy a life of luxury; now they sell out to stay afloat.

Making more money means leading a different working life. The tiny handful of careers that are surefire routes to the top of the income distribution—management consulting, corporate law, investment banking—are neither enjoyable nor fulfilling for many creative, educated people. This is not to say that no one's true calling is to become a corporate tax attorney, but merely to assert that few talented college freshmen, let alone talented toddlers, tell their parents they want to be corporate lawyers when they grow up. A life singularly devoted to the overwork and over-consumption enshrined by corporate America holds little appeal for many liberally educated people. Their voting behavior bears this out—in the 2000 election, anticorporate crusader Ralph Nader outpolled MBA-toting George W. Bush among Yale undergrads. So do opinion surveys that show government and public service as the areas in which the majority of top college graduates would ideally like to work. Certainly big money can be as addictive as cocaine, but why do so many try it in the first place? Because a whole host of middle-class careers that are often enjoyable and fulfilling—teaching, writing, music, art, activism, government service—no longer buy the lives they once did. As a result, these fields have been relegated to a mix of moral giants, mental midgets, and trust-fund babies.

In 1970, when starting teachers in New York City made just $2,000 less than starting Wall Street lawyers, people who wanted to teach taught. Today, when starting teachers make $100,000 less than starting corporate lawyers and have been priced out of the region's homeownership market, the considerations are very different. It may be counterintuitive, but talented young people actually have less control over their lives in a society in which they can get rich quick because, in such a society, the consequences of not getting rich quick become much more serious. When a middle-class income no longer buys a middle-class life, things that rarely or never make one rich become harder and harder to pursue. When it comes to the distribution of wealth, you're freer when it's flatter.

In our nation of self-financed higher education, tenuous health-care coverage, and out-of-control housing costs, Adam Smith's "invisible hand" has hardened into an invisible fist. When you realize a modest existence costs a not-so-modest sum of money, attainable only through a narrow range of unfulfilling jobs, that pang you feel is the invisible fist—and it's giving you an invisible beatdown.

◆

In an America that is bifurcating into "winners" and "losers," it is easy to dismiss the problems of those not stuck at the bottom as irrelevant, the whining of a pampered generation. According to the conventional wisdom, as long as you can get yourself out of the predicament facing those at the bottom, you don't really have any problems. A non-college-educated Wal-Mart worker with no health care who can't afford to send her gifted son to the best college that accepts him is widely understood to be underprivileged, if not exploited or oppressed. The Wal-Mart worker goes without through compulsion, not choice. But a college-educated freelance photojournalist with no health care who can't afford to send her gifted son to the best college that accepts him has made a choice. With her skills, she could surely land a job at an ad agency where a high salary and health care would be provided. As long as there is choice involved, we are told, it's all good.

But examined from a larger perspective, it's not all good. America is the only developed country where an individual has to choose between the career she desires and the health care and education her family needs. The predicament facing this individual is bad enough—but even more serious are the repercussions for society. A dynamic and decent society would offer the talented the widest possible range of choice over their careers, the greatest possible freedom over their lives. In a more egalitarian society, individuals would be freer to follow their callings and speak their minds, and America would be better off for it.

The same concentration of wealth that holds back the young person from becoming what she wants to be holds back the country from becoming what it wants to be. Surveys show fully two-thirds of Americans support universal health care. The chief reason we don't have it is not because it lacks popular support, but because the insurance and pharmaceutical companies hold too much wealth and power for such a proposal to pass on Capitol Hill. As the late Supreme Court justice Louis Brandeis put it, "We can have a democracy or we can have great wealth concentrated in the hands of the few. We cannot have both." When wealth and power are so concentrated, both personal and political choice are rendered irrelevant. What people want—as individuals from their lives or as a community from their government—no longer matters.

◆

Claire could be speaking for her entire generation when she admits, "I'm not sure how I got into this position." Somewhere along the line, back when she and her peers were too young to notice, someone changed the rules. But to change the system that constricts Americans' life choices, we must understand its origins. The transformation of America into a country where wealth is concentrated in the hands of a few has been slow and steady but nonetheless dramatic. The upward redistribution of wealth that has transformed American society began with the Reagan Revolution, a slow-motion revolution, but a revolution nonetheless—with real, pervasive, negative implications for human freedom.

Today's inegalitarian America was intentionally built—or more accurately, another America was intentionally destroyed. In the decades after World War II, America became a middle-class society of broadly shared prosperity. Teachers and factory workers and lawyers often lived in the same neighborhoods as progressive taxation pushed incomes closer together. (Even executives' pay was brought down from the stratosphere; GM CEO Charles Wilson's 1950 paycheck of $586,100 was whittled down to $155,750 after taxes.) The GI Bill meant that a bright young veteran from a modest background could attend any college in the country debt-free—each veteran got an annual grant of $500 in an era when Harvard tuition ran $400 a year. Widespread unionization ensured that a rising tide lifted most boats. Jobs with pensions and health care were common and attainable. Eventually, long-overdue efforts to make American institutions meritocratic and open to women and minorities began to build a truly egalitarian nation.

Conservatives saw what America looked like in the 1960s, with the most equal distribution of wealth in its history and liberals sitting-in and marching for even more, and they didn't like what they saw. The wealthy were being taxed to open up their elite colleges to bright middle- and working-class students. These students were questioning authority, not cozying up to it in hope of landing a job. They were seizing on the freedom offered by America's egalitarian prosperity to further social progress—to expand the economic equality seen throughout white America to the nation at large.

Looking at this America, a small cadre of conservatives vowed to turn back the clock. At the time, conservatism had been in decline for years. Hoping to breathe life into a moribund ideology, a young Yale graduate named William F. Buckley Jr. founded *National Review* as the publication that stands "athwart history, yelling 'Stop!'" Slowly gaining influence within the Republican Party, conservatives were able, in 1964, to nominate Arizona senator Barry Goldwater for president, a candidate who shared their view that America was going off the rails.

"The tide has been running against freedom," Goldwater warned in his nomination acceptance speech. Goldwater and his intellectual offspring redefined individual freedom as the power to spend more of the money you earn free from government taxation and regulation. These policies, they insisted, would un-leash the gifted and ambitious. "In our vision of a good and de-cent future, free and peaceful, there must be room for the liberation of the energy and talent of the individual," Goldwater declared. To this end, the market should be trusted to provide not merely things some of us might want, like the latest kitchen ap-pliances, but the things we all desperately need, like health care. Government programs to assure equal access to basic necessities would drain people of initiative and enforce a soul-crushing Soviet-style conformity, Goldwater argued, and progressive taxation to more equally distribute wealth penalized success. As Goldwater put it, "Equality, rightly understood, as our founding fathers understood it, leads to liberty and to the emanci-pation of creative differences. Wrongly understood, as it has been so tragically in our own time, it leads first to conformity and then to despotism." For Goldwater, postwar America's growing eco-nomic equality was a threat to freedom, not its guarantor.

While Goldwater lost the 1964 election, Ronald Reagan was able to implement his governing philosophy in the 1980s, slash-ing top tax rates, cutting student aid, and busting labor unions. Most of Reagan's substantive policy changes were left in place by George H. W. Bush and Bill Clinton, and have been pushed even further by George W. Bush.

And yet, as is plain to see, the conservative philosophy is wrong. Conservative economic policies have not merely stopped the social progress that was making American freedom real for those further down the socioeconomic ladder. They have begun rolling back freedom for everyone but the independently wealthy—even for the talented and fortunate few who have at-tained a top-notch education. The America conceived by Gold-

water and Buckley and built by Reagan and Bush has con-
strained a generation of talented individuals, enforcing conformity, not unleashing creativity. Their true stories of diminished
freedom fill this book.

A free-for-all society does not set people free. Instead, it sets
in motion a moral race to the bottom reminiscent of the savage
state of nature described by seventeenth-century British political theorist Thomas Hobbes in which simply surviving becomes
the overarching goal of human life and all higher aspirations
must be stifled. "No Arts; no Letters" was Hobbes's stark
phrase. Yet any civilization worth living in depends on having
some talented people who opt not to maximize their earning potential and instead pursue less lucrative creative and service
professions.

Ironically, Goldwater's warning is once again called for, this
time in order to describe the nation created by the very policies
he endorsed. The tide is indeed running against freedom. The
tide of conformity continues to rise as the talented are corralled
into a narrow swath of careers, forced to stifle their altruistic impulses and retreat from public life. We ignore the predicament
faced by today's brightest young people, the coal-mine canaries
of Reaganomics, at our peril.

◆

With the ascendance of today's extreme form of American capitalism, the Right flatters itself that it has vanquished the Left
and won a grand war of ideas. In reality, it has merely amassed a
staggering amount of power—power that is cunningly self-
reinforcing. The Left hasn't disappeared; it is merely in hiding.
In a sense, a variant of Senator Joe McCarthy's paranoid fantasy

has come to pass. Corporate America is riddled with secret dissenters, though the system may be powerful enough to contain and co-opt them all.

The most audacious triumph of Reaganomics has been its creation of a system in which individual ideological opponents like Pam Perd are enlisted in the Right's unrelenting crusade to increase corporate power. Traditional institutional opponents, like the Democratic Party, are similarly co-opted; hobbled by corporate campaign donations, the party has ceased to oppose rising inequality.

On a cultural level, Reaganomics has created a society in which the Discover Card company has the chutzpah to sponsor a reading of "Howl" in Tompkins Square Park. From where does such chutzpah spring? Perhaps from an understanding on the part of the Discover Card executives that they have so much power, they have nothing to fear from a little anticorporate rhetoric in the park. When they really need to, they can silence even their strongest opponents. They can buy a top-notch PR expert—even one like Pam, who disdains everything they stand for. If need be, they could even buy a liberal senator. In fact, they have.

As First Lady, Hillary Clinton convinced her husband to veto a credit card company–backed bill to make it harder for Americans to declare bankruptcy. Inspired by Harvard Law professor Elizabeth Warren's speech about the devastating impact the legislation would have on single mothers and their children, Hillary informally lobbied the president on what she termed "that awful bill." Yet a few years later, Hillary, now in the Senate with the help of copious contributions from the credit card companies, voted for the same bill. "The financial services industry is a big industry in New York, and it's powerful on Capitol Hill," Warren explained. "It's a [testament to] how much influence this industry group wields in Washington that . . . they can bring to heel a senator who obviously cares, who obviously gets it, but who also obviously really feels the pressure in having to stand up to an industry like that."

As Princeton philosophy professor Harry Frankfurt observed, "One of the most salient features of our culture is that there is so much bullshit. . . . The realms of advertising and public relations, and the nowadays closely related realm of politics, are replete with instances of bullshit so unmitigated that they can serve among the most indisputable and classic paradigms of the concept." To state Frankfurt's claim another way—more constructive albeit less entertaining—we live in a system in which people don't believe their own public pronouncements, in which deeply held convictions can be stifled with a campaign contribution or a paycheck. Whereas in the past companies purchased people's physical labor, today they purchase public personae or, in the parlance of young people, their "souls." A first-year student at Hillary's alma mater, Yale Law School, recently mused in the stairwell just outside the library, "Why does a corporate law job pay $70,000 more than a nonprofit job? What is that $70,000 buying? It's buying your soul."

Knowing that the system is fixed, but not knowing how to fix the system, most young people try to make the best choices they can within the social context they have been born into. Many sell out. As one social critic put it, they "act affirmatively within the channels cut for them, cutting them deeper, giving the whole a patina of consent and weaving complicity into everyone's life story." A few live saintly lives, giving up the chance to own a home or raise children in order to do what they believe is right. But rather than just lamenting that the system is fixed, we can collectively fix the system. This will take an understanding that the old maxim "The personal is political" still applies. And it will take work to undo the failed policies of false freedom that created the hard realities we all now face.

Some may dismiss change on this order as impossible, just as naysayers tried to dismiss the young conservatives who questioned America's egalitarian path in the years after World War II. Yet the Goldwaterites were willing to stake out unfashionable positions, take on a consensus that seemed immutable, and ultimately change America. Whatever one thinks of their ideas, one has to admire their chutzpah—and learn from it. As William F. Buckley put it in the introduction to his first book, *God and Man at Yale*, "I have some notion of the bitter opposition that this book will inspire. But I am through worrying about it."

1

THE RISING STICKER PRICE
ON THE AMERICAN DREAM

Connecting the Dots

Just about everything you need to know about the rising sticker price of the American Dream gets plunked down on your doorstep each Sunday. In a recent Sunday paper, there might have been a human interest story on the so-called boomerang kids—young college grads so saddled with tuition debt they move back in with their parents. The business section might have run an article describing how rising health insurance premiums are making health care less and less attainable for the middle class. The arts pages might have had a melancholy piece on a downtown dance troupe squeezed out of its rehearsal space by gentrification.

To some extent, the tale you're told will vary based on where you live. Rising higher education and health-care costs affect all Americans equally; housing costs vary by region, though most metropolitan areas have seen similar declines in the number of middle-class neighborhoods in recent decades. If you were reading the Sunday *Oregonian,* you might learn that teachers have been priced out of two-thirds of Portland-area homes; if you were reading *The Boston Globe,* you'd find the starker figure of 90 percent. In bellwether metropolises like New York, San Francisco, and Washington, D.C.—centers of business, culture, and government—you'd find the problem at its most extreme.

Reading the Sunday paper, you would learn everything you need to know about the problem except the thing that's most important: why it's happening. None of the articles would link the issues they are describing to rising economic inequality. The "boomerang kids" would treat the college tuition spike that nailed them as an immutable, if regrettable, fact of life. In the health-care story, the middle-aged professional laid off by a local company and rehired as a benefits-free temp would blame his company for his predicament, not the national health-care system. The evicted performers would attribute the real estate boom that squeezed them out to a drop in crime and the proliferation of fancy restaurants downtown, not the creation of a new economic overclass. It's hard to imagine the dancers dropping econ stats to explain their plight.

This is not to say that America's recent and dramatic rise in economic inequality will be ignored by the paper. Any regional newspaper of record will surely include a story on the new census numbers, showing how both the nation and the local metro area are seeing a larger and larger gap between rich and poor with fewer and fewer people in the middle. On the opinion page, two columnists may slug it out, the liberal fretting about the unfairness of the new inequality, the conservative celebrating the triumph of a perfect meritocracy. The paper itself may weigh in with an editorial taking one side or the other. But rising economic inequality will never be linked to the "boomerang kids" or the health-care mess or the real estate squeeze. It's time to connect the dots.

The Geography of the New Inequality

In a clever turn of phrase, social critic David Callahan dubs America's post-Reagan political-economic order the "Banana Republic economy." America's level of inequality, he argues, already greater than in any other developed country, is headed in the direction of the Third World's so-called banana republics. Actually, some parts of America have already hit those levels. Data from the 2000 census show that Manhattan, where the top fifth of earners rake in an average of $365,826 a year while the bottom fifth scrape by on $7,047, had income disparities on a par with the African nation of Namibia, the most unequal country in the world according to a recent UN Human Development Report. Berkeley, California, and Washington, D.C., were not far behind.

But Callahan intends a double entendre. In each of the four hundred outlets of the chain clothing store Banana Republic, a subsidiary of Gap, Inc., there is only one employee, the store manager, who makes a middle-class income, enough to support a family. The retail workers toil away at or near a minimum wage that has lost 20 percent of its value since Reagan's 1980 victory. It would take these workers an entire day's wages just to buy a single Banana Republic polo shirt, priced at $42. It doesn't take a Wharton MBA to figure out that high prices and low wages make for big profits. And where do those profits go? To the shareholders, to Gap, Inc., founder Donald Fischer, a billionaire several times over and a major Republican Party donor, and to the salaries of the high-end professionals at Gap, Inc., headquarters—the marketing gurus, sales number-crunchers, and financial deal-makers who manage the company.

What is missing in Callahan's analysis of the redistribution of wealth is a geographic component. While most Americans now own token amounts of stock, more than 40 percent of all shares are owned by the wealthiest 1 percent of Americans. The top 5 percent own about two-thirds; the top 10 percent, more than three-quarters. Needless to say, the wealthiest Americans are not equally distributed across the nation, but are clustered in fancy urban neighborhoods like the Upper East Side of Manhattan, in tony suburbs like Palo Alto, California, and in exclusive rural enclaves like Aspen, Colorado. Similarly, while Banana Republic has stores all across America, the vast majority of its managerial positions are located in its headquarters, which, like so many other "hip" corporate headquarters, is in San Francisco.

With so many well-heeled young professionals working in San Francisco, the local cost of living there goes up for everyone else. It's not just Gap and Banana Republic. Bay Area corporate behemoths founded in the past forty years include Oracle, Cisco Systems, Restoration Hardware, and Williams-Sonoma, to name a few. In 1984, the cost of housing in San Francisco was 63 percent higher than in the average American locale, proverbial Peoria. Today San Francisco's housing costs are three times higher than Peoria's. The median home price in the Bay Area is well over half a million dollars. As the wealth of the country has been redistributed since the 1980s, the percentage of income a household has to spend on housing has *dropped* in almost every part of the country, save the cosmopolitan metro areas on the coasts where it has skyrocketed—the very places that draw ambitious, creative young people.

It is comforting to hope that the decline of the metropolitan middle class in places like San Francisco is the temporary result of a speculative—and soon to be deflated—housing bubble, but examining rents should temper that optimism. Although home sales prices can become susceptible to "irrational exuberance," rents don't lie. They present an accurate picture of the month-to-month housing market in a city. In San Francisco, for example, rents rose 76 percent from 1995 to 2002. The *San Francisco Chronicle* calls its column on the local property market "Surreal Estate."

When housing costs go up, people get squeezed. Some get squeezed out, literally evicted and forced to move elsewhere. Others get squeezed metaphorically: squeezed into a narrower set of options on what they can do with their time. And this imperils the American Dream in both its classic forms—the talented individual from a modest background who blossoms in her chosen field, and the family that, through honest, hard work, reaps the benefits of a middle-class life, with homeownership and good schools for the kids.

Growing Up Absurd

Though it is economically less hospitable, young college grads with artistic or intellectual ambitions still flock to San Francisco, the golden-gated community whose allure enchants even as its cost of living ensnares.

After graduating from Yale in 2003 with a double major in film studies and gender studies, Tara moved to San Francisco to pursue queer documentary filmmaking. She settled in the Castro district, the historic epicenter of American gay culture, and quickly discovered plenty of enticing projects. "There were lots of opportunities to do film and to help people with their films, but no one had any money to pay me so I did a lot of volunteering and part-time work," she told me in a Castro coffee shop. "Everyone's working on their own dream projects that they're funding through credit card debt." In an ironically circular effort to pay the rent, Tara got a gig as the personal assistant to a high-flying San Francisco real estate agent before biting the bullet and getting a full-time corporate job to support her outrageously expensive habit of being an interesting person in an interesting neighborhood.

A friend encouraged her to apply for a job at his company, Google, one of the few blue-chip Silicon Valley companies still hiring in the dot-com aftermath. The application process involved an exhaustive screening procedure. She divulged her SAT scores, took a writing test, and submitted to three separate half-hour interviews where she put on the feigned-enthusiasm routine demanded by corporate America—all for a temp job. "When they asked me about my resumé, they were like 'Wow, it looks like you're really interested in film.' And I was like, 'No, it's just a hobby. What I'm really interested in is customer service.' And they bought it."

But the joke was on Tara. By moving to San Francisco to get serious about film, to make it more than just a hobby, she had rendered it just that. Had she stayed in her native Portland, Oregon, the lower cost of living might have afforded her the time to work on film but would have kept her from making the contacts she needed to get noticed. Like her entire generation of creative young people, Tara was damned if she moved to a creative center, and damned if she didn't. Who's to say whether Tara would be the next great documentary filmmaker; not everyone who wants to make films for a living succeeds. But a fair and dynamic society would let the talented rise to the top rather than limit competition to those with trust funds.

Tara was hired at Google, the search engine giant with the informal corporate motto "Don't be evil." Firings were routine; there was no job security whatsoever. "Every Friday, they would tap some [temps] on the shoulder and they would be gone. It was really horrifying. Every Friday. Everyone was freaked out."

While Google, which generated $3.6 billion in profits on $8.5 billion in revenue in 2005, sells itself as a "family," Tara told me, "this large percentage of the family is getting shit upon." That was how she felt temping away for two of the richest men on the planet without basic benefits like health insurance or paid sick days, let alone Silicon Valley goodies like stock options. "Sometimes they would take us out to movies for free, but no one had health care!" she explained, as if describing some insane social experiment. Yet this is the American economy people like Tara have grown up in. Talk about "growing up absurd."

Tara worked for a Google department called AdSense that placed ads on other companies' Web sites. (Tech companies don't seem content just to repeal the social contract—they have to repeal grammar as well.) Tara reviewed Web sites for content that would disqualify them from working with Google, like obscene material—a peculiar job for an aspiring queer documentary filmmaker, to say the least. Minute by minute, a program would relentlessly feed a new site to her computer for screening in a kind of twenty-first-century manifestation of the Ford assembly line. In Tara's estimation, "Monkeys could do it." But what disturbed her most was that the longer she did the job, the more simian she became, losing her most human quality. "I had films that I was working on—my own stuff—but you were just so tired at the end of the day and so fried that you couldn't do anything creative." She started having nightmares in which she was at work, sitting in front of her computer screening Web sites for Google.

Despite the New Economy trappings, including what Tara conceded was "the most amazing snack room with incredible organic gourmet food," the job left her not unlike the factory workers of an earlier age. "I would go to a bar, usually directly from work, with my coworkers and complain about our managers. I would complain a lot about the hierarchical system. I feel like if there's anyone in need of a union, beyond service workers and people who are not getting paid very well, it's temps because the kinds of problems that temps have are the kinds of problems that all people at the lowest level have, because they're so expendable. A hundred people a day are applying to Google, so everyone is so expendable. It doesn't matter what your problems are, they can just get rid of you."

But unlike twentieth-century factory workers, none of her Google coworkers seriously spoke of organizing. Moving up or moving on were the easiest ways out. Those who get hired full-time, according to Tara, "forget how sucky it was to be a temp because now they're invited to all the secret beer-and-sushi meetings." Tara decided to move on, gaining acceptance to UC Berkeley's doctoral film studies program—a more intellectually rewarding way to scrape by in San Francisco, but no more likely to lead to a full-time job with benefits than working at a tech company.

Housing Projects for the Upper Middle Class

To the casual observer, Meadow Park, a new affordable housing development in Novato, California, about thirty miles north of San Francisco, looks like any other "new urbanist"-style subdivision. There are the neat little town houses, the communal open spaces, schools, and day-care centers within walking distance. Touring the development reminded me of the HOPE VI public housing developments, which replaced crime-plagued high-rises in cities like Chicago and Philadelphia with walkable, human-scaled neighborhoods. Except there was something besides the palm trees that distinguished the subsidized Novato development from those in the Chicago and Philadelphia ghettos—families with six-figure incomes could qualify to live there.

"From my office, there were a few people who applied, but they were at the clerical level—secretaries and people in accounts payable. So when they started talking about it, I said let me go on the Internet and see if I qualify. I was very surprised," explained Rajiv, who moved to the United States from India in the mid-1990s to work in the tech industry. "In Marin County, 'low income' is very high. It would be 'high income' in other places." With a five-person household of himself, his wife, two sons, and mother-in-law, Rajiv could make up to $123,000 a year and still qualify for one of the subsidized units. Because his company, a national upscale retailer where he works as a computer systems manager, is located in Novato, his application took precedence over all but those of city and school district employees.

The qualification formula is derived from the median income for a family of four in Marin County—nearly $100,000. Even with the high incomes, all but the very rich are priced out of homeownership in the county, where the average sale price for a home is $925,000. Marin County, with its easy access to San Francisco, natural beauty, and superb park system, has always been an expensive area, but a generation of economic policies that have made the rich both richer and more numerous has, for the first time, rendered entire counties, even entire regions, unaffordable to the middle and even upper middle class. Today, with a less egalitarian economy and a less progressive tax system, the lid has come off. In the market-rate subdivision just a few blocks from Meadow Park, I saw a For Sale sign on a starter home and grabbed a flyer. "Offered at $869,500," it read. The subsidized homes across the way cost about half as much— relative bargains at just over $400,000.

Before landing a home at Meadow Park, Rajiv tried to buy in nearby Petaluma, with its well-reputed school district. "We were outbid four or five times in the Petaluma school district. Let me give you an example: A ten-year-old condo came in at $449,000. We bid $477,000. And the condo went for $510,000," Rajiv recounted. "Wherever the school district is good, the housing prices are very high."

In his 1991 magnum opus, *Savage Inequalities*, Jonathan Kozol exposed unequal school funding as a national scandal. The inequalities are particularly savage in California, where a conservative antiproperty tax referendum passed in 1978 has starved schools of money for decades. With state funding woefully inadequate, wealthy districts have created "local education foundations," nonprofit organizations that fund "extras" like art and music classes in well-to-do districts. In a particularly perverse twist, contributions to these foundations are tax-deductible, allowing wealthy parents and local businesses to further withdraw from any attempt to give other people's children a quality education. In Novato, the local foundation is called School Fuel. Its Web site crows, "Funding to Novato Public Schools from the state of California will never be what it should be for a stimulating, quality education. Support your local public school and students by donating today!"

The upward redistribution of wealth in recent years has made the gap between rich and poor districts even more pronounced—and has raised housing prices in strong school districts to levels that are unaffordable to anyone who doesn't work in the upper echelons of corporate America. Just as private school tuition has skyrocketed, the real estate boom in public school districts that teach music and art and offer AP classes has raised the de facto "tuitions" for good public schools as well. As home prices climb, teaching, by definition a profession for those who value education, becomes a less and less desirable career. After all, how could you possibly raise your own family in a good school district on a teacher's salary?

At Meadow Park, teachers make up the highest percentage of home buyers, no surprise considering a National Association of Home Builders study that showed that teachers were priced out of 99.7 percent of the census tracts in the San Francisco metropolitan area. Jason Eckl, a twenty-six-year-old music teacher at Novato's Sinaloa Middle School, recently moved into a town house there. He heard about the development from a flyer in the school staff lounge announcing "something like, 'low-income housing for teachers and public service employees,'" he recalled. At the time Eckl, who grew up in a small town in California's Central Valley, was renting an apartment near his school in downtown Novato. Many young Sinaloa teachers who had grown up in the area were living at home with their parents. If not for Meadow Park, "I would have kept going slowly broke from renting. Because

I was a single guy living in a not-so-nice apartment I was surviving. I was paying twelve hundred dollars rent for a one-bedroom apartment," he said. "That was over half my salary."

Eckl's career choice was inspired by his high school music instructor. "It's the only thing I ever wanted to do. I decided I wanted to be a music teacher when I was fourteen," he said. But upon earning his certification, Eckl was snagged by the catch-22 that hits a generation of public school teachers: work in a wealthy district, where he'd have the resources to do his job but would have to struggle financially, or work in a poorer district, where he could afford to live but would have to constantly deal with school budget shortfalls. In Novato, School Fuel makes his job viable. "The district pays for my salary as a schoolteacher but that's where it stops," he explained. "School Fuel pays for the instruments, music stands, school trips. It's up to me to fund everything else." Through grant writing and fund-raising, Eckl finds the money he needs. Because the school is in a wealthy area, he said, "bake sales are just where it starts." A local corporation donates its luxury skybox to Giants baseball games, which the music department then raffles off. "When I need a tuba—that's a three-thousand-dollar instrument—it would take me maybe a year to fund-raise. In the [poorer] East Bay, if they could ever get to that point it would take years."

Despite a handful of subsidized developments like Meadow Park, residency in much of the Bay Area has become contingent upon stifling impulses toward altruism and public service. In 2005, Half Moon Bay mayor Sid McCausland resigned his post because he could no longer afford to live in the town. The *Los Angeles Times* headlined its piece on the situation, "Priced Out of Public Service." The small agricultural town had mutated into a seaside retreat for Silicon Valley executives, pushing the average home price into the seven figures. A few years earlier, the former mayors of San Carlos and Cupertino, both in Silicon Valley, also left their communities for financial reasons.

A development like Meadow Park in a county like Marin, long a wealthy enclave, may seem an isolated phenomenon, but projects like it—housing projects for the upper middle class—are springing up in metropolitan areas all over America, though in nowhere near the numbers needed to keep metropolitan America from becoming a middle-class-free zone. At first it is hard to see what the regions that include the Bay Area, Boston, Brooklyn, and Burlington, Vermont, have in common. They are all places where cultured, well-educated people have settled in the hopes of finding a middle-class lifestyle that offers more than just a house with a white picket fence—stimulating places with free parks, nature trails, university lectures, inexpensive cafes, and museums. While in a typical suburb each home has to be equipped with a giant "media center" just to have something to do on a Saturday night, in these lifestyle meccas a vibrant public culture makes private consumption largely superfluous to living a full life. As a longtime middle-class Manhattanite mused, "New York has always attracted people who aren't just interested in money—people interested in culture and poetry and music and dance." But those little Brooklyn co-ops and Bay Area bungalows now cost more than exurban McMansions.

With a subsidized multifamily Meadow Park town house in his name, Rajiv says he can plow more of his earnings into college savings accounts for his two sons. "I couldn't go to Harvard or Stanford, but one of my kids is surely going to do that," he declared with the brash confidence of a new American. Indeed, with his professional job and close-knit family, Rajiv should be living out the classic American Dream. But these days, for all his hard work, he can afford neither a house nor higher education at the going rate. To go to college, Rajiv's children will have to go into debt. This is a far cry from his own experience growing up. In India, his education was "awesome," he said, sounding every bit the Californian. For his master's degree, he paid about $1,600. "It's subsidized by the government, so it was pretty cool." Despite India's extreme poverty, its government provides a top-notch education for its brightest citizens. And despite America's extreme wealth, our government does not.

The Futures Market

"I'm shocked that there's no price resistance anymore." *New York Times* Sunday Styles reporter Guy Trebay caught this quote from a Barneys executive under the Bryant Park tents at 2005's fall fashion week. The exec was flummoxed over the seemingly endless stream of people willing to plunk down $4,000 for the season's must-have jacket. But Trebay surely could have gotten the same quote seventy-five blocks uptown from an undergraduate dean at Columbia, where students who had won the ever-fiercer competition for the privilege of purchasing a six-figure education were moving into their dorms. "The triumph of upper America," as political analyst Kevin Phillips crowned the Reagan era and its aftermath, triggered price spirals not merely for superfluous luxury goods like haute couture fashion but also for highly coveted public goods like higher education, which, through the peculiarities of the American economic model, are privately purchased. According to Duke University economist Charles Clotfelter, "The improvement in the well-being of those at the top of the income distribution fueled their demand for consumption of many kinds, including elite higher education."

In 1980, undergraduate tuition at the prestigious University of Chicago ran $5,100 a year ($12,600 in current dollars). Today it costs over $31,500. Stunning and yet entirely typical— Chicago's peer institutions, elite research universities and liberal arts colleges, all experienced similar tuition spikes over the past twenty-five years. As any aspiring Ivy League parent knows, the schools' tuitions are all suspiciously within a few dollars of one another, regardless of location. The only thing that costs as much in New Hampshire as it does in New York is an Ivy League BA—Dartmouth's tuition is within $500 of Columbia's.

But why did universities aggressively raise their tuitions after 1980? The short answer: they could. As one irate observer told a reporter for *The Atlantic*, university trustees are "incredibly rich and can't understand why anybody would think forty thousand dollars a year is a lot to send your kid to school." Surprisingly, this rabble rouser was Mark Heffron, a senior vice president at the leading consulting firm for university admissions offices. Heffron is right that the return to Gatsby-era wealth distributions has brought with it a return of let-them-eat-cake attitudes, but increasingly out-of-touch trustees are a symptom of the problem that led to the college tuition boom, not its cause. The problem is the upward redistribution of wealth.

In part because their tuitions are high enough to scare off nonwealthy applicants and in part because of the savage inequalities of America's secondary schools and their guidance departments, elite colleges have long drawn the bulk of their students from the upper echelons of society. Though these trends were ameliorated during the 1960s, the high point of American egalitarianism, they have been getting worse since the 1980s. To pay for tax cuts for the wealthy, Reagan and George W. Bush reduced federal student aid and shifted the aid from grants to loans. As a result, colleges have been forced to set up their own individual mini-welfare states, using price increases for parents who can pay as a way to make up for the missing government financial aid. But all indications are that colleges are losing their battle. As the nation has become less equal, its campuses have become less economically diverse. Fully 74 percent of students at America's top 146 colleges and universities now come from families in the top quarter of income earners. Only 3 percent of students come from the quarter of American families with the lowest incomes. At the renowned University of Virginia, in 2004 just 8 percent of students came from the bottom half of the income distribution—an embarrassing statistic for the school founded by Thomas Jefferson to be a place where top students "whose parents are too poor to give them further education [can be] carried at public expense through the colleges and university."

As the benefits of America's economic growth have been diverted to the top, whatever caps once existed on what wealthy households were willing to spend on education have been lifted. As the return on an elite college degree has risen (assuming the graduate pursues the handful of fields where salaries have boomed), college has become a better and better investment, no matter how high the sticker price. And as top students—and the corporate recruiters who pursue them—have concentrated at elite schools, the stakes have been raised to attend one. Students who in earlier generations would have gone to the honors program at their state's flagship campus are applying to top schools all over the country. Companies that once looked locally for talent now look nationally.

R. Owen Williams, a retired Wall Street investment banker, sat me down in the grand living room of his tasteful Tudor mini-manse near Westport, Connecticut, and explained what he'd observed at Salomon Brothers and Goldman Sachs over the years. "When I got into the business in 1976, most people on the trading floor had worked previously in the mail room and worked their way up from the back office to a low-level position—a clerk or sales assistant—on the trading floor. By proving themselves there, they would move up to a trading job. Most of them didn't have BAs. In 1970, there were thirty-nine partners at Salomon Brothers and seventeen of them had gone to college and twenty-two of them had not. Ten years later, it would have been inconceivable that someone without a college degree could become a partner."

Not only did going to college become important, going to the right college became key. "It was pretty overt. It was an obvious screening mechanism," Williams said. By the 1980s, Ivy Leaguers were common on the Salomon Brothers trading floor—young bankers like Princeton grad Michael Lewis, a Williams underling who wrote the best-selling 1989 tell-all chronicle of life at the firm, *Liar's Poker*.

But Williams regarded the credentialist trend as a mistake. "The truth is, most folks on a trading floor are not doing anything that's really sophisticated mathematically, technically, analytically. It's just not that difficult," he told me. "This notion of emphasizing a person's education and their intelligence, the emphasis that's placed on that is a little bizarre and hard to understand when you realize how difficult the work *isn't*."

Compounding the unfairness of the new screening system was an astounding rise in take-home pay. Williams recounted, "In 1979, the highest-paid salesman at Salomon Brothers made two hundred thousand dollars a year. By 1989, the highest-paid salesman at Salomon Brothers made a million dollars. And by 1999, the highest-paid salesman would have been north of five million dollars."

With these kinds of rewards available in corporate America, taking on debt to go to one of the elite universities where top companies come knocking makes economic sense. But as the return on educational investment increases if one pursues finance or a handful of other corporate fields, so too does the penalty for anyone who wishes to pursue another path. In 1980, it was inconceivable that a University of Chicago student's first job—even as a social worker or editorial assistant—would pay less than her annual tuition. Today, it is entirely conceivable, indeed probable, that students who take jobs as social workers or editorial assistants will earn less than their tuition bill. An idealistic University of Chicago graduate from the class of 1980 who opted to stay on the South Side and teach in an inner-city public school would have earned $13,770, more than two and a half times her $5,100 senior year tuition. Today such a student would earn $38,851, only 23 percent more than her senior year tuition of $31,500.

Because elite universities are determined to educate at least a few poor or working-class students—if only to bolster their increasingly dubious claim to reward the merit of the applicants rather than their parents' social standing—they offer very generous aid packages to those at the very bottom. But such plans don't relieve the pressures for most students. For the first time in history, most American college students now graduate in the red.

Students who graduate from the University of Chicago or Columbia know they won't work at Wal-Mart; they know their incomes will likely never be low enough to get their children a full ride. If they pursue a middle-income job, becoming a social worker or a city councilman, they know their children's lives will be hemmed in by debt. If they want their kids to get a full ride, they'll have to provide it themselves. And to do so, they'll have to sell out.

The Futile Attempt to "Live Richly"

In 2001, Citibank launched an advertising campaign with the tagline "Live Richly." On billboards and phone kiosks, the world's largest financial institution sent out the seemingly heretical message that money isn't everything. "Collecting interest does not count as a hobby," one ad proclaimed. "For a guaranteed return on investments, try buying flowers," read another.

The ad campaign, still going strong five years later, must have struck a chord. The ads were successful because they expressed an idea many metropolitan professionals had surely come to on their own: to focus on the important things in life, you have to be financially secure enough not to be constantly worrying about money. (This, of course, is where Citibank comes in.) Not surprisingly, the company targeted the ads geographically, running them only in San Francisco, Los Angeles, New York, Chicago, Miami, and Washington, D.C.—a short list of the metropolitan areas where financial security has become a six- (or seven-) figure proposition.

But the promise of the Citibank ads is illusory. To not constantly worry about money in one of America's most influential cities, you have to work sixty-hour weeks in a high-paying field that offers so little free time you might want to console yourself with the thought that collecting interest actually *is* a hobby—

since then, at least, you can claim to have one. Achieving real work-life balance would require that we join together to build a society in which a home and good schools are not luxury goods.

Political policies have created the current situation and only collective action can get us out of it. Despite Citibank's propaganda, some people are beginning to realize this: a local tagger defaced the "Live Richly" billboard in San Francisco's Mission District subway station with a graffito reading "Labor City," suggesting that there are ways to attain basic economic security that don't entail investing with Citibank—working together through unions and through government. In a nation as wealthy as ours, there is surely a way out of the bind that, as Citibank tells us, "the most exciting growth charts are on the pantry door" but those little marks are the only evidence you have children, tucked in long before you return home from the office.

Yet, rather than working together to change society, we too often accept Citibank's slogans and fend for ourselves. The company's campaign adopts the same reactionary, solipsistic prescription that lies at the heart of President Bush's Ownership Society initiatives—that the personal is *not* political.

"Be independently happy," Citibank tells us.

Good luck.

2

HOME AND HEARTH

If you marry, you will regret it; if you do not marry, you will also regret it.

—Søren Kierkegaard, *Either/Or*

The Mutual Martyrdom Marriage

I hate to say all these things because we have, like, a $135,000 combined income," Johanna apologized after running through the new math of raising a family in Washington, D.C. "But it's fucking ridiculous."

Johanna finds her family's cash-strapped, six-figure (pretax) existence particularly fucking ridiculous because she grew up working class and is seemingly living the social mobility dream. "My mom works in a fish factory and my dad's a construction worker," she told me. She grew up in Denmark where "even being working class, you're not that bad off. The minimum wage is close to twenty dollars an hour and there are lots of social benefits." Through the free, high-quality public education system, Johanna ultimately earned a master's degree in international development and environmental studies. While doing development work in South Africa in 1998, Johanna, who is blessed with her homeland's standard-issue good looks, met the man she would marry, then a Harvard Law School student. Having settled in D.C., Johanna works at a nonprofit that lobbies on Third World water rights issues. She calls it her "dream job." Her husband, Brendan, works at a law firm that represents municipal governments.

It has been quite a shock for Johanna that her financial life is more trying as a master's degree–toting professional married to a Harvard-educated lawyer in the capital of the richest nation on earth than it was as a daughter of the Danish working class. "I definitely grew up thinking that part of social justice is you can grow up in your own dwelling and afford some pretty basic things like decent schooling." But she has discovered that in metropolitan America, attaining those basics is a struggle for all but the wealthiest.

Her husband had been working at the public interest Center for the Study of Responsive Law, but switched to the local-government law firm to earn a $100,000-a-year paycheck—enough to buy a house. The firm was a compromise, midway between the work he wanted to do and the salary he needs to earn to start a family. While an Ivy League lawyer can easily make loads in D.C.—Brendan recently turned down a $200,000-a-year job offer from the firm defending Enron—he went to law school to do public interest work, not to defend corporate crooks. Though Brendan is free to turn down $200,000 jobs, he and Johanna still have to compete in the housing market against whoever takes those jobs.

The career change has taken its toll on Brendan. "Every week we'll have a conversation about how he had to compromise," Johanna said. "But he was like, 'You know what? All our friends have houses. All our friends have kids. I'm getting too old for this shit.'" Brendan's compromise job has allowed the couple to go from renting a $1,500-a-month one-bedroom in thoroughly gentrified Adams-Morgan to owning a $600,000 house in a slowly gentrifying D.C. neighborhood. In Johanna's estimation, "Our neighborhood is still a little rough. We definitely have gang activity." Still, she exulted, "We lucked out and got a cheap house," using definitions of "luck" and "cheap" that bespeak our age of diminished expectations.

Now that they own a home, the couple—Johanna is thirty-three, Brendan thirty-four—can imagine having children. "I'm at the age where I'm like, I'm going to have children. I'm not going to wait too much longer," Johanna said. But having children adds a whole new list of expenses beyond a monthly mortgage payment. "All of our friends who are our age have had children and they find it extremely cheap if they're paying twelve hundred dollars a month in child care. And that's illegal-immigrant child care. That's the cheapest you get, and I ask everybody." This is particularly jarring to Johanna because her sister, a lawyer in Denmark, has four children and relies on legal, high-quality, government-regulated and subsidized child care. "She pays less for four children than I would pay for one child," Johanna noted.

For Johanna and Brendan, a large family is out of the question. "One kid would be fine economically, but if we had two, I would really start to worry," she said. "It would make less sense for me to work. As a woman in a nonprofit, if you have two kids, the salary that you're pulling down is hardly paying for child care." Thus the martyrdom becomes mutual. First the husband quits the job he loves in order to start a family. Then the wife quits her dream job because the cost of child care means it no longer makes economic sense for her to work. All of a sudden, a progressive couple like Johanna and Brendan is forced back into 1950s gender roles, with the husband an unfulfilled breadwinner and the wife an unfulfilled stay-at-home mom.

In contemporary America, the idea that a woman can "have it all"—both a full career and a full family life—is now regularly dismissed as a 1970s-era fantasy. Indeed, without government-mandated maternity leave and subsidized day care, it is. The life led by Johanna's sister, both lawyer and mother of four, is almost inconceivable in the United States. Despite living in a culture that famously celebrates choice, the most an American woman can hope for is a choice between a fulfilling professional career and a large family. Having both is not an option.

Johanna is not fully inured to these realities yet, but she has lived in America long enough to begin regarding family members as financial instruments as well as loved ones. In a deadpan tone she explained, "Child care costs scare me a lot more than a house because a house, you can sell it. If you can't afford it, you can get rid of it. You might have to take a loss. But with a child, it's not like you're going to give it back. You lock yourself in." Sadly, in the current political climate, it seems more likely that conservatives will propose a "market-based solution" to allow hard-up couples to sell their kids than that liberals will propose a universal child-care system that affords couples the freedom to balance work and family as they see fit.

Even once their child is old enough for school, Johanna and Brendan won't be out of the woods. The local public school is considered merely middle of the road even by the degraded standards of our nation's capital. Johanna has vowed to try to improve it. "We sort of have this pact" with the neighbors, she said. "We're lobbying all of our neighborhood folks with little kids to get involved in the school and make it better." But not everyone is on board. One of their neighbors plans to stay only until their newborn is ready for preschool, despite the community efforts. Johanna's debate with this neighbor closed with the remark, "Well, you don't have kids. Wait till you get pregnant. Would you want your kids to go to that school?" As Johanna admitted, "I can imagine having my own kid and loving this kid and being like, I don't think the school is good enough. We're well educated. Are we going to give the best possible to this kid if we stay in this neighborhood? I don't know. I feel this is testing our ideology of social responsibility involving our community. It is something I would really, really like to do. But I can't promise."

If the local public school proves inadequate and irreparable, further martyrdom is in store. Johanna and Brendan will stare down three options. They could give up on the local public school in favor of a private school, though, on moral grounds, Johanna says, "I really, really despise the idea." It wouldn't just be an ethical dilemma, but an economic one as well. "Sure, we're wealthy now," she said, "but are we wealthy enough to afford a private school? Some of my husband's friends who are earning a lot of money are sending both of their kids to Georgetown Day. Twenty-five thousand dollars a year per kid. Twenty-five thousand dollars. That's what I make [after taxes]. Suddenly he's going to have to make two hundred thousand dollars." Private school would mean that Brendan would no longer have the choice to turn down jobs defending the Enrons of the world. A second option would be to move to a suburb with good public schools. At their current salaries, Johanna and Brendan would be priced out of the inner-ring suburbs, which would mean "buying a place that takes two hours to drive to work." Johanna is quick to acknowledge that lifestyle would "decrease the value of our family life." The last option: relocate to a less expensive part of the country. That would mean giving up the high-impact public interest work the couple loves. They could move to Cleveland, but it's unlikely Johanna's nonprofit would move there with them. This is where Johanna's personal problem becomes a problem for America, for all of us. When the best and the brightest can't afford to dedicate themselves to the public service, everyone suffers.

All in all, it's enough to make you want to work in a Danish fish factory.

A Tale of Two Generations

While the savage inequalities of America's public school system have long marked it off from other developed countries, the inability of many well-educated parents to insulate themselves from those inequalities is new. As the rich have proliferated and gotten richer, both private school tuitions and housing prices in suburban districts with good public schools have skyrocketed. In America's major metropolitan areas, the rules of the game have changed.

Rachel grew up in the 1980s on the Upper West Side of Manhattan, the daughter of a city housing department lawyer and a City University of New York English professor. "They never indulged my desire for designer jeans," Rachel said, "but they poured a lot of money into my education and my brother's education." The local public school wasn't particularly strong, so, as Rachel recounted, "after first grade, my dad walked over to the private school Dalton, to the admissions office, and said, 'I'd like for my daughter to go here.' And they said, 'Fill this out.' I guess they had the results of some test I had taken. The tuition at the time was like three thousand dollars," she said. Today, the Upper East Side prep school charges $29,000 a year.

The life Rachel's parents lived is no longer possible. A generation ago, professionals who wanted a cosmopolitan existence could attain it without selling out. The only sacrifice entailed was giving up the snob appeal of a Park Avenue apartment and a Nantucket summer home. Instead, Rachel's parents lived on the blue-blood-deprived West Side and had a summer home on Candlewood Lake in Connecticut, a lovely spot even if it lacked the cachet of the Hamptons. As long as they weren't hung up on the social pecking order, any two-income professional family could be more than satisfied with this lifestyle.

Today Rachel, who holds a bachelor's from Vassar and two master's degrees from NYU, is a French teacher at a New York City private school. Her husband is an artist who teaches art full-time as well. They have two sons, aged one and four. The family lives in a rent-stabilized apartment in a new lower Manhattan building where 20 percent of the units are set aside for "moderate-income" families, defined as households making between $68,000 and $94,000 a year. The capped rent on their apartment is $2,000 a month. A market-rate parking space in the building costs $650 a month.

Rachel is hoping to get her children into the private elementary school where she teaches, but even that is no fait accompli. Despite the explosion in the number of rich young parents in New York, the public schools remain underfunded and inadequate. This has created a spike in demand for private education that has pushed up both tuitions and the competition for admission. At the school where Rachel teaches, "there have been teachers whose children have not been accepted. For twenty-eight or thirty spots, there are probably three hundred applicants."

Staying in the city is a priority for Rachel. She grew up there and the location makes it possible for her mother to help her out with child care—a necessity when the going rate for New York nannies is $100 a day. Being in the center of the art world also helps her husband's career.

With home prices at their current levels, moving to a suburb with good schools will not solve the family's financial bind. Rachel has a sense of why. The financial district employees who live in the market-rate apartments in her building, she told me, "seem to have a house in Westchester that they go to on the weekends, and this is their city house." In the suburbs, she'd be competing with these same people for housing—but without government programs like the developer set-asides that allow a handful of middle-class people to squeeze into her city building. In Westchester County, where the median home price is $675,000, municipalities largely ignored a county plan to build 5,000 units of affordable housing during the 1990s. Only 1,640 units actually got built.

Back to the '50s . . . the 1850s

> Economics are the method but the object
> is to change the soul.
>
> —Margaret Thatcher

The affordable units in Rachel's downtown building are spread throughout the development to maintain the anonymity of the lesser-heeled neighbors. In our inegalitarian age, apparently, the merely middle class are supposed to be ashamed. Indeed, Rachel admitted, "We do feel self-conscious sometimes. At this lobby party the other night, everybody works in finance. And they're paying the market rent of close to five thousand dollars a month. And we're paying two thousand dollars." Still, "I feel like we're no different from them. I went to a private school and a private college. I could have gone into finance but I just didn't. I wasn't interested. I don't feel different from a person making $400,000 a year in terms of my ability to talk to them at a cocktail party." She added, "Education is more of a calling card than your profession in a lot of ways," before admitting, "that's just the way I like to reassure myself."

Although it would be reassuring to imagine that the unprecedented level of inequality among people with similar levels of education has few social implications, it would be wrong. Mixed-income cocktail parties are the least of it; you can always go home at the end of the night and snarkily debrief with your significant other. The more insidious problem is how the new inequality influences whom you go home with.

Emily, a teacher in Northern California, recounted, "Talking with my other friends who are teachers who aren't married, most of them are saying 'I'm a girl—' er, 'I'm a woman, I'm a teacher, I don't make that much money. I better marry someone who makes at least this much or I won't be able to buy a house.'" More than just being a dehumanizing, arbitrary force keeping potentially happy couples apart, Emily feels the new economic terrain is undoing the gender equality produced by the women's movement. "It pisses us off that we feel like we have to get married in order to buy a house. Society's saying that I have to get married in order to buy a house. That's crap. Why can't I be a single person and have a house? Why can't I live where I grew up without having to get married?" Emily's "I'm a girl" is exactly on point, a Freudian (or a Friedanian) slip: can you really be said to be a woman—an adult—if you are still dependent on others for the basic necessities of life?

In the egalitarian economy of the 1950s, a single female teacher willing to buck the social pressure to marry could buy a house on her own. Despite our modern mores, in many parts of the country, this is no longer the case. Today's wealth distribution resembles that of the Victorian Age more than the 1950s, and it is shaping social life accordingly. Many of Emily's unmarried teacher friends live at home with their parents and, in true Victorian fashion, move out only upon pairing off.

While Emily is uncomfortable admitting that these calculations figure into deciding whom to date, she admitted that "it's definitely in the back of your mind, especially in this area" where housing prices are so high. And considering the childcare math, female teachers, who are likely to drop out of the workforce when they have children, are forced to seek a traditional breadwinner husband. A male teacher at Emily's school told me he didn't think his female colleagues were dating with an eye toward men's finances. Ignorance is bliss.

Oblivious men notwithstanding, after a brief moment of women's liberation, the culture of the "good catch" is back with a vengeance. Appropriately enough for an age in which "kissing a frog" has made such a comeback, the wealthiest man in America actually looks like a frog. (Sorry, Melinda, we know he looks like a million bucks to you.)

When a trio of economists examined Internet dating data, they found that a leading predictor of a man's success in attracting e-mails was a high income. As they wrote in their wittily titled paper, "What Makes You Click?: An Empirical Analysis of Online Dating," the only thing women found more attractive than high incomes was, well, actually being attractive. Men are reacting accordingly, retuning to traditional breadwinner occupations. The proportion of men in the teaching profession is at a forty-year low. From 1961 to 1986, about one in three schoolteachers was male; today, one in five is.

The only way out of the bind for women is to preemptively sell out. As a highly paid female mergers and acquisitions lawyer on Wall Street proclaimed, "Now I can marry for love!" She uttered it with the gusto one might expect of a peasant girl from Pakistan, not someone raised in a Western nation where what the Pakistanis call "love marriages" (as opposed to the "arranged" variety) have long been the norm. Indeed, doing corporate mergers and acquisitions is now one of the few ways a professional woman can avoid regarding her own personal life as an exercise in mergers and acquisitions.

While a few female M&A lawyers can marry for love, more and more couples retreat into the Victorian ideal, in which the husband serves as breadwinner and the wife manages the household and does good works on the side. Journalist David Brooks described this as the "predator-nurturer" marriage. A friend of mine put it even better, describing a couple he knows: "She's his prosthetic conscience."

The return of Victorian wealth distributions and social relations is now so full-blown that Cheryl Mendelson could write a wholly believable novel set in contemporary Manhattan and consciously model it on the novels of nineteenth-century British author Anthony Trollope. In a city where, among all but the corporate class and those like Rachel who luck into subsidized housing, land is inherited rather than purchased, finances weigh more and more heavily on romantic relationships. In Mendelson's 2003 novel, *Morningside Heights*, a lawyer-turned-Episcopal-priest worries that by adopting his new low-paying vocation, he'll never find a woman who'll marry him. Another character bails on a potential liaison because, the narrator tells us, "she wasn't pretty enough to get him to jump over the class line for her." The tale gets a happy ending when the cash-strapped musician family at the heart of the story inherits a rich widow's condominium. But the happiest part is the author's embrace of the prevailing notion that class is about manners and attitudes, not money. Mendelson reassures her readers in much the same way Rachel reassures herself. The neighborhood may no longer be affordable to the idealists and intellectuals who once populated it—save those who fortuitously inherit rich widows' condos—but the corporate types who now inhabit their apartments are charmingly self-effacing, not haughty. Never mind that pesky little detail that the new tenants devote their lives to making money, not music. As Mendelson writes on the final page, "The building and neighborhood were remaking the newcomers, molding them to their own ways rather than the other way around."

The Retreat into Epicurean Selfishness

I interviewed Rachel sitting at her contemporary-looking dining-room table, which, being in a New York apartment, was located in the living room. At the end of our conversation, I asked if the table was from Ikea. "You noticed?" she asked, surprised.

I hadn't noticed the table from the catalog or the store, but I had noticed that Rachel and her husband were members of the Ikea class—young people with elite educations but without elite incomes. It's more that Ikea had noticed *them*—an enormous demographic group with a sophisticated sense of style but little more disposable income than many discount shoppers. (A pair of New York City bus drivers, for example, would earn an income similar to Rachel and her husband's but, quite likely, cultivate a different taste in home furnishings.)

It isn't just Ikea. A whole slew of retailers have grown wildly successful by noticing what mainstream economists and pundits have missed: although education and income often track together, for a whole class of people they don't. This class's incomes are usually lower than their education levels would suggest because their values lead them toward public interest work or creative pursuits. Seeking high-brow goods at modest prices, they furnish their homes at Ikea, feed their families at Trader Joe's, and buy everything else they need at Target.

For years, people have jokingly pronounced Target *en français,* as "Tar-zhay." The company tellingly sponsors quintessential high-brow, low-income events like New York City's free Shakespeare in the Park and free Friday night admission at the Museum of Modern Art. Other times of the week, adult tickets to MoMA run $20—money better saved for your next trip to, well, Target.

The most successful retailers understand that to win over this demographic, they need to offer not merely good economic values—reasonably priced goods—but also good moral values—products that are environmentally sensitive and sweatshop-free. Some top-selling products succeed by merely being sophisticated without being expensive, say Target's $40 teapot designed by postmodern architect Michael Graves or Trader Joe's eminently drinkable Charles Shaw wine, priced at $1.99 a bottle (nicknamed "Two-buck Chuck"). Others, like "fair trade" coffee, for which coffee plantation workers are paid more than the starvation wages doled out by the invisible hand of the market, succeed by embodying a progressive political and ethical outlook.

Despite their colossal success, few outside of the corporate marketing departments of these companies seem to understand their strategies. In 2005, when Target monopolized all the advertising space in a single issue of *The New Yorker,* an unprecedented ad buy in the eighty-year history of the magazine, the mainstream media were at a loss to explain why Target had done it. After all, *The New Yorker's* usual advertisers are strictly high-end—Fifth Avenue fashion boutiques, top-shelf liquor, luxury cars. What was a discount retailer doing there (aside from that perennial advertiser, John Helmer, an Oregon-based purveyor of $10 European berets)? As the media accounts all noted, Target didn't even have a store in Manhattan, the magazine's hometown and home of all things highbrow and high-priced. Thus the *New York Times* pontificated that Target must be hoping to "burnish the image of its stores among fashionistas in the garment district and burnish the image of its corporate parent on Wall Street." The online magazine Slate ventured that Target was "making discount acceptable for the rich and famous, and, hence, everyone else." The writer for Slate even found a Manhattanite who claimed she took the subway to Brooklyn to shop at the nearest Target and "then if I buy too much stuff, I call a car service to pick me up at the store."

But a million-dollar ad buy to win over a few Park Avenue princesses? Perhaps Target was taking out ads in *The New Yorker* for the same reason any retailer takes out ads in any publication: in hope of getting the magazine's readers to shop at its stores. Sometimes a cigar is just a cigar.

What defines *The New Yorker's* readership is its education

levels more than its income levels. It is a must-read publication among academics, curators, journalists, and book editors—the highly educated, modestly paid professions that make up the core of the Ikea class. In the New York area, most of these people, long priced out of Manhattan, already live near Target's Brooklyn store. Sure, some wealthy business types read *The New Yorker* too, but unlike in the faculty lounge no one's getting mocked on the trading floor at Bear Stearns for missing David Denby's latest movie review. A year after the all-Target issue, *The New Yorker* tacitly conceded Target understood its demographics better than its own publisher did. The magazine began offering subscriptions on an installment plan—four easy payments of $11.75 rather than a hefty $47 up front.

Target, Ikea, and Trader Joe's all offer enlightened domesticity at a reasonable price. Together, they facilitate the retreat into domestic life that has become the standard response of well-educated progressive people to contemporary America. Many older observers have been floored by the renewed interest in, and devotion to, the domestic sphere among the generation they raised on feminism. But when fulfillment in the public sphere proves unattainable, searching for it in the domestic sphere is the natural reaction. Each member of the Ikea class strikes a balance between sainthood and sellout-dom in the world of work, but at home all embrace a sophisticated style befitting their elite educations and an ethic of ecological and humanistic concern befitting their politics.

What homeschooling is to evangelicals in the heartland, organic cooking is to progressives on the coasts. Evangelicals may not be able to get the Supreme Court to put prayer back in the public schools, but they can pull their children out of them. Similarly, progressives may not be able to get Congress to ban genetically modified foods, but they can ban those foods from their kitchens. Both are motivated by the same impulse: a desire to separate themselves from a nation whose values they reject. Both are attempts to provide a hedge of protection around their children. Both seek to hide from the world rather than transform it.

Although enlightened consumerism is a contemporary phenomenon, the urge to hide is not new. It ensues whenever social progress is turned back, whenever grand hopes for *we* give way to a narrow obsession with *me*. Way back in 1799, as Napoleon rose to power, Samuel Coleridge wrote a letter to his friend William Wordsworth suggesting he write a poem "to those who, in consequence of the complete failure of the French Revolution, have thrown up all hopes of the amelioration of mankind, and are sinking into an almost epicurean selfishness [disguised as] domestic attachment."

Today's materialism disguised as progressivism springs from the dashed hopes of the American century: the failure to consummate the egalitarian revolutions of the New Deal and the 1960s and build the "beloved community" of Martin Luther King Jr.'s dream. As Coleridge's letter notes, the political is also personal; just as the revolution failed in the political world, there is a corresponding failure of the revolution in the life of each sympathetic individual. Abandoning hope in "the amelioration of mankind" takes a psychological toll. So do the inevitable compromises people make to survive in a reactionary time. These compromises foster a need to re-create one's dashed hopes for the world in the only place one has the authority to do so—in one's home.

Instead of following Gandhi's wisdom to "be the change you wish to see in the world," today people hide the change they wish to see in the world in their homes. Instead of turning the personal into the political, they turn the political into the personal. They drink their fair-trade coffee and raise free-range, vegetarian-fed children. Many opt to live in liberal enclaves like Burlington and Berkeley, replete with recycling bins and nature trails. But the attempt to erect a cordon sanitaire is futile. As inequality has grown, selling out has become the price of living in such an enclave. Eventually, even the loved ones they are trying to protect are reduced to lines on the profit-and-loss statements of Me, Inc. We can't shop our way out of this mess. But trying to is nothing new.

Karl Marx, living and writing in Victorian England, theorized that consumer goods were inordinately alluring because they served as a substitute for the fulfillment lost in work. By spending wages to purchase commodities, a worker attempts to regain that part of himself he has poured into the products he creates but does not own. Marx dubbed this phenomenon "commodity fetishism." Today we call it "retail therapy."

The echoes of the nineteenth century in our high-tech era— Internet daters conforming to Victorian notions of the "good catch," the retreat into the domestic sphere—may be surprising, but they shouldn't be. The intellectual forefathers of Reaganomics were quite explicit about their intentions to turn back the clock. William F. Buckley vowed to stand "athwart history, yelling 'Stop!'" And in his 1979 book, *Free to Choose*, the economic mastermind of Reaganomics, Milton Friedman, hailed nineteenth-century Victorian England as "a golden age."

All is proceeding according to plan.

3

THE ROAD TO MICROSERFDOM

The 1960s: Freedom Summers

In the summer of 1960, invitations went out to scores of leading campus conservatives inviting them to become charter members of a conservative youth movement. The founding conference was to be held at the family estate of their recently crowned hero, William F. Buckley Jr. "America stands at the crossroads today," the invitation read. "Will our Nation continue to follow the path towards socialism or will we turn towards Conservatism and freedom? The final answer lies with America's youth."

On a sunny Saturday, September 10, nearly one hundred of the young conservatives gathered at Great Elm, in Sharon, Connecticut, so named because the family's grounds boasted the state's largest elm tree. Many of the attendees had already met that spring in the unsuccessful Youth for Goldwater for Vice President campaign. Their platform was simple: laissez-faire capitalism at home and militant anticommunism abroad. For their name, they chose Young Americans for Freedom. They decided to use "Americans" rather than "Conservatives" because the word *conservative* then was what the word *liberal* is today. During the years of broad-based prosperity following the New Deal, the C-word had become an epithet.

There was little debate over using the word *freedom*. One member convinced others that using it would safeguard the word against liberals, who had already managed to capture "democracy." The young conservatives all agreed on what freedom meant. In global affairs, freedom meant fighting the Red Menace. Domestically, it meant restraining federal power—especially progressive taxation and regulation of business—to unleash individual talent and initiative.

The view of these young men and women stood in sharp contrast to that of most of their fellow Americans, whose views had been shaped by the policies of Franklin Roosevelt. FDR had proposed that government power be used to level the playing field, to make the promise of freedom real for all Americans. Under Roosevelt, tax-funded educational benefits made college accessible to the bright, not merely the wealthy. Labor organizing enabled workers to strike fairer deals with corporations. Under Truman, Eisenhower, and Kennedy, FDR's approach was expanded, albeit timidly, to encompass race. Federal power began to be used to ensure that southern blacks enjoyed the same rights as whites. For the black students attending a newly integrated high school in Little Rock or the scores of Americans who'd gone to college on the GI Bill, the increase in federal power was the key to their growing freedom.

But to young Buckley and his followers, freedom was the power to spend your money free from interference from the government. Under that definition, America in 1960 might have looked less than fully free. The top marginal tax rate was 91 percent. Not that this "confiscatory taxation" was creating too much hardship for Buckley's family. In 1955, when at age twenty-nine Junior founded *National Review,* his father chipped in a cool $100,000 from the family fortune, built on oil and real estate in Latin America. Yet the YAF founding convention made clear that conservatism had the potential for mass appeal to middle-class strivers. Few of the students who met at Sharon were rich; the majority of them had fathers who hadn't gone to college.

While often ignored by the 1960s media in favor of the New Left, YAF boasted far more members than Students for a Democratic Society, whose tactics they often cribbed. YAF became known for staking way-out-in-right-field positions. Its members picketed in *favor* of the House Un-American Activities Committee's witch hunts and organized a petition drive *against* the Limited Nuclear Test-Ban Treaty. They took a hard line against, of all things, the Peace Corps, which was attracting tens of thousands of applications from their public service–oriented New Frontier generation peers. Many adopted Buckley's penchant for humorous hyperbole and hijinks. One YAF activist broadcast a conservative program on his liberal college campus titled "Radio Free Williams" after the U.S. government–funded broadcasts over Soviet-occupied Eastern Europe; YAFers taunted hunger-striking Vietnam War protesters at a New York City rally by stuffing their faces under a banner reading "Better Fed Than Red!"

During the 1964 Republican primaries, YAF activists flocked to the Draft Goldwater Committee. In Goldwater, the young conservatives saw a kindred spirit, a man who shared their vision of freedom—one greatly at odds with the egalitarian vision of the Freedom Riders and Freedom Summer activists on the left.

At the peak of labor's power, Goldwater had assailed the movement from his perch on the Senate Labor Committee, championing the brilliantly named, antiunion right-to-work laws. While Democrats fought to root out union corruption, Goldwater took on the labor leaders, like Walter Reuther of the United Auto Workers, most responsible for harnessing America's industrial might to build a broad-based middle class. "I would rather have Hoffa stealing my money than Reuther stealing my freedom," the Arizona senator snarled.

Goldwater also railed against the progressive taxation that he felt was stealing the cold, hard freedom of American businessmen. He ingeniously attacked the progressive taxation ushered in under Roosevelt—perhaps the only factor as important as the labor movement in building the economic equality of the postwar period—as an affront to (get this) equality. "Government has a right to claim an equal percentage of each man's wealth, and no more," Goldwater wrote in his 1960 best-seller, *Conscience of a Conservative*. But while Goldwater was a master of rhetoric, his own life story, like that of Buckley, weakened his case. There was only so long average voters could listen to a department store heir argue that progressive taxation "penalizes success" before asking, "Whose success? Your dad's?"

Others on the right seized on Goldwater's knack for redefining words. A proposed constitutional amendment to repeal the income tax was dubbed the "Liberty Amendment." Opponents of the civil rights movement tried to claim *freedom* for themselves: to support a 1964 ballot proposition to override the California state legislature's recently passed prohibition of housing discrimination, the California Real Estate Association put up signs reading "FREEDOM: RENT OR SELL TO WHOM YOU CHOOSE."

Obsessed with horse-race politics, few in the media noted the importance of the Right's rhetorical shift. When four thousand YAF activists welcomed Goldwater to the Republican National Convention in a rally at the San Francisco airport, Walter Cronkite quipped, "They're Young Americans for Freedom but I don't know what *kind* of freedom." He was referring not to their political views but to the hysterical, Beatlemania-caliber reception the young conservatives gave to the perpetually suntanned, impossibly square-jawed Arizona senator. Veteran print reporter Theodore White was one of the few journalists with a handle on the changing terms of political debate. He asked civil rights protesters and Goldwater backers how they interpreted "freedom" and wrote, "It is quite possible that these two groups may kill each other in cold blood, both wearing banners bearing the same word."

In his acceptance of the 1964 presidential nomination, Goldwater invoked the words *free, freedom,* and *liberty* forty times. Though the speech became known for the hot-button declaration, "Extremism in defense of liberty is no vice . . . and moderation in pursuit of justice no virtue," the central refrain was Goldwater's ominous warning "The tide has been running against freedom." Looking out over 1960s America, Goldwater made his diagnosis: the problem plaguing the nation was conformity. "Equality, rightly understood, as our founding fathers understood it, leads to liberty and to the emancipation of creative differences. Wrongly understood, as it has been so tragically in our own time, it leads first to conformity and then to despotism."

It would seem an odd conclusion. In hindsight, 1960s America is viewed as the high-water mark of nonconformity. College students, floating on a sea of broadly shared prosperity, were turning a philosophical eye to the world, staking out positions from the YAF right to the SDS left. Campuses erupted in vigorous debates over everything from civil rights to hair length. But Goldwater couldn't make sense of these phenomena from behind the blinders of his conservative ideology, particularly his devotion to Austrian economist Friedrich August von Hayek. In his 1944 book, *The Road to Serfdom,* Hayek argued that government policies to encourage greater economic equality would force people to conform to the dictates of government bureaucrats and ultimately lead to totalitarianism. Who was Goldwater to disagree?

Hayek's ideas had been popularized in America in University of Chicago economist Milton Friedman's 1962 book, *Capitalism and Freedom.* In his opening, Friedman puts forth his theory that creative geniuses flourish in societies where the government butts out and lets markets do their thing. He lists a group of innovators from Sir Isaac Newton to—perversely—Chicago settlement house founder Jane Addams, who worked to ameliorate the most savage outcomes of the unregulated free market, and concludes that none of them "opened new frontiers in human knowledge and understanding, in literature, in technical possibilities, or in the relief of human misery in response to government efforts. . . . Governments can never duplicate the variety and diversity of individual action." Governments require conformity; markets unleash diversity. Thus, for devotee Goldwater, America was haunted by the threat of conformity—even if the only issue Americans expressed conformity on was that he couldn't be trusted with the presidency.

Goldwater's political heir, campaign volunteer Ronald Reagan, would carry the conservative torch—as well as a heavily annotated volume of Hayek—to Sacramento and Washington.

With a name famous courtesy of the silver screen, Reagan had been recruited as an orator of the Right by conservative business interests. In 1961, he had recorded an album mailed to doctors' wives by the American Medical Association, which was then working to stop a health-care reform bill in Congress that would provide nursing home care to the elderly. "One of the traditional methods of imposing statism or Socialism on a people has been by way of medicine," Reagan claimed, blithely conflating any government program designed to guarantee citizens' human rights with Soviet Communism. If the health-care legislation passed, he purred, "you and I are going to spend our sunset years telling our children and our children's children what it once was like in America when men were free."

In support of the Goldwater campaign, the conservative pitchman gave a last-minute nationally televised speech, a week before Election Day. While Reagan shared the nominee's off-the-charts reactionary views—he once referred to JFK as Karl Marx with a "tousled boyish haircut"—Reagan had undeniable charm and an inspirational life story. A self-made man could champion tax cuts in a way a department store heir never could. Parting with FDR's view that activist government programs would unleash individual freedom—he later described his youthful self as a "near hemophiliac liberal"—Reagan endorsed the conservative party line that government activism is antithetical to liberty. In his national debut speech Reagan posited, "There is no such thing as a left or right. There is only an up or down: up to man's age-old dream, the ultimate in individual freedom consistent with law and order; or down to the ant heap of totalitarianism." In 1966, Reagan would run for California governor on a platform of replacing the liberals' Great Society (and its idealist-stuffed offices) with his own "Creative Society," in which the government deferred to individuals to solve social problems in the hopes of unleashing, rather than stifling, human initiative.

But in 1964, the Gipper's appeal wasn't enough. Even Willam F. Buckley had written Goldwater off. Addressing a YAF convention in New York City, Buckley offered an inspiring funeral oration for the Goldwater campaign: "The point of the present occasion is to win recruits . . . not only for November the third, but for future Novembers: to infuse the conservative spirit in enough people to entitle us to look about us, on November 4th, not at the ashes of defeat, but at the well-planted seeds of hope, which will flower on a great November day in the future."

The 1970s: Things Fall Apart

Conservatives hoped that "great November day" would come in 1968, but the more moderate Richard Nixon beat out Reagan for the presidential nomination. Nixon went on to win the presidency by speaking on behalf of the "silent majority," Middle Americans who turned the counterculture's "Tune in, turn on, drop out" slogan on its head. They had tuned in to the counterculture (on the nightly news at least), got turned off by what they saw, and dropped out of the Democrats' New Deal coalition. Sensing the national shift to the right, many progressive young people looked for smaller ways of making change, outside of the federal government. Some flocked to Ralph Nader's consumer rights campaigns, run through groups like Public Citizen, founded in 1971. Others went into public interest law, social work, and teaching—career paths that in those days were still compatible with owning a home and raising a family anywhere in America.

But while Nixon fanned the flames of resentment at liberals, smearing them as "effete snobs," his administration's domestic policies were moderate. In substance, if not style, they fell to the left of those the Clinton administration would back a quarter-century later. The Nixon years saw the creation of the Environmental Protection Agency (EPA) and the Occupational Safety and Health Administration (OSHA); his administration seriously considered providing all Americans with a minimum annual income. Nixon spoke for many when he called the antitax crusaders at YAF "about as nutty as the [New Left] militants."

But Nixon's centrism sparked a concerted effort by big business to pull the country back to the right. In 1971, Virginia corporate lawyer Lewis Powell sent a confidential, five-thousand-word memo to the U.S. Chamber of Commerce arguing that "the time had come—indeed it is long overdue—for the wisdom, ingenuity and resources of American business to be marshaled against those who would destroy it." He saw enemies everywhere. Not just campus radicals, but professors, journalists, and politicians who "stampede to support almost any legislation related to 'consumerism' or the 'environment.'" Fighting back effectively, Powell counseled, "lies in organization, in careful long-range planning and implementation, in consistency of action over an indefinite period of years, in the scale of financing available only through joint effort, and in the political power available only through united action." The following year, the Business Roundtable, an organization of CEOs "committed to the aggressive pursuit of political power for the corporation," was founded. Conservative philanthropists answered the call as well, setting up right-wing think tanks like The Heritage Foundation, founded in 1973, and the Cato Institute, founded in 1977.

In a few years, the Right's antitax crusaders looked far less nutty—and not just because they had new think tanks handling their PR. The inflation of the 1970s pushed more and more middle-class Americans into higher income tax brackets. In the early 1960s, nearly nine in ten Americans essentially paid a flat tax of 22 percent; by the end of the 1970s, as a result of "bracket creep," nearly half of Americans paid more than that. Yet the Democrats, firmly in power in the aftermath of Watergate, dropped the ball, refusing to recalibrate the tax code to preserve its mild-on-the-middle-class, soak-the-rich progressivity. Oddly enough, a major change in the social contract had been put in place through policy inaction rather than action. More than a decade after a Goldwater for President poster asked, "Are You the Forgotten American?" the sentiment began resonating with more than just the right-wing fringe. The poster had answered the question: "Of course they remember you. At tax time."

In 1978, Californians passed the property tax–slashing Proposition 13 by a two-to-one margin. It provided an all too late wake-up call. Jimmy Carter enacted a cut in the capital gains tax, agonizing even as he signed the bill that it would favor the rich. But the reductions, targeted to the wealthy, were misdirected; they did little to appease the "Forgotten Americans." The conservatives' "great November day in the future" came at Carter's expense, in 1980.

The 1980s: Winners and Losers

Does the federal government need laboratories full of Nobel laureates, legal offices full of the top graduates of the best schools, administrative offices staffed with MBAs from Wharton, or policy shops full of the best and the brightest

whatevers? I think not. . . . The private sector [is] the true
vehicle for prosperity, social cohesiveness, and national
welfare, and the place where we ought to encourage our best
and brightest to migrate.

—Terry Culler, Associate Director for Workforce
Effectiveness and Development, U.S. Office of
Personnel Management, Reagan administration

Upon taking office, even Ronald Reagan was hard-pressed to
claim that America was no longer the land of opportunity. In
1979, American CEOs already made twenty-nine times what
their average workers earned—a higher ratio than in many European countries today. Still, Reagan saw no reason not to take
preemptive action against the phantom threat: "What I want to
see above all is that this remains a country where someone can
always get rich."

Having steamrolled Carter in the election, Reagan rode to
power with a mandate for tax cuts. The Democrats rolled over.
Political analyst and Nixon administration veteran Kevin
Phillips observed, "The party of the little man and of progressive
tax rates agreed to reduce top individual tax rates for millionaires
from 70 percent to 28 percent. . . . In accepting these 'reforms'
Democrats not only voted for top rates contrary to their political
traditions but lost the right to criticize tax policy as a source of
concentration of wealth."

"The Reagan Revolution required a frontal assault on the
American welfare state," was how Reagan's economic policy
czar David Stockman put it. In what amounted to an undeclared
class war, the plunder was lavished on the wealthy as tribute. In
addition to slashing the top marginal tax rates, Reagan ended
the policy of taxing unearned income at a higher rate than
earned—a policy initiated by Richard Nixon. He lowered the es-

tate tax paid by the rich while raising the payroll taxes that hit ordinary workers. By allowing the minimum wage to fall below the poverty line, he created the "working poor." Reagan personally destroyed the air traffic controllers' union, putting the bully back in bully pulpit and ushering in an open season on organized labor that continues unabated to this day. To boost defense spending while cutting taxes, the Gipper gutted social programs that benefited the poor and middle class, including college students' financial aid. Financing the federal budget through debt further redistributed wealth to the top, as the wealthy bought up government bonds and then enjoyed lowered taxes on the returns.

The further one went up the socioeconomic spectrum, the larger the gains; the further one went down, the greater the losses. As Park Avenue penthouses became ever more coveted, so too did the steam grates on Manhattan's sidewalks that kept the homeless alive on winter nights. Supply-side guru George Gilder maintained in his 1981 book, *Wealth and Poverty*, that "a successful economy depends on the proliferation of the rich. . . . To help the poor and middle classes, one must cut the taxes of the rich." But Reagan's help all seemed to flow one way. On Reagan's watch, the number of households with incomes over $50,000 doubled, the number of millionaires nearly tripled, and the number of billionaires quadrupled. By the time Reagan left office, the CEO-to-worker pay ratio had jumped to ninety-three to one. It is impossible to say by what factor homelessness increased under Reagan; before he took office, homeless people were so rare in America no one had thought to count them since the end of the Great Depression.

When his 1981 tax bill passed, Reagan sent a considerate thank-you note to his old friends at YAF. "Cutting government spending and reducing taxation have always been YAF goals. To-day, they're government policy," the president wrote. But by the 1980s, the group was dwindling; politics no longer had the hold on young Americans it had enjoyed in the 1960s and '70s. Sur-veys showed that making money had become the overarching obsession of American college students. The Reagan Revolution made it easier for those at top colleges to cash in—and harder for them not to since relying on underfunded public services like city schools was becoming less and less of a viable option. A concerted effort to "defund the Left" reduced job opportunities for the remaining idealists by cutting government funding to the nonprofit social service agencies that employed many of them. Under Reagan, the federal human resources office explicitly sought out the mediocre, hoping to push the most talented into the private sector.

Not that they needed a push. The growth of the deregulated financial sector produced scores of new investment banking jobs for number-crunching grunts fresh from the Ivy League. At Yale, half the members of the graduating class of 1986 applied for the same entry-level investment banking job title at First Boston. The number of big-firm corporate law jobs doubled dur-ing the Reagan years, and the starting salary for new associates jumped from $35,000 to $67,000. The proliferation of high-pay/no-experience jobs crammed metropolitan America with a new type of young person: the yuppie.

Ironically, considering Goldwater's earlier predictions and Friedman's idea that free markets foster nonconformity, the young i-bankers and corporate lawyers were known for a con-formism not seen among young people in decades. While the new generation of business types came in both genders and all colors, "the big questions were how red were your suspenders, how yellow was your tie, and how green was your wallet," journalist Hendrick Hertzberg quipped in his 1988 article, "The Short Happy Life of the American Yuppie." As Hertzberg noted in his anthropological study, published in an issue of *Esquire* magazine that featured Michael J. Fox, a.k.a. Alex P. Keaton from TV's *Family Ties*, eating sushi on the cover, the biggest yuppie put-down was saying "the guy's a complete loser." The conformism in the taunt is implicit: everyone wants to be like us (i.e., winners). Anyone who isn't like us has simply failed in his quest. Appropriately enough, the *Wall Street Journal* named Ronald Reagan America's "most aged yuppie."

The 1990s: Ineffectual Interlude

By the end of the Reagan era, the country seemed ripe for a backlash. A Times-Mirror survey found 82 percent of Americans supported raising taxes on those making over $80,000 a year. If ever there was a winning political issue, this was it—even Mom, the flag, and apple pie don't poll that high. Perhaps with this in mind, George H. W. Bush centered his campaign on social issues, ostentatiously reciting the Pledge of Allegiance and calling for a constitutional amendment to ban flag-burning. His opponent, Michael Dukakis, took the bait. He got bogged down talking about his opposition to the death penalty and his (gasp) ACLU membership, and failed to propose a single tax increase. Bush, who had long ago made his peace with what he had mocked in the 1980 Republican primaries as "voodoo economics," won with a substantively identical if better-packaged platform—his famed "Read my lips: no new taxes" pledge.

Social critics, and even the general public, were quicker to sense the upward redistribution of wealth than economists were to track it. As Tom Wolfe observed in his decade-capping novel *The Bonfire of the Vanities,* competition for condos in the Upper East Side's "Good Buildings" was intensifying; a million dollars just didn't buy what it used to. When solid academic research firmly established that the benefits of the past decade's economic growth had been siphoned off by the rich, the Bush administration's economists tried to discredit it.

With the trends toward ever greater concentration of wealth at the top continuing, by 1992, Democrats positioned themselves to win with a new "if you can't beat 'em join 'em" strategy, showing they could kowtow to big business just as well as the Republicans did. The strategy helped the Democrats raise campaign money and win the presidency, but it also gutted the party of its long-standing role as a counterweight to corporate power and entrenched wealth. It seemed a different party entirely from the one that, in the last period of extreme inequality, railed against "a new industrial dictatorship [that renders] political equality . . . meaningless in the face of economic inequality." As a pair of U.S.-based British journalists observed, in the 1990s, "The Democrats [became] marginally less addicted to corporate largesse than the K Street conservatives at the helm of the Republican Party, but only in the way that a cokehead is in less trouble than a heroin junkie. . . . All this political money inevitably drags the Democrats to the Right."

Tax policy professor Michael Graetz observed that Bill Clinton "disguised himself as Robin Hood." On the stump, candidate Clinton attacked the Reagan tax cuts for the rich. Upon election, his promised middle-class tax cut was quickly abandoned. With the Democrats finally in a position to repeal the

Reagan tax cuts, Clinton timidly pushed up taxes on the rich by only 10 percentage points. Polls showed most Americans thought he had raised their taxes (perhaps a reaction to his broken promise to lower them) and the Republicans swept the 1994 midterm elections. In 1995, Clinton threw in the towel, shook hands with Newt Gingrich, and declared that "the era of big government is over."

On Clinton's watch, the rising inequality and deregulation of the Reagan years continued. Tax loopholes allowed many companies to pay no federal income taxes at all. If you paid any income taxes in 1999, you paid more than Microsoft or Cisco Systems. As social critic Thomas Frank observed, the Democratic Party had given up on checking corporate power and inequality: "The opposition literally ceased to oppose."

While the NASDAQ soared, the yuppies' little brothers and sisters began making their way in the world. The libertarianism of Hayek and Friedman found new expression in the joint ventures and joints lifestyles of Silicon Valley. Tech pioneer Jaron Lanier summed up the views of his peers: "The libertarian view of capitalism has become so exalted among tech types and bright young people that it isn't even contested anymore—it is just the common air we breathe." The key goal sought by young dot-commers—to retire by thirty—was seen as a testament to the opportunities of the era, not its perversity. By the late 1990s, after decades of deregulation and growing inequality, retiring rich had become the only way for a well-educated private-sector professional to attain any leisure time at all. While the rest of the developed world worked less and less, Americans were working more and more, victims of unchecked corporate power. That the tech industry was centered in the San Francisco Bay

Area, an earthly paradise where a life sentence of 24/7 service in an air-conditioned cubicle seemed the cruelest of all fates, only added to early retirement fantasies. It's no surprise that the Golden Gate Bridge is the world's leading suicide location.

The Turn of a New Century: Making the Pie Higher

> You bet I'd cut the taxes at the top. That encourages entrepreneurship. What we Republicans should stand for is growing the economy. We ought to make the pie higher.
>
> —George W. Bush,
> South Carolina Republican Primary Debate,
> February 15, 2000

It has been observed that a gaffe in politics is when a politician accidentally speaks the truth. This was certainly the case when George W. Bush said "we ought to make the pie higher." Bush was grasping for the common phrase that we should "make the pie bigger" (i.e., grow the economy). But making the pie higher is the perfect image for understanding the economic policies he has put in place as president. As wealth has become more concentrated at the top, the American dream has become more expensive, requiring higher and higher incomes to attain it. Tuition goes up, health care becomes more elusive, metropolitan rents and housing prices jump through the roof—the proverbial pie gets higher and higher. As a result, the rising generation, famous for its volunteerism and civic engagement, finds its altruistic impulses stifled at graduation.

George W. Bush came into office arguing that the federal

budget surplus demanded tax "relief." In 2001, he signed a bill to lower the rate of each tax bracket, with the largest reductions going to the highest bracket, a cut from 39.6 down to 33 percent. The bill also phased out the estate tax on inherited wealth—a levy that applied to only 2 percent of estates. In 2003, a second round of tax cuts reduced the capital gains and dividend taxes of stockholders. Since most stock is owned by the wealthiest 5 percent of Americans, again the vast majority of the cuts flowed to the already wealthy.

Yet, the Bush tax cuts were popular with middle-income Americans. This was partly the product of misleading rhetoric from the White House. Promoting the first tax cut, the administration demonstrated how a "typical" American family earning $40,000 a year with two children would get a $1,600 break. What they didn't reveal was that this was the best-case scenario. Poorer families would get nothing or next to nothing. A family with fewer children or grown children would get far less. Only the rich could count on a windfall.

The deeper explanation for their popularity, from Princeton political science professor Larry Bartels's, is that while polls showed Americans were concerned about growing inequality, they didn't connect the proposed tax cuts—even the slashing of the estate tax on the wealthy—to the problem. Bartels's article, "Homer Gets a Tax Cut," included a drawing in which TV's Homer Simpson, holding two one-dollar bills, shouts "Woo-hoo!" while his boss, Mr. Burns, stands in front of a pile of money bags and thinks to himself, "Sucker." Most Americans don't connect tax cuts that favor the rich to the country's growing inequality not because they lack Bartels's expertise, but because no one—that is, the Democratic Party—is making the point. Some

Democrats are indifferent to rising inequality; others talk about bringing up the bottom; no one speaks of holding down the top. Today, the top 1 percent of the country controls more wealth than the bottom 90 percent and yet only 1 percent of Americans believe taxes are too low.

George W. Bush pushed his tax cuts with slogans like "They trust the government, we trust the people!" and "It's not the government's money, it's your money!"—rhetoric that echoed Hayek's argument in *The Road to Serfdom* that the power to spend money *is* the power to choose. (Hurricane Katrina gave the lie to this argument. When those imprisoned by poverty and neglected by the federal government, without the "choice" to leave town, ended up starving or dead, one critic mocked the Bush administration's response as, "It's not the government's hurricane, it's your hurricane!") But it's not just the poor for whom rising economic inequality restricts choice. With every passing year of growing inequality and misguided federal policy, choice becomes more limited to those at the very top, and for all but the independently wealthy the choices keep getting narrower. Social mobility in America—the raison d'être for these policies, Reagan's hope that "this remains a country where someone can always get rich"—has dropped below that in socialist Scandinavia. Economic mobility is now no higher than in Great Britain, the nation whose ossified class hierarchies we rebelled against in the first place.

Those at the bottom are stuck; those with the education needed to get ahead are trapped: do what you need to do to support a family at the ever-rising going rate or do what you want to do and give up the American Dream. For young educated Americans, the nation is fast becoming the land of compulsory yuppiedom. And the pie gets higher every year. Today, just paying the bills in metropolitan America requires that most educated young people join up with one of those undertaxed corporations like Cisco or Microsoft or the law, banking, and consulting firms that keep them undertaxed. The best you can hope for is to become what novelist Douglas Coupland termed a Microserf.

4

SELLING THE BODY POLITIC

The Dream and the Nightmare

While in college in the late 1990s, I took part in labor protest at a hotel in Fairfield County, Connecticut. The hotel workers had voted to form a union, but management was dragging its feet negotiating the first contract, a standard union-busting tactic all but endorsed by America's ineffectual labor laws. Yale students, attending the institution that is by most measures the nation's most oft-struck employer, had no shortage of on-campus activism. But for many, getting off campus had its allure. There was a certain thrill in taking to the streets amid the country clubs and country-club Republicans of Fairfield County, the historic stomping grounds of the Bush clan and Ann Coulter (whose father was a union-busting corporate lawyer). As the mostly black and brown workforce was bolstered by a smattering of liberal college students, all stared down by the conservative white locals, the picket line at first took on a 1960s feel. But that all changed when management's union-busters appeared, an egalitarian mix of men and women, a perfect portrait of multicultural diversity in finely tailored suits. In terms of race and gender, they were indistinguishable from the workers. Not one of them could have been Ann Coulter's dad. This wasn't in the script.

Some restricted Fairfield County country clubs may still try to hold on to a dying WASP world, but these union-busters represented the elite of the future. While the diversification of the elite was often resisted by the Far Right, which opposed affirmative action, it was embraced by most on the Left. Somewhere along the line, much of the Left had stopped fighting for a more egalitarian society and begun fighting for a more inclusive elite.

The Connecticut protest looked very different from the Memphis sanitation workers' strike, with its all-black workforce and all-white management, which Martin Luther King Jr. was supporting when he lost his life. But what was unfolding in Fairfield County was hardly a scene out of King's dream. This was not little black children and little white children sitting down together at the table of brotherhood. It was black women and Asian men sitting down at the table in the boardroom to plot how to keep the maids' children from receiving health-care coverage.

When King stood at the Lincoln Memorial at the culmination of the March on Washington for Jobs and Freedom, he accused America of not making good on its promise by leaving racial minorities out of the social contract of the New Deal. That social contract promised the American Dream to whites only, essentially reading, any white man willing to work forty hours a week for forty years could raise a family in a home he owned, in a safe neighborhood with good schools, and receive a lifetime of health-care and retirement benefits from his employer, his union, and his government.

While some conservatives fought King with dogs and fire hoses and bullets, others fought him more subtly, by redefining the American Dream as the chance for a handful of Americans to get fabulously wealthy while the rest struggled for the basics. Many on the Left came to accept this redefinition—with the caveat that at least a few women and minorities be among those getting fabulously wealthy, too. By the time the 1990s boom came around, with all its gains going to those at the top, this new vision of the American Dream was so firmly entrenched in the national imagination that few could remember it had ever been any other way. Those who were living the dream, the mainstream media showed us, lived in Silicon Valley mansions, not Levittown subdivisions.

The Diversity Myth

There have been times in this country when liberals worked to redistribute wealth and power to build a more egalitarian America. Following the late Supreme Court justice Louis Brandeis's counsel that a democracy cannot function when wealth is concentrated at the top, New Dealers mixed labor organizing, an expanded social safety net, and progressive taxation to build a more equal society. The civil rights and women's movements worked to expose and address the racial and gender disparities that still plagued the nation despite its New Deal progress. In response, corporate America co-opted the 1960s movements and began to roll back the New Deal by championing diversity in lieu of equality. For big business, the threat to their wealth and power was a more equal America, built with progressive taxation, regulation, and organized labor; expanding the hiring pool to include talented women and minorities might have made a few crusty old white executives squirm, but it was a boon to the bottom line. Too many on the Left took the bait. The diversification of the elite in terms of race, gender, and sexual orientation is a real-world reflection of the fantasy that we can fight inequality without more equally distributing wealth and power—indeed, that we can fight it even as we continue to further concentrate wealth and power. Today we are building a society that each year, as more women and minorities are welcomed into the upper echelons of corporate America, appears to be more equal even as the hard economic data show it is becoming less so.

It would be comforting to think the new inegalitarian America was born out of an ideological conflict, that both the Right and the Left presented their arguments and the Right's arguments were just more convincing. But the success of the Right has primarily been a function of the acquiescence of the Left. It's not that the Left stopped sparring with the Right—the culture wars of the 1980s and '90s were often contentious affairs—it's that the Left took its eyes off the prize of building a more egalitarian society and instead worked, often quite successfully, to integrate the elite. As one commentator put it, today's mainstream liberalism endorses "a multicultural caste system in which people of all races, creeds, genders, and sexual orientations eat dinner at the same upscale restaurant . . . while people of all races, creeds, genders, and sexual orientations eat dinner out of the garbage Dumpster out back."

Progressive social critic Walter Benn Michaels put it another way: "Multiculturalism [went] from proclaiming itself a subversive politics to taking up its position as a corporate management technology in about ten minutes." But which ten minutes? As with any change in society, it is difficult to trace it to an exact moment, but the 1979 leadership change at the Ford Foundation, the nation's largest philanthropic institution, is as good a moment as any. That was the year Kennedy administration brain-truster McGeorge Bundy retired and was replaced by Franklin Thomas, a Columbia-educated, African-American poverty lawyer who had been working in Bedford-Stuyvesant, the inner-city Brooklyn neighborhood where he'd grown up. As a basketball player at Columbia, Thomas had set a rebounding record that still stood when he was named president of the Ford Foundation. In politics, his best move would be fake left, go right.

Thomas became the first black president in the history of the foundation, replacing Bundy, a veritable walking WASP stereotype complete with a last name as first name. (True to form, he went by a sporty prep school nickname, Mac, that stuck for life.) In stark contrast to Thomas's Bed-Stuy roots, Bundy grew up in the exclusive Back Bay section of Boston and summered at his family's enormous "cottage" in Manchester-on-the-Sea before being packed off to Groton. Despite the aristocratic ethos of his upbringing, his character was tempered by an honest desire to understand the world beyond his sheltered circle.

Bundy viewed his mission at Ford as working for the public good—even at risk to his personal stock portfolio and those of the foundation's donors. He understood that markets do not always serve the best interests of society and, when they don't, government and civil society must step in. After CBS, choosing ad revenue over the public good, opted to broadcast reruns of *I Love Lucy* rather than live coverage of congressional hearings on the Vietnam War, Bundy worked to found the Public Broadcasting Service (PBS). More important, he made funding the nascent consumer and environmental movements a major Ford Foundation initiative, helping to create the emerging field of public interest law.

Bundy's support for checks on the power of concentrated corporate wealth did not always endear him to Ford Foundation funders. Henry Ford II, the founder's son, resigned from the board of trustees in 1976. In his letter of resignation, Ford wrote: "The Foundation exists and thrives on the fruits of our economic system. [It] is a creature of capitalism. . . . Perhaps it is time for the Trustees and staff to examine the question of our obligations to our economic system."

Apparently, it *was* time. In September 1979, soon after taking the reins, Thomas eliminated Ford Foundation funding for public interest law firms. That Thomas was retreating in the face of business pressure was clear to all observers. The *Washington Post* ran its story on the changes at Ford exactly where it belonged: the front page of the "Business & Finance" section. Under Thomas, the group would focus on education and minority programs, giving minority youth a better shot at joining the corporate elite rather than checking corporate power. Worse, Thomas effectively complied with the Reagan administration's request that private entities step up as the federal government slashed funding for programs to help the poor, becoming a collaborator in policies that would ultimately hurt the very inner-city youth Thomas claimed as his central concern.

Now, nearly three decades after Thomas was tapped to run the Ford Foundation, corporate profits are rising to new heights while the ghetto has become a seemingly intractable fixture of urban America's landscape. The conservative alternative to eliminating poverty altogether—allowing a fortunate few to get rich and get out—has been accepted by most liberals. One who got out, Bed-Stuy-born hip-hop impresario Jay-Z, paid homage to this philosophy when he named his music label Roc-a-Fella Records, after the nineteenth-century robber baron. Mad props to the Gilded Age, yo!

The New Republicans, a.k.a. the New Democrats

When Bill Clinton took the White House in 1992, he did so with the backing of corporate donors who had no interest in reducing inequality and under the spell of a group of intellectuals who had doubts about government's capacity to reduce it. Among the thinkers was Mickey Kaus, a *New Republic* senior editor, whose book, *The End of Equality,* argued that rising economic inequality is an immutable fact of the modern economy.

A central idea of liberalism, until Kaus and the centrist New Democrats scrapped it, was that economic inequality was a necessary evil. Each individual has the same basic needs—for food, clothing, shelter, employment, health care, and education—but some degree of inequality is necessary because it spurs people to work. The rule of thumb for liberals was that inequality should only be tolerated to the extent that it serves this purpose. The need for economic growth must be balanced against the ill effects of inequality; otherwise you would get the type of growth we've seen in recent years, that only benefits an elite minority.

Inequality is dangerous for social and political reasons as well. As Franklin Roosevelt and Justice Brandeis explained, when inequality grows too great, individual freedom and even democracy itself are imperiled. Workers are reduced to slavish dependence on their bosses and entrenched interests overpower the popular will. As we have seen in recent years, those near the top of the labor pool are not immune from the ill effects. As inequality distorts markets for housing and education, an epidemic of selling out ensues and private gain trumps public good.

But there's no need to catalogue the merits of a more egalitarian economy, Kaus concludes, since equality is just not possible anymore. While only 30 percent of American jobs require a college degree, Kaus dismisses the prospect that we could make the remaining 70 percent pay a living wage. Kaus explains, "For an American autoworker, a strong back was once a valuable attribute," but today only "brainworkers" can demand decent wages.

Thus Clinton's prescription: create more brainworkers. "You want to reverse income inequality in this country," Clinton said in a 1994 speech, "there is an education premium, and we had better give it to every American who is willing to take it. That is the only way to do it." While this rhetoric sounds compassionate, it is little different from Reagan redefining poverty as a personal shame rather than a national one. Clinton's rhetoric subtly shifted responsibility for inequality from society to the individual.

More troubling, his argument was fallacious. While there is a large gap between what high school graduates earn compared to college grads, Clinton's suggestion that if everyone were a college grad everyone would have a higher income is simply not true. In a global economy, having a well-educated workforce can help bring in high-skill, high-wage jobs, but only to an extent.

One of the fastest-growing fields in information-age America is janitorial work. Economist Michael Zweig explains, "If college education becomes universal, [employers will require] that a janitor have a college degree." Another economist, James K. Galbraith, notes that when you create an economy with a few huge jackpots at the top, giving out more lottery tickets—college degrees—simply means creating more losers. To create more winners, the economy has to be flattened out and prosperity more broadly shared. Education ought to be accessible to all, but what America's janitors need is a union card, not a university diploma. If American labor law were reformed so that today's service workers could effectively organize—a 2000 Human Rights Watch report documented that the right to organize exists only on paper in the United States—the ranks of the "working poor," America's latest peculiar institution, would dwindle, creating a more equal society. After all, American autoworkers didn't win living wages because of their valuable backs, as Kaus suggests, they won it because of their invaluable solidarity.

But policies to build a more equal America were not high on the New Democrats' agenda or that of their corporate backers. The tried-and-true changes that other developed nations have successfully used to limit inequality—steeply progressive taxation and a much higher minimum wage—were nonstarters in the Clinton White House. Hardly radical, the economic model of the prosperous, diverse United Kingdom is so similar to that of the United States that even free marketeers like *New York Times* columnist Thomas Friedman often lump our systems together under the rubric Anglo-American capitalism. Yet in Britain, with a minimum wage nearly twice ours, only one in twenty people earns below 35 percent of the median income; in the United States one in six does. The United Kingdom's top tax bracket of 40 percent—higher than our own, though lower than nearly every other developed nation—does some work to limit the top.

Despite a few timid policy proposals, Clinton essentially retreated into diversity-in-lieu-of-equality liberalism. He defended affirmative action in the face of a conservative backlash and succeeded in creating a cabinet that "looked like America," but on his watch the growing economic inequality of the 1980s continued.

In selling the American people on the idea that pushing up the bottom and holding down the top is not a legitimate goal of public policy, Clinton sold out the best of the Democratic Party's New Deal and civil rights movement traditions. By the time John Kerry "reported for duty" at the 2004 Democratic National Convention the word *equality* was missing in action. He used it only once in his entire acceptance speech, in a reference to gender, not economics.

Diversity was a game even an archconservative like George W. Bush could play. When it came to administrative appointments, Bush outdiversified even Clinton. For Bush, multiculturalism meant nominating Linda Chavez, a Hispanic woman who opposed minimum wage laws and affirmative action, for Secretary of Labor.

But it didn't take George W. Bush to realize that end-of-equality liberalism is not liberalism at all. In a surprising *National Review* piece on Kaus's book, the critic lavished praise on the author's political views, inviting the *New Republic*an into the right-wing ranks. In a statement brimming with Buckleyesque editorial hauteur, the reviewer wrote, "Welcome, Mr. Kaus, to social conservatism."

Dr. Pangloss, or How I Learned to
Stop Worrying and Love the New Inequality

With the acquiescence of the Democrats, in recent years the debate on inequality has shifted from the political realm to the press. But as the policymakers abandoned the subject to the policy scribblers, the debate has come to focus not on what we should *do* about rising economic inequality, but on how we should *feel* about it.

When left-wing critic Barbara Ehrenreich chronicled the lives of those on the bottom of the growing class divide in her 2001 best-seller *Nickel and Dimed*, she told her university-educated professional readers who live in "a magical world where needs are met" that they ought to be ashamed. On the right, conservatives like *New York Times* columnist David Brooks celebrated the educated elite that sits atop the new class chasm with a chuckle: "Wherever they have settled, they have [made] life more enjoyable (for those who can afford it)." Reading Brooks, one can't help but think of Dr. Pangloss, the farcical philosopher in Voltaire's *Candide* who constantly reassures all that, despite its manifest injustice, we live in "the best of all possible worlds." Neither Brooks nor Ehrenreich seriously entertains the notion that rising inequality could have any ill effects on those in the educated class who think themselves spared.

While the baby boomer Brooks concerns himself with his generation's hippies turned yuppies, the self-consciously hip Richard Florida focuses on the younger generation of wired professionals. Florida's 2002 tome, *The Rise of the Creative Class*, conveniently distills the conventional wisdom of hundreds of issues of *Fast Company* and *Wired* into one handy reference book replete with gee-whiz charts and graphs. Working hundred-hour weeks in a Silicon Valley office with a Ping-Pong table, and grabbing the occasional day off to mountain-bike to an art opening with a same-sex domestic partner, today's high-end professionals surely enjoy a lifestyle epitomizing American freedom. They pour out their souls for corporate America, Florida tells us, because they want to, because creative work is its own reward. In the new "flexible" American workplace that Florida describes, the threat of being fired simply doesn't exist. But as advertising firm chairman Lee Clow says, "Sometimes I'm asked what I say to people to get them to work on Saturday or Sunday. We don't say anything. But our creative people know what we expect from them."

This ever-present albeit unspoken threat, coupled with the new gulf between the "haves" and "have-nots," are what make modern professional life so frequently demeaning. In interviews for this book, I've heard about a banker who was forced to cancel her honeymoon when an office project came up and a corporate lawyer who was ordered to work through the weekend, missing a friend's wedding. (The law firm generously offered to reimburse the cost of his plane ticket, so no harm done.) In Florida's world, employees devote themselves to work not because ever more powerful bosses demand it, free from union contracts and government regulations that limit the workweek and mandate paid vacation, but because they want to. ("A honeymoon sounds nice, dear, but on the whole, I'd rather spend the week after our wedding putting in some face-time at the office.")

Florida gives us a pseudo-academic gloss on the trend toward overwork: "The long trajectory of modern capitalism has involved the relentless extension of the working day across time and space—first through electricity and electric light and now via the personal computer, the mobile phone, and the Internet."

But there is nothing exactly modern about working long hours. In fact, early capitalism is usually associated with the endless workday: before the rise of the labor movement and modern workplace regulation, the workday was often twelve hours long. Today, in modern capitalist countries, working hours have been dramatically reduced—the big exception is America. Here, professionals—Florida's so-called Creative Class—are working longer and longer hours, as are the working poor, who often put together two full-time minimum wage jobs in a futile attempt to make ends meet. Americans work 3.5 weeks more per year than the notoriously hardworking Japanese, 6.5 weeks longer than the British, and 12.5 weeks longer than the Germans. Should Florida travel to any of these places, he might be surprised to find they too have cell phones, personal computers, and Internet access—though the technology has not tethered them to the office.

As a thoroughly office-tethered management consultant at the elite firm McKinsey & Company explained to me, generously giving me an hour of a summer Sunday away from the office, in the absence of government regulation or the right to organize, white-collar employees engage in an overwork arms race, a Hobbesian war of all against all. "If there's one person who's willing to work harder, everybody else has to," he said. And it's not just the eager beavers hoping to make partner; this consultant was actively looking for other jobs, but still routinely logged sixty- to seventy-hour weeks. He connected overwork to a larger trend of eroding job security in corporate America—a trend fueled by those sixty-hour-a-week McKinsey consultants with their reams of reports on streamlining companies and squeezing employees. "You see today people working much harder than they used to in corporations. I think it's that everyone is worried about what's next and what could happen. So you have enough people who are trying to match the hardest workers and that just sets the bar higher for everybody else who wants to be average. So at the end of the day everyone is working more." For the working poor, the rise in corporate power means stagnant wages; for professionals, it means more and more hours. The only people the new inequality benefits are corporate bosses and wealthy shareholders—the people who were doing just fine already.

Rather than calling for some limits on corporate power or rebuilding the social safety net, Florida states, "There is no corporation or other large institution that will take care of us . . . we are truly on our own," as if repealing the social contract was just hunky-dory. It's not a coincidence that Florida's safety-net-free "Creative Economy" so eerily echoes Ronald Reagan's 1960s vision of a "Creative Society."

The Cultural Contradictions of the Creative Age

A computer-code writer living in a downtown loft apartment above a coffee shop may flatter himself that he's living in the golden age of creativity. But he's really living, as a 2006 report from the investment bank UBS put it, in "the golden era of profitability," a time of unprecedented corporate wealth and power. Wealth is, among other things, the power to employ—"to make use of someone" as the dictionary definition puts it. So while more people may be using creativity on the job, they have less and less control over the ends to which their creativity is directed.

The more the upward redistribution of wealth pushes up the cost of living in metropolitan America, the more corporate-directed creativity is demanded and the less independent, self-directed creativity is possible.

Florida cites urbanist Jane Jacobs's aphorism, "New ideas must use old buildings," to celebrate how Amazon.com has moved its offices into a former hospital complex in downtown Seattle. But Jacobs didn't mean that there is something about old buildings that fosters new ideas, that all that inhaled dust somehow stimulates big thoughts. What Jacobs meant was that new ideas must use *cheap* buildings. In her bohemian Greenwich Village neighborhood of the early 1960s, old was synonymous with cheap. The new buildings uptown were expensive and dedicated to corporate offices; the old buildings downtown had lower rents, which accommodated artists and writers. In a nation in which old neighborhoods are no longer cheap, in part because tech companies like Amazon have moved in, new ideas—especially noncommercial ideas—get snuffed out. As David Brooks writes, not noting how tragic this is, young people today "have never known a world without $4 million artists' lofts . . . and the rest of the accoutrements of the countercultural plutocracy."

In his obituary for Jacobs, *New Yorker* architecture critic Paul Goldberger noted that "Jacobs could not afford to live on her beloved block of Hudson Street today." In life too, Jacobs warned of the threat of gentrification—an astonishing feat of foresight considering her *Death and Life of Great American Cities* was published in 1961, long before the "Manhattanization" of San Francisco or Boston, let alone Manhattan. "So many people want to live in the locality that it becomes profitable to build, in excessive and devastating quantity, for those who can pay the most," she wrote. "Families are crowded out, variety of scene is crowded out, enterprises unable to support their share of the new construction costs are crowded out."

In a plutocracy, countercultural or otherwise, independent creative work becomes a luxury for the wealthy. Professor Florida mentions all the rich kids he knows pursuing art, music, and writing and concludes, "Creative Class people no longer define themselves mainly by the amount of money they make. . . . In interviews and focus groups, I consistently come across people valiantly trying to defy an economic class into which they were born. This is particularly true of the young descendants of the truly wealthy—the capitalist class—who frequently describe themselves as just 'ordinary' creative people working on music, film or intellectual endeavors of one sort or another. Having absorbed the Creative Class value of merit, they no longer find true status in their wealth and thus try to downplay it." Now that ordinary people can no longer move into an old building in Jacobs's neighborhood and think up some new ideas, the only people who can—CEOs' trust-fund children—go around telling us how "ordinary" they are. God bless the egalitarian values of the new inegalitarianism!

When thinking for yourself becomes a privilege for the superrich, what do the rest of us get to do? Why, we get to think for the superrich. That's where all these so-called creative professionals come in. With power shifted more and more to corporate America, big companies can hire more and more creative proles to do their bidding.

I first read *The Rise of the Creative Class* in preparation for an interview with Florida for a newspaper story. I remember being flattered that I, not a novelist or poet but a mere nonfiction writer, made the cut to be in what Florida calls the "Super-Creative Core," the very vanguard of the creative class. But I was puzzled. The creative class he was defining was enormous. "Creative Class" may be a memorable catchphrase, I thought, but he just means professionals. Even accountants are part of the creative class?—I snickered, as I read his book. Creative accounting?—You've got to be kidding me. Little did I know that "creative accounting" would soon be making its way into the American lexicon, coined during the string of scandals that hit Enron, WorldCom, and other corporations when accountants were charged with cooking the books, covering up massive fraud, and outright theft. Sure, they used their creativity—to break the law and enrich the already rich at the expense of everyone else. The last section of Florida's book is titled "Creativity to What End?" To what end, indeed. While the author admits that much of what the private sector directs our creativity toward is "trivial, vulgar, and wasteful," he never muses on how creativity might be put toward more self-directed or socially worthwhile ends. Florida advises that "we must carefully consider the ends to which we direct our creativity," as if "we" were the ones who get to decide.

Having the time and ability to direct their own creativity and having enough money for a modest lifestyle are all most creative people desire. As German essayist Walter Benjamin observed, "Writers are really people who write books not because they are poor, but because they are dissatisfied with the books which they could buy but do not like." In Florida's reading, Benjamin's lesson is that creative work is its own reward, regardless of who is directing it or to what end. He fails to see that creativity is only its own reward when it is self-directed or when the goals of the directing person or organization coincide with that of the creative person.

For Florida and his followers, the institutions that direct our creativity are irrelevant; our creativity is by definition self-directed. "While people can be hired and fired, their creative capacity cannot be bought and sold," he states. So though it may appear that we are forfeiting more and more control to corporate America—even before the Enron scandal fully 72 percent of Americans thought corporations had too much power according to a *BusinessWeek* survey—we are rapidly approaching a Marxist utopia. Florida writes: "Karl Marx had it partly right when he foresaw that workers would someday control the means of production. This is now beginning to happen, although not as Marx thought it would, with the proletariat rising to take over factories. Rather, more workers than ever control the means of production because it is inside their heads; they *are* the means of production."

To show how wrongheaded this is, consider another fulfilling human function, one arguably even more basic and rewarding than creativity: sex. As with creativity, the conditions in which sex is given are crucial. Sex given out of love is edifying; sex given out of economic necessity is degrading. It is not for nothing that people who do creative work they don't believe in are called corporate whores, or that as prostitution is described metaphorically as "selling my body," many in the business world speak of "selling my soul."

You can easily imagine Richard Florida hosting one of his famed focus groups (his consulting companies are Catalytix and the Richard Florida Creativity Group) with a panel of prostitutes. "You must feel so lucky," he would tell them. "You get to do something you love—and you get paid to do it!"

And talk about being the means of production.

Freedom *or* Equality vs. Freedom *and* Equality

The idea inherent in the much-ballyhooed "rise of the Creative Class"—that individual freedom can blossom alongside growing inequality—is so firmly entrenched that it is no longer just conservatives who make the argument. Richard Florida is, after all, a Democrat. From Clinton onward, Democrats have not merely given up on fighting rising inequality, but they have bought into the Right's framework for the debate.

In 1997, as a member of the Liberal Party of the Yale Political Union, I went on the group's annual trip to New York City to meet-and-greet various Democratic politicians. In the morning, we were hosted by former New York governor Mario Cuomo, now an attorney at a corporate law firm. Sitting around the conference table overlooking Midtown Manhattan, he asked us what we wanted to be when we grew up. When "professor" and "politician" and "activist" came up over and over, he made a point of encouraging at least some of us to go out and make as much money as possible—and then donate it to the Democratic National Committee.

In the afternoon we piled into New York City Councilman Tom Duane's cramped office. An openly gay man who represented Chelsea, the heavily gay neighborhood on the far left side of Manhattan, Duane was known as one of the city council's most reliable progressives. He'd never heard of the Liberal Party or the Yale Political Union, so to get a sense of our politics he took an informal straw poll.

"Who among you favor freedom over equality?" he asked. A slight majority of hands went up. "Who among you favor equality over freedom?" he asked. The other hands went up. "Ah, the real leftists," he said with a smile.

I didn't realize it at the time, but Duane's poll illustrates almost everything that is wrong with American politics. Duane was buying into a core conservative idea in accepting that freedom is a value of the Right and equality a value of the Left, and that one must choose between them in a zero-sum game. That government action to increase equality restrains freedom is a central tenet of Hayek and Friedman, Reagan and Bush. And it is a fundamentally antidemocratic belief, one that forsakes the promise of modern democracy—that a human society can be based, as an early rallying cry put it, on *liberté, égalité, fraternité.*

But it's not just Duane. The idea that freedom and equality are competing values has become so widespread in contemporary America that mainstream historians have begun suggesting that even Thomas Jefferson himself believed them to be incommensurable. In a 1997 Ken Burns PBS documentary, popular historian Joseph Ellis offered an executive summary of the Declaration of Independence, blithely betraying the revolution on prime-time TV: "Part of Jefferson's genius was to articulate at a sufficiently abstract level these principles, these truths that we all *want* to believe in. The level is sufficiently abstract so that we don't have to notice that these truths are at some level unattainable and, at another level, mutually exclusive. Perfect freedom doesn't lead to perfect equality. It usually leads to inequality." This interpretation puts the cart (freedom) before the horse (equality). More upsetting, it grafts Hayek and Friedman's argument back onto Jefferson's principles. For Jefferson, only equality could ensure freedom; only by guaranteeing a base level of equality could each individual be given the freedom to blossom—to pursue happiness. To put these principles into practice, Jefferson founded the University of Virginia, a free, tax-funded college intended for what he called the "natural aristocracy"—the bright and talented rather than the well-born. Tax-funded equalizing institutions, like free public universities, could extend freedom beyond the rich and their children; without them, he feared a hereditary aristocracy would arise despite the trappings of democracy. Today, Jefferson's vision has been forsaken, as it has been in other eras of extreme inequality. Our current intellectual consensus is all but identical to that of the last Gilded Age, in which, as historian James MacGregor Burns wrote, "the fatal and false dichotomy [of] freedom against equality . . . deranged American social thought."

Four years after meeting with Duane, I was in another modest office with another progressive politician, Mikael Damberg, a Social Democratic member of the Swedish parliament. Although conservatives argue that the taxes which ensure free public education for all take away people's freedom to use their money for whatever they see fit, Damberg asks rhetorically, "Aren't you more free when you have the rights through the welfare state to higher education without fees?" These days, it takes a European to make the liberal retort. Sadly, the Jeffersonian ideal of free higher education is in place in Sweden but not in Jefferson's own country. When education is free, graduates can pursue whatever career suits them, unburdened by debt and the pressure to save hundreds of thousands of dollars to educate their own children. Similarly with health care, conservatives claim that making people work for their health care breeds self-reliance while government guarantees breed sloth and dependency. But aren't you freer and more independent to, say, change jobs or strike out on your own, when health care is guaranteed? "The freedom debate is crucial," Damberg concluded. "Sometimes the conservatives win the freedom debate. Sometimes we win the freedom debate."

In the United States, where progressives have accepted the conservative shibboleth that freedom and equality are competing values, we don't have the freedom debate. And historians who are busy erasing the historical record that this nation was founded on Jefferson's vision, not Friedrich August von Hayek's, are ensuring we never will. Since Goldwater, the Republicans have pushed their vision of freedom based on low taxes, low regulation, and low government benefits—or, in the area of parental leave, no benefits at all. The Democrats have yet to respond.

For the thirty-one-year-old Damberg, the freedom offered through redistributive, egalitarian government benefits was real on a personal level, not something generously bestowed by Stockholm upon the great unwashed. In a few months, he told me, he would take a leave of absence from his position in parliament to raise his two baby girls. Like all Swedish parents, the government would pay him 80 percent of his current salary while he was on leave. In the United States, if a new father wanted to take a leave of absence from work he would have to be wealthy enough to finance it himself. He certainly couldn't be a public servant like Damberg. Yet another reason for young Americans to follow Cuomo's advice to skip the public service and sell out.

Two Visions of Freedom

Liberals have won the fight for equality in the past, and they could win it again. But to do so, they need to revive the freedom debate.

Franklin Roosevelt showed how it's done. For FDR, the concentration of wealth in the 1920s—a concentration we have once again matched—was a threat to individual freedom. In an earlier America, among white men at least, one could always set out for the frontier. The Homestead Act, a conscious government program to build a society of economically independent citizens, gave out free land in the West. But in the age of a closed frontier and a shrinking agricultural sector, most Americans began to rely on corporations for their livelihoods. Without proper safeguards, Roosevelt believed, the individual could easily become tethered to "economic royalists" in a situation of such servile dependence that real freedom was quashed. As Roosevelt put it in a 1932 campaign speech at the Commonwealth Club in San Francisco, "Property rights might so interfere with the rights of the individual that the government, without whose assistance the property rights could not exist, must intervene, not to destroy individualism but to protect it." According to James MacGregor Burns, "Roosevelt was asserting that individual political liberty and collective welfare were not only compatible, but they were mutually fortifying."

Ronald Reagan's stated goal was strikingly similar to FDR's, though his policy methods could not have been more different. He too called for unleashing the individual. As he put it early on in his political career, "The American dream that we have nursed for so long in this country and neglected so much lately is not that every man must be level with every other man. The American dream is that every man must be free to become what God intends he should become." In order to fulfill this vision, Reagan slashed the social safety net, viewing government guarantees of excellent free public education and universal health care as antithetical to human freedom. For Reagan, a society in which private wealth had no limits was the best way to unleash individual creativity.

The historical record speaks for itself. The years when FDR's vision was in place were years of growing social mobility, robust democracy, and cultural creativity. The past twenty-five years of Reagan's vision have yielded the opposite. Inequality has sky-rocketed. Social mobility has declined. Progress on addressing racial and gender disparities has stagnated. While Reagan called his vision the Creative Society, the policies he enacted have placed even our potentially most creative citizens on a treadmill of educational debt, health-care coverage worries, and out-of-control housing prices that turns their creative capacities into wholly owned subsidiaries of corporate America.

But the pendulum is swinging back. Of late, the inchoate consensus has grown stronger, enough so that Democrats could win a round of the freedom debate without even showing up. In 2005, without even the slightest hint of leadership from the Democrats, President Bush's plans to privatize Social Security unraveled in the face of public skepticism and hostility. When Bush began selling his plan, polls showed 58 percent of Americans viewed his proposal favorably. After a year of presidential salesmanship, support had dropped to 27 percent. The more people knew, the less they liked it. The president touted the freedom to move your retirement money around the stock market, drawing on Milton Friedman's view that "the citizen of the United States who is compelled by law to devote something like 10 per cent [sic] of his income to the purchase of a particular kind of retirement contract, administered by the government, is being deprived of a corresponding part of his personal freedom." But most Americans didn't see things that way. They decided to stick with the freedom that comes from knowing they will never be destitute in old age even if it means renouncing the freedom to play the market today. It is that "freedom from want," as Social Security's founder FDR called it, which affords people the freedom to take more risks during their working lives. As today's Democrats should be reminded, this is such rhetoric as landslides are made on.

The defeat of Social Security privatization signaled a larger defeat for George W. Bush's Ownership Society agenda, essentially Reaganomics rebranded for a new century. As companies increasingly back out of the social contract—of using layoffs only as a last resort and bargaining in good faith with their employees over wages, health insurance, and working hours—the government must step in. The Ownership Society programs that transfer even more risk from government and business onto individuals are the opposite of what the public is clamoring for. Half a century after William F. Buckley exhorted Americans to stand "athwart history, yelling 'Stop!,'" it is high time we stand athwart history, yelling "Forward!"

5

START UP, SLIP DOWN:
SELF-EMPLOYMENT WITHOUT A NET

Capitalism with a Human Face

Business partners Josh Koplin and Samuel Reeves look and sound like a comedy team in the classic Laurel and Hardy/ Abbott and Costello mold. Josh, short and stocky with a full beard and mane of blond hair, sported camouflage shorts and sandals the day I dropped by the office. Reeves, his tall, skinny straight man, wore a button-down shirt, and would be almost impossible to imagine in anything less formal. Sitting at a conference table in the Weiss Tech House on the University of Pennsylvania campus, a pattern soon developed: Koplin would shoot off his trenchant, often profanity-laced observations, leaving Reeves to clean up the mess.

Koplin grew up in Philadelphia and went to Hampshire College, the New England school for kids who find Wesleyan too straitlaced and Bard too uptight. He'd gone on to study architecture and design at Pratt, the well-regarded Brooklyn art school. Reeves, a seventh-generation Texan, had gone to Wharton. His grandfather, he told me, had fought for the independence of the Lone Star Republic at the Battle of San Jacinto, which he pronounced in true Texas style, with an anglo *J*. Had their accountant fathers not become friends, it's unlikely the two would ever have met.

After college, Koplin and Reeves both took self-directed paths, rejecting the corporate route laid out for them in school. Hoping to use their talents to do good and do well, today they are pioneering a new technology to clear land mines.

"Freshman year, if you had asked me, I would have said 'I want to be an investment banker. I want to be big on Wall Street,'" Reeves told me. Over his first two summers at Wharton, he interned at Texas Pacific Group, a major private equity firm. Despite the perks of the high-end corporate life—he attended the founder's $12 million, Robin Williams–emceed birthday party, which featured a live performance by the Rolling Stones—something was missing. A fat paycheck, he concluded, couldn't make up for a lack of autonomy and creativity on the job. A career in i-banking, he decided, would be "horrendous." Today, most of his college friends are "grunts" in New York investment banks. "I had lunch with one of them on Sunday who was saying, 'They're treating me so bad. I hate this job.' So I'm like, 'So, are you going to take their full-time offer?' And he says, 'Probably.' I just threw up my hands."

Surprisingly, Koplin faced similar pressures to sell out at art school. With the upward redistribution of wealth, the brightest members of the once-comfortable upper middle class—be they quantitative whiz kids like Reeves or creative types like Koplin—have all faced mounting pressure to enlist in the ranks of a new high-end servant class for the superrich. As New York has come to be solely dominated by the wealthy, even art schools like Pratt have embraced the preprofessional orientation formerly found only in business schools. In the past decade, gentrification has swept the Brooklyn neighborhood surrounding Pratt, pushing up the cost of living and increasing the need for students to land corporate jobs upon graduation. While Koplin was drawn to creative projects with public interest applications at the school, "People looked at me as if I was out of my fucking mind." At Pratt, he said, "the goal was to become a corporate stylist." ("He doesn't use 'corporate' with any disdain," Reeves immediately piped up. "We are a corporation after all.") When I asked Koplin what the faculty wanted him to pursue, he replied, "Perfume bottles. We had a class on that. I had an advanced product studio where we designed cell phones."

Over the summers, Koplin worked as a carpenter designing and building high-end furniture, but the work left him unfulfilled. "I was more interested in how do we actually solve a world problem as opposed to how do you offer a product to the world that some people can afford." After graduation he eschewed the traditional route for young designers. "Throwing me into a typical architecture firm would have driven me crazy. It's driving all my friends crazy," he said, echoing Reeves's take on his classmates. "I'd be unhappy. I'd be designing minimalls in the middle of New Jersey and maybe the odd fancy house for a rich person up in Connecticut, neither of which appeals to me."

During school, Koplin started keeping a sketchbook of all the ideas he was discouraged from pursuing at Pratt. In February 2004, while traveling through the former Yugoslavia, he became fascinated by land mine clearance. "I was going through Croatia," Koplin recounted. "I spent a few days there. Basically, everywhere in Philly where you see a homeless person, in Zagreb you see a land mine victim. They're doing the same stuff: begging for change. No legs, no arms, no eyes. Just kind of sitting there. Street beggars with all sorts of wounds and pins. After a few days there, I was on my way off to Italy. I pulled out my sketchbook and scrawled down this idea that kind of hit me for how to get rid of land mines, which was to take a fifty-gallon drum, put a little robotic mower on the back, and push it around by remote control. That was the original idea we started with. And a lot of research later we ended up here." When I visited their offices in the summer of 2005, they showed me a prototype—a small vehicle with a roller on the front made out of steel pipe cut into sections.

A big hurdle for Koplin was getting Reeves, with his business expertise, to join him on the venture. "I was always needling Sam, asking, 'What's the point of just working for A. G. Edwards or whatever the fuck?'" Koplin said.

After winning over Reeves and winning a few small grants and free office space through university engineering and business competitions, the two went to work. A grant from an NGO in Geneva allowed them to travel the world—Afghanistan, Cambodia, the former Yugoslavia—researching land mine clearing methods. The PennVention prize entitled them to five hours of free legal work from a leading intellectual property law firm. They incorporated their business as Humanistic Robotics and patented their invention.

Their device is surprisingly low-tech—and that's the point. The hope is to produce a land mine–clearing vehicle for $50,000 rather than the going rate of $250,000. Since land mines plague some of the poorest countries on Earth, existing technology is often prohibitively expensive, leading people to attempt to clear the mines on their own, an incredibly risky endeavor.

"If you don't have a million dollars to put down for machines," Koplin explained, "you get the locals together, put some body armor on them. You give them a metal detector and a screwdriver. They walk through the fields, get a beep, crouch down, dig up whatever it is—sometimes it's a bottle cap or a bullet or a mine—and they take it somewhere else and set it off." As Reeves added, "Nobody really likes manual demining. Everyone wants to do machine demining—but it's really expensive." The pair dismiss another emerging demining method: using African pouch rats to sniff out mines. In trials, the two said, the rodents identified only about 50 percent of mines and, as Reeves put it, "It's not the kind of business where fifty percent is okay." Using a remote-controlled device would reduce the risk of injury and death common when using either the expensive manned vehicles or the low-tech demining methods, where people and animals scour the ground.

While there is some money in demining—humanitarian NGOs from wealthy countries often purchase demining equipment and donate it to poor countries where it is used—demining is not profitable enough to attract the usual investors. "We're not going to return 5 times, 10 times their investment in three years like the companies they want to invest in," said Reeves of venture capitalists. Instead, they hope to find some investors more interested in improving the world than in improving their net worth. When I spoke to them, they were still looking.

"We're not coming up with a new form of saccharin that's worth forty billion dollars," Koplin said, explaining why venture capitalists don't return their phone calls. Not that their pitch couldn't be improved. As Reeves explained, "Josh always says something that makes potential investors very nervous. He always says, 'We're in business to put ourselves out of business.'"

Too young to have any major assets, such as homes, a conventional bank loan is out of the question. As "those of us who read between the lines" learned at Wharton, Reeves quipped, "bankers only loan you money if you don't need it." The irony isn't lost on him: "This is entrepreneurship at its best"—thinking outside the box, building a better mousetrap—and yet it's been nearly impossible to find funders.

Without a traditional start-up model, the only reason Reeves and Koplin can pursue their dream is that they're young, healthy, and come from upper-middle-class families. Koplin's parents put him through school and Reeves has just a small amount of educational debt; Koplin is living on savings while Reeves works part-time for the Small Business Administration to pay the bills. Without preexisting health conditions, both buy relatively inexpensive health-care coverage on their own. (They also benefit from being male—in some states, including Pennsylvania, insurers are allowed to charge higher rates to young women than to young men, since pregnancy necessitates so many doctor visits.) With a parental safety net, donated work space from the university, and Philadelphia's unusually modest cost of living (multi-million-dollar condos are a recent—and still rare—phenomenon in the City of Brotherly Love), the pair's existence resembles those of Silicon Valley entrepreneurs a generation ago, who came out of school financially unburdened and could afford homes with garages for tinkering. But Koplin and Reeves's fortunate situation is becoming rarer and rarer. Entrepreneurship of this sort, with its humanitarian aims and modest financial rewards, is something few Americans, no matter how driven or talented, could pursue. Once you've "contracted a wife, and a kid, and two dogs, and three cars," it wouldn't be a realistic option, said Reeves, speaking of marriage and family in terms most people reserve for pneumonia. While it is tempting to chuckle at Reeves, a bachelor zealously guarding his independence, the fact of the matter is that for many, the holes in the American safety net, health care chief among them, make entrepreneurship and family life mutually exclusive.

Without a Net

Despite the risks, some will stake all for their entrepreneurial dreams. I met Jeremy in his loft office in the South of Market section of San Francisco, the heart of the dot-com industry. When he had the chance to become a founder of a new Web-based consumer applications start-up, he took the leap, leaving that rarest of Silicon Valley gigs, a contractor position with benefits at Yahoo. Tall and trim and decked out in a daringly fashion-forward suit, Jeremy looked the very picture of a confident, healthy, young tech entrepreneur. But he is not. While at Yahoo, he was diagnosed with prolonged QT syndrome, a congenital heart condition whose symptoms include fainting, cardiac arrest, and sudden death. "When I was diagnosed with this, I was covered really well," he told me. He took "a stress EKG which means you put on all the EKG stuff and then run on a treadmill up to 90 percent of your capability. They have four doctors there for that and it takes about an hour, so you can imagine what the price is."

Leaving Yahoo, he had the option of continuing his health-care coverage by paying roughly $500 a month out-of-pocket through the federally mandated program known as COBRA. When setting up health-care coverage at the start-up took longer than anticipated, Jeremy decided to apply for benefits. He discovered he had missed the deadline. "I thought it was ninety days but it's not. It's like sixty days." With dark humor, he conceded there's not much even the best health-care coverage can do if your symptom is sudden death, but he realizes he's risking bankruptcy should he suffer cardiac arrest and regain consciousness under the defibrillator paddles in the emergency room.

For Jeremy, buying coverage on the open market would be impossible. Even before he'd been diagnosed with his heart condition, he'd had trouble obtaining health insurance during a previous stint of self-employment. "I applied for an independent plan and I was rejected flat out," he recounted. "I originally got rejected because they said that I went to the hospital too much and my weight was wrong. I had been to the emergency room once in my life. It was in Germany because I had cut my foot. It was great. It was twenty-five dollars. It was the best health care I'd ever had. It was really incredible, and the Germans complain about it. And I said I was six foot two and weighed one-seventy which was true. And they said that was wrong. So I changed it. I said I weighed one-eighty-five and they gave me insurance. So I can see that with a heart condition I'd never get independent insurance."

Jeremy's business partner, Lars, is also counting the days until his company gets its first health-care plan. To get group coverage, he explained, "you have to be perceived as a real company, and for that you need incorporation, you need to either show several months of pay stubs or tax filings." He figured his gap in coverage will end up being about three or four months. Until then, he, his wife, and their four-year-old child have no health insurance. (In California, insurance companies can reject individuals, but they are required to offer plans to small businesses, even when they have high-risk employees like Jeremy.)

Like so many in the tech industry, Lars is a libertarian on most issues. "I think the government's role is, in general, to stay the hell out of things," he said, expressing a typical Silicon Valley attitude in a typical Silicon Valley dress-down Wednesday outfit. But he calls health care "a classic case of where the government needs to step in and lead." Even though he was willing to shoulder the risk, he suspects that some who share his entrepreneurial calling won't take the leap: "I think there's a portion of people who because of pressures—their wives don't want their family to have worse insurance—may be somewhat less likely to start a company."

Jeremy realizes that he and Lars, enduring just a few months without insurance as they form their company, don't face the same challenges as many self-employed people who face the prospect indefinitely. Jeremy's sister, who started a landscaping business out of the back of her car and now owns a tree store, went without health insurance for years. She now receives her coverage through her domestic partner's employer.

Every situation is different, but the problem is universal. All Americans, weighing their career dreams against the hand they were dealt health-wise, and cognizant that half of American bankruptcies are the result of health-care bills, must strike their own balance between ambition and foolhardiness.

The Great American Entrepreneurship Mystery

It's a truism that American culture celebrates entrepreneurs. The opinion polls show exactly what you'd expect: Americans are incredibly entrepreneurship-minded. A 2005 survey showed that 28 percent of Americans have considered setting up their own businesses, compared to only 15 percent of Europeans. Yet the employment statistics reveal that Americans are far less likely to actually do it—14.7 percent of the European workforce is self-employed, compared with only 7.3 percent of Americans. American entrepreneurs are clearly being held back from pursuing their dreams.

The difference is evident to the casual observer—stroll around a piazza in Rome and you will pass innumerable independent bakeries and cafes; walk down an avenue in Washington, and you will find Starbucks after Starbucks after Starbucks. In America, sectors of the economy that were once dominated by independent businesses—drugstores, barbershops, even veterinary practices—are being replaced by corporate chains (Walgreens, Supercuts, VCA Animal Hospitals). Our self-employment rate is now at its lowest level in decades.

What explains the paradox? In Europe, working for yourself doesn't affect your health-care coverage. Preexisting conditions, marital status, and number of children are irrelevant. Public spending creates a safety net that lets the ambitious few strike out on their own even if it means having a rough first year or two. In America, the ambitious many are held back. Our "safety net," geared toward the elderly, disabled, and desperately poor, is not even worthy of the name. The metaphor, after all, comes from the piece of circus equipment that lets the trapeze artist attempt the most daring feats.

Yet the American health-care debate is framed as an issue of whether those at the bottom of the labor market—say, Wal-Mart workers—should be given health care out of some charitable impulse. The predicament of the self-employed is completely ignored. America is thwarting the very ambition that has long defined its people.

For George W. Bush, the self-proclaimed champion of entrepreneurs (and veteran failed entrepreneur himself), universal coverage is a nonstarter. In his mind, simply cutting taxes on the rich, by definition, encourages entrepreneurship. But the Bush model of low taxes and low government benefits grudgingly distributed only to those who merit his "compassion," never to the college-educated middle class, stifles entrepreneurship.

This simple fact, understood the world over, is nowhere to be found in the American debate. Take a 2006 feature story on Berlin in the *Financial Times*, the ardently pro-business British equivalent of the *Wall Street Journal*: "With its low [real estate] costs and generous welfare net, Berlin is an entrepreneurs' heaven, where barriers to entry are low and failure rarely entails personal ruin. In the past two years, twenty-seven thousand companies have been created." Amazingly, when Bush pushed through his draconian bankruptcy "reform" law, with its harshest provisions reserved for middle-class debtors, rather than the poorest of the poor, few called him on its disastrous effects on would-be entrepreneurs. In America, now more than ever, small business failure entails personal ruin (unless you happened to be the independently wealthy son of a president, in which case it may well lead to the White House). Restraining would-be entrepreneurs not only runs against the principles conservatives claim this country is all about, but it is bad economic policy. We are shooting the goose that lays the golden eggs. Under the cloak of supporting entrepreneurs, conservative economic policies make would-be entrepreneurs slavishly dependent on their current bosses for their lives, not just their livelihoods.

Like so many of America's social problems, the lack of national health insurance is maintained by our unprecedented degree of corporate power. Surveys demonstrate overwhelming support for universal health insurance. A 2005 poll by the Pew Research Center found that 65 percent of Americans favor providing health insurance for all Americans even if it means raising taxes. Yet no serious proposal for national health insurance has been offered since the insurance companies destroyed the 1993 Clinton administration plan. The health insurance and pharmaceutical companies that have grown rich on America's insanely expensive, inefficient, and ineffective health-care "system" now constitute the leading industry for political donations, starving potential reformers of campaign funds and co-opting them with contributions once they're elected.

Organizing for a "New New Deal"

New York's Freelancers Union isn't waiting for Washington to come to the rescue of the self-employed. It is creating smaller-scale programs to improve its members' lives in the here and now. The group provides health insurance for thirteen thousand independent workers—everyone from actors to yoga instructors—who live in the tristate area. Founder Sara Horowitz takes her lead from an earlier generation of New York City workers, who didn't wait for Roosevelt's election to start improving their lot. "There had been a whole social movement pre–New Deal that really built a movement on self-organization and mutual aid," she told me in the group's Brooklyn office.

A lifelong Brooklynite, Horowitz grew up in the type of intellectual, politically progressive, middle-class family that defined New York before its Reagan-era bifurcation into rich and poor. (The formerly rent-stabilized Brooklyn Heights apartment where Horowitz grew up is now a luxury apartment building.) Horowitz's father and grandfather were both labor leaders. Her grandmother lived in a cooperative housing development on the

Lower East Side built in the late 1920s by the Amalgamated Clothing Workers union for its members—a development aimed at taming the New York real estate market during America's last period of extreme inequality. While many progressives have come to see government programs as the answer to all social problems, Horowitz's upbringing tied her to the idea that democracy only works when people band together to create their own self-run organizations that, she says, embody the "Jeffersonian ideal of decentralization."

Initially a labor organizer, Horowitz had her first run-in with the challenges faced by independent workers soon after finishing law school, when the ostensibly radical labor law firm she was working for reclassified her and her fellow attorneys as independent contractors. "They didn't want to give anybody benefits. There were two of us who were married and our husbands had benefits and one who just went without. I thought it was despicable." Despite her organizing experience, Horowitz didn't see an easy way to remedy the situation, so she quit the job for a master's program at Harvard's Kennedy School of Government in 1994. As a parting gag gift, her coworkers presented her with letterhead for the "Transient Workers' Union." According to the mock letterhead, Horowitz was the union president.

At Harvard, Horowitz concluded that the Transient Workers' Union idea was in the "crazy enough it just might work" category and began sketching out her first plans for what became the Freelancers Union. "Independent contractors weren't really contemplated as a group when the New Deal–era labor laws were written," she explained. In addition to being ineligible for benefits such as health insurance, freelancers lack many of the rights taken for granted by most American workers— antidiscrimination protection and unemployment benefits. "As a freelancer, you're not eligible for unemployment insurance," she said. "That doesn't really make sense, because if you're an employee for six months, you can be eligible for unemployment whereas if you freelance on a gig for six months, you're not." While traditional unionism was based on a large number of people working full-time for a single employer, today, fewer and fewer workers fit this model. A new model of unionism was needed for an economy in which 20 million Americans work as freelancers or independent contractors.

"It's not like employers now need any more or less flexibility than they needed then. They just need it in a different way," Horowitz continued. "In the New Deal, there was an agreement between government, business, and labor. Back then we said it's not fair to foist that all onto workers and we collectively made a system," which, for example, provided unemployment benefits to workers who were laid off during downswings in the business cycle. This outdated system remains in place, Horowitz said, only "because there isn't an organized constituency that's saying this is completely ludicrous."

To make the Freelancers Union more than just a Kennedy School term paper, Horowitz needed start-up funding. But the AFL-CIO—a seemingly natural ally—turned her down. Horowitz then turned to the foundation world, but their grant-makers' compassion seemed to dry up when it came to serving people who were not living in dire poverty. "This group is falling out of the safety net," Horowitz told them, but they were unmoved. In the midst of the repeal of welfare, foundations felt they had to focus on the most vulnerable members of society.

"They thought contingent workers were rich and that was kind of hard to take. It just became this sanctimonious thing where I felt like I was supposed to apologize for caring about people who earn a living and are educated." Remembering the single lawyer at her office who went without health insurance, Horowitz argued that people were affected regardless of their income and education level. "To me a worker is a worker is a worker. I'm not impressed if someone's poor or if they're rich."

Many in the world of Democratic politics dismissed Horowitz on the grounds that "people who earn between $25,000 and $50,000 in New York City earn too much for me to care about." Others were hung up on whether freelancing was a choice or a necessity dictated by the labor market. To Horowitz, that was beside the point—freelancers should be entitled to certain benefits and protections regardless. As the feisty, diminutive Brooklynite put it, "To me, some freelancers are miserable and some are happy, but it doesn't really matter because none of them are eligible for antidiscrimination laws. None of them have health insurance. Let them have a glass of wine and let them talk about whether they're happy or not happy. I really don't care. I just think that we have to be building institutions that make sense."

Fortuitously, the field of social entrepreneurship was budding just as the foundations were telling Horowitz to look elsewhere. The concept was based on funding nonprofits in the same way venture capitalists fund companies—with start-up funds that support the group until it can support itself. It was "a happy coincidence," she said. "I was just looking for money and they were like, 'You have a good idea, here's some money.'" For Horowitz it was perfect; she always intended the Freelancers Union to ultimately become self-sufficient through membership dues.

The trick was figuring out how to organize freelancers. In a normal organizing drive, a labor organizer stands outside the factory gate or office parking lot and talks to workers as they change shifts. But freelancers work all over the place, often from home. The solution, Horowitz realized, would be to provide health insurance. Then the freelancers would come to her.

Five years after its 2001 founding, the union had 38,000 members and was able to expand to issues beyond health insurance. In 2006, the group was working on a legislative agenda to change New York law to make it into a model state for independent workers. That would mean changing antidiscrimination laws so that they cover "workers" rather than "employees" and creating some kind of retirement system for freelancers. More than half of the union's members have no savings at all, despite their middle-class incomes. "It used to be when you had a job that paid $50,000 your employer was paying something into your pension," Horowitz explained. But she worries that taking on the biggest problem facing New York–based freelancers—the cost of housing—may be too difficult. "I've looked into housing, but when you do the math, you have to raise several million dollars and then you've housed twenty families, raising it to a much higher policy level." When the Amalgamated Clothing Workers decided to build housing, they were in a better position, having nearly 200,000 members.

Despite the Freelancers Union's success in securing health insurance for its workers—two-thirds of its members were either uninsured or transiently insured before joining the group— Horowitz believes only a federal commitment to universal coverage will permanently solve the health-care woes of independent workers. The least expensive coverage available through the union—a bare-bones plan with a $10,000 deductible—costs over $1,000 a year for individuals and over $4,000 for families. Horowitz supports a voucher system in the mold of the GI Bill, in which people would receive guaranteed coverage through a mix of public and private health-care providers. Health insurance would no longer be tied to a job. The current system, in which people primarily obtain coverage through their employer or spouse's employer, seems as if it were cunningly crafted to stifle independence. As the Freelancers Union's subway ads proclaim: "It's time for a new New Deal."

Who's Afraid of an Independent Artist?

> The artist should be the freest individual in our society. He should set an agenda for personal liberty and intellectual investigation.
>
> —Bill T. Jones, choreographer

Short of a new New Deal, Freelancers Union members make do with the benefits the union can provide. For Nigel, a thirty-two-year-old photographer, who was uninsured until he joined the union, the group's insurance plan helps, but his main health-care costs remain uncovered. He was recently diagnosed with bipolar disorder (manic depression). Neither his psychiatric sessions nor his $200-a-month prescription drug bill is covered by the health plan.

But Nigel is luckier than most freelancers; he has a safety net should he need one. Born in Great Britain, he moved with his mother to the United States at age four after his father died. Today, Nigel has a green card but remains a British subject. "If I was in England, I would get access to the national health insurance. My plan when I didn't have insurance was that if I got really sick, I would go to Europe. That's still probably the case. I plan on leaving if I ever have children because of the cost of education," he said, with no trace of a British accent.

In college, Nigel decided he wanted to become an art photographer and gained acceptance to a graduate program at Pratt. He has always used commercial photography assignments, mostly advertising and fashion shoots, to pay the bills, but his art income is now almost equal to his commercial income. If that keeps up, he hopes to quit commercial work entirely. "I'm not a religious man," he said, "but God willing."

When he spoke of his corporate gigs, it was easy to see why he was hoping for divine intervention. "With my advertising clients, you have no creative control. They have what they want and you just have to make their vision a reality." Working with fashion magazines is no different: "Fashion editorial is really 'advertorial.' You have to put all the advertisers in the magazine in the shoots, which leaves very little room for up-and-coming designers." While close ties between the business and editorial sides of a publication would be a scandal in a news magazine, Nigel observed, de facto payola is an open secret in the fashion media. "They're completely up front when you're working with them that the advertisers have to be represented in the shoots."

Nigel's art photography is strikingly at odds with his couture shoots, which often celebrate the gloriousness of spending $15,000 on a dress. For a recent project, he shot portraits of the latest heirs to America's great fortunes. Some of the portraits are charming throwbacks to what looks like a lost world. Others are less flattering. His extreme close-ups of overly made-up elderly women border on the grotesque. The purpose of the series, according to Nigel, is to ask the question, "How can we have an aristocracy in a democracy?"

It is the kind of work that makes you understand why the Right pays lip service to self-employment while going to such great lengths to thwart it. Nigel wouldn't be much of a gadfly if he were working full-time for a fashion magazine, without a union card or the safety net provided by his British passport. Making the world safe for plutocracy requires creating a world in which only the independently wealthy can afford to be independently employed.

6

FROM *PARTISAN REVIEW* TO PARTISANS REVUE: INTELLECTUALS IN THE POST-ACADEMIC AGE

> I used to think. Now I just read *The Economist*.
>
> —Larry Ellison, CEO, Oracle

Eviction Notice: The Demise of Bohemia

In 1929, Lionel Abel, a young aspiring intellectual, did what all aspiring intellectuals did in the days before the GREs: he moved to New York City. Abel lived briefly with his extended family before landing his first book deal. Advance in hand, he rented an apartment in Greenwich Village. The book would be a translation of Rimbaud's poetry.

The idea that someone could live in New York City on an advance for a work of translated poetry sounds like a tall tale. Yet this world is not as distant as it seems. As late as the 1960s, cultural critic Ellen Willis could support herself in the East Village for months on the fee from one mainstream magazine feature.

As our once broadly middle-class society has split into rich and poor, city neighborhoods have as well. Historian Russell Jacoby observed in the 1980s, "Economic exigencies reshaped

New York into a city of extremes, a city that could no longer sustain bohemians who were neither rich nor poor." While people mourned the death of the Greenwich Village bohemia for generations—for the old guard, things were never as good as they used to be—the pace of gentrification has accelerated to the point where bohemian communities can no longer take root in major cities like New York. The Greenwich Village bohemia lasted for decades, SoHo for ten years, the East Village for five, Williamsburg for two. The game is over. The unofficial death knell came in 2005 when the *New York Times* redubbed the South Bronx, trendy "SoBro."

The rising cost of living in major cities snuffs out the forms of noncommercial intellectual creativity for which our most cosmopolitan metropolises have long been known. "So many of the people who kept American cities alive and creative through dark decades, when capital abandoned the city, have become victims of capital's recent triumphant return to the city," writes urbanist Marshall Berman. When rents were low, cities were inclusive. People of various income levels could move in; any commercial or retail tenant—upscale or downscale, nonprofit or for-profit—could set up shop. But as rents went up, that diversity was destroyed. More and more, only the rich could move in; only the upscale and for-profit could set up shop. As architectural theorist Kyong Park mused upon leaving New York: "Each generation should be able to build its own city, and I'm not sure that New York can do that [anymore]. I don't think it has unclaimed peripheral or open spaces where the time period and generation can be redefined."

Today, bohemia lives on in style, not substance, as hyper-gentrification has rendered "alternative" neighborhoods no cheaper than the traditional stomping grounds of the business elite. Thus membership in an alternative neighborhood becomes contingent upon a corporate job. In an earlier San Francisco, for example, the corporate climbers occupied Nob Hill while the poets lived in North Beach, but today the corporate climbers live in both. Yet today's unenthusiastic servants of the corporate elite hang on to the neighborhood distinctions. As people sell out, taking jobs that do not reflect their identity, they search for self-definition through what they buy—the most crucial purchase being which city and neighborhood to live in. Where one lives, the only lifestyle choice with any meaning for those who leave work only to sleep, takes on greater and greater importance. Thus a "corporate tool" who works at McKinsey might live on Nob Hill, while an "intellectual" McKinsey consultant would live in North Beach; the fact that North Beach was once beatnik territory psychologically compensates for working hundred-hour weeks for the system Allen Ginsberg derided as "Moloch whose mind is pure machinery." On a free Sunday afternoon the fauxhemian consultant could even slip on a pair of clunky black glasses and wander the aisles of North Beach's City Lights Books, which first published Ginsberg's poem. How cool is that?

An activist (and law school applicant) told me about her corporate lawyer and health-care consultant housemates in the seemingly bohemian Lower Haight neighborhood of San Francisco: "They're both corporate and lefty. The consultant who works in health care believes that the health-care system in the United States is absolutely broken and we have to figure out what a single-payer health plan for all U.S. citizens would look like. And the lawyer works for an insurance firm and he hates it. Hates it. But he's paying off his student loans." Today's "bohemians" may dress like Beat poets, but they're actually health-care consultants.

Yet the mainstream press insists on assuring us that the kids are alright in pieces like the 2005 *New York* magazine cover story on what it calls the "trickle-down effect of ridiculous, ostentatious wealth." The story argues that the colonization of New York by a new class of superrich is really in everyone's interest. We are instructed to "consider, for example, the sommelier at a four-star restaurant who makes about $90,000, edging into six figures when Wall Street bonuses are up. This sommelier, let's say, lives in one of those rapidly upscaling Brooklyn neighborhoods, renting a brownstone floor-through that not so long ago was inhabited by a $30,000-a-year secretary who feasted on Cup-a-Soup three nights a week." The article neatly overlooks the full implications of gentrification by making our displaced Brooklynite a $30,000-a-year secretary with a penchant for ramen rather than a $30,000-a-year poetry editor with a flair for Thai cooking. If apartments are no longer affordable to people making $30,000 a year, both are squeezed out. *New York* fails to mention that Brooklynites, struggling to live a middle-class life in a city where it is no longer possible, are now the most house-poor people in the nation: the borough has a higher percentage of residents spending more than 30 percent of their income on mortgage payments than any county in America. As urbanist Rebecca Solnit notes in her book on the subject, even the word *gentrification* has become inadequate to describe what has befallen places like New York and her beloved San Francisco. Gentrification connotes the transformation of a single neighborhood, not the transformation of an entire city or region.

Yet the Sunday real estate section of the *New York Times*

crows that "Yes [Virginia], There Are Apartments Out There for $1000," pointing to one-bedroom offerings in Queens and the Bronx. But to rent a $1,000-a-month apartment, as any financial planner will tell you, you should have an income in excess of $48,000. Needless to say, spending 25 percent of your income on rent is one of those rules that was made to be broken, but there's only so low you can go. The catch-22 for today's aspiring intellectuals is that you can have the time to do creative work or the money that affords a place to do it, but not both. The only way to make $1,000 monthly rent payments is to work a day job (translating Rimbaud won't cut it); the only way to spend less than $1,000 is to have roommates. The prerequisite for the writing life, what Virginia Woolf famously named "a room of one's own," is now hopelessly out of reach for young writers hoping to tackle any subject more substantive than how Opal Mehta got a life.

Rather than sign a New York lease, today's aspiring intellectuals sign up for the GREs.

God and Mammon at Yale

The squeezing out of intellectual life from urban bohemias would not be as tragic if not for the transformations the academy has undergone in recent years. As early as the 1950s, intellectuals began jumping from the leaky ship of bohemia for comfortable berths in the university. Today, those berths no longer exist.

The postwar higher-education boom, coupled with the opening up of academic posts to radicals, Jews, and women, created new opportunities for aspiring intellectuals. The number of college professors in the United States increased tenfold from 1920 to 1970. To the surprise of many, the working-class students admitted to college on the GI Bill flocked to liberal arts courses, not preprofessional majors. Buoyed by an American economy of broadly shared prosperity, even for those of modest backgrounds, college was a place to explore ideas. To aid in this exploration, many writers who had begun their careers publishing in intellectual journals like *Partisan Review* and *Dissent,* and even popular magazines like *Fortune,* moved into academic posts. In a move that would be unthinkable in the contemporary credential-obsessed academy, Daniel Bell was awarded a PhD by Harvard University for his 1962 book, *The End of Ideology,* a well-regarded anthology of previously published magazine articles. It was hardly a PhD thesis. Even Irving Howe, who famously wrote, "No one who has a live sense of what the literary life has been and might still be . . . can accept the notion that the academy is the natural home of the intellect," took a job at Brandeis when the offer came.

As the country moved to the right in the 1980s, jobs in the nonprofit sector dried up, a casualty of a conservative push to defund the Left. As a result, universities became safe havens for left-leaning youth, those whom Yale professor David Bromwich described as "people who in a better time would be doing political work." The trend was so widespread that the Right began to mock the academy as the province of "tenured radicals." Contrary to the hopes of Bromwich's subjects, when it comes to politics, you can run but you can't hide. Soon, conservative economic forces began to shake the ivory tower.

Unlike their grandparents, who could afford to delve into the plays of Shakespeare and the dialogues of Plato, the generation that came of age in a nation with a widening gap between rich and poor came to regard college, by necessity, as the beginning of the "real world" rather than a respite from it. According to UCLA's annual survey of American freshmen, the number of college freshmen who view "being very well off financially" as "very important" has risen steadily since the 1970s. It's not that today's freshmen are congenitally more materialistic than freshmen in 1970, but that being very well off has actually become much more important as the price of the American Dream has risen. Fittingly, the year of Reagan's election, 1980, was the first time the life goal of being very well off polled higher than "developing a meaningful philosophy of life."

In recent years, the prevailing notion that all the world's a rat race and all the men and women merely rats has leached into childhood itself. It's not just Kaplan Test Prep anymore—though the company's revenues have increased more than fifteenfold in the past decade. Today's parents nurture their toddlers' test-taking skills with toys like the Elmo Picture Quiz.

The narrowing of students' horizons is so blatantly apparent that even some of the conservative movement's cheerleaders have grown concerned. In an *Atlantic* cover story on the current crop of Princetonians, David Brooks called the undergraduates he found the "Future Workaholics of America." Scheduled to the hilt, the young men he interviewed said they found time to shave every day, but had no time to devote to more passionate pursuits: arguing politics, discussing literature, staging a protest, even having a serious romantic relationship. The undergrads call themselves "tools"; their professors call them "professional students." "Nowhere did I find anybody who seriously considered living any other way," Brooks reported.

Brooks's visit to Princeton eerily echoes Betty Friedan's 1959 visit to her alma mater, Smith College, where she perceived a similar absence of intellectual ferment. "Nobody, except a few faculty members, sat around talking in the coffee dives or the corner drugstore," she wrote in *The Feminine Mystique,* published in 1964. "We used to sit for hours arguing what-is-truth, art-for-art's-sake, religion, sex, war and peace, Freud and Marx, and all the things that were wrong with the world." At Smith in the late '50s, the culprit was a raft of reactionary social norms; for today's youth, reactionary economic policies are to blame. When the merit-based admissions policies of the 1960s are combined with the winner-take-all income stratification of the 1980s, students are turned into "tools"—crafted at university for use by corporate America after graduation.

As student priorities have changed, so have their majors. While the number of bachelor's degrees granted increased 50 percent between 1970 and 2002, the number of English majors fell in absolute terms. Today, the top field is business, pursued by 22 percent of undergraduates, compared with 13 percent in 1970. In the late 1960s, most students earned arts and sciences degrees; today a hefty majority of undergrads pursue preprofessional majors like marketing and accounting.

But it's not just the students who have been bowled over by conservative economic forces. College administrators have been, too. Surrendering the university's age-old stance as an independent sphere untouched by the pressures of the market, administrators have abandoned the notion that universities differ from private businesses (except when it comes to their beloved tax exemptions). Students are merely customers and professors are merely workers—and both are treated accordingly.

If demand for liberal arts courses has decreased, the thinking goes, so should the supply of people who teach them. Thus, as

Harvard Magazine observed, the disciplines that "make money, study money, or attract money" are flourishing, while those that do not are floundering.

Consider philosophy, once exalted as the cornerstone of all intellectual inquiry; it is now on its knees. A 2001 graduate of the top-ranked University of Pittsburgh philosophy doctoral program told me she was the only person in her class still teaching philosophy. Everyone else took one look at their job prospects and headed to law school. And Pitt's is arguably the top department in the country. The situation is even more dire at less elite graduate programs.

If professors are just workers, then why not cut back on their wages, benefits, and job security just as employers in the private sector have done since the Reagan Revolution? More and more, universities rely on part-time, benefits-free instructors. Most are paid by the course, usually less than $3,000 a pop. In 1970, a mere 22 percent of college faculty were part-timers; today, nearly half are. Tenured faculty has dropped from 37 percent in 1975 to 24 percent and tenure-track positions have shrunk from 20 percent to 11 percent of the total. The Modern Language Association estimated that today's entering English PhD students have only a 25 percent chance of coming out with a tenure-track job. Professors routinely discourage their most promising students from pursuing graduate degrees. It is the only responsible thing to do.

But with the bohemian option off the table, many aspiring intellectuals still press their luck with the academic lottery, even though the odds of winning keep getting worse. Thus administrators are able to keep graduate programs large and use the graduate students as low-wage teachers and graders. On campus after campus, in an attempt to turn entry-level college teaching into a real job, graduate students have tried to form unions. Organizing efforts have often won bread-and-butter results. After students at New York University unionized, stipends jumped from $10,000 to $18,000 a year. But in 2004, Bush appointees at the National Labor Relations Board came to the aid of NYU administrators and revoked teaching assistants' right to organize, accepting the contention that graduate students are apprentices, not workers. Considering the academic labor market, one is tempted to ask, apprentices for what? Law school?

Even those lucky few who end up finding full-time employment within the academy are more and more likely to end up as de facto employees of corporate America. To defang their critics, corporations have adopted a kill-them-with-kindness strategy, endowing institutes at prestigious universities with the expectation that they will turn out favorable research. Most infamously, the Enron-funded Harvard Electricity Policy Group issued thirty-one reports supporting energy deregulation in California. HEPG research director William Hogan explicitly advised the state to adopt the "Enron model"—a policy with disastrous consequences for everyone save Enron's executives. At Stanford, ExxonMobil, the leading global warming skeptic among the Fortune 500, and other benefactors of the Global Climate and Energy Project actually decide which academic projects to fund.

With corporate funding playing an ever-larger role, only those fields that are of use to corporate America can thrive. The university was once a place where all disciplines were equally valuable, where the metaphors of Molière or the minor prophets were considered as worthy of study as the investment strategies of Deutsche Bank or Morgan Stanley. Those days are over. The salary gaps that have developed in the American economy generally have been imported into the academy, surely having the same routing effect seen in the economy at large. Not only are there more tenure-track jobs for associate business professors than for associate English professors, but they pay more than twice as much. Associate law professors earn nearly 70 percent more than the English professors, while economics profs enjoy a bonus of 50 percent. At the top of the new academic order are superstar professors who rarely teach, never grade, and earn as much as half a million a year, as well as university presidents who have begun to see CEO-style inflation in their near-seven-figure pay.

The most reactionary fantasies of Adam Smith and William F. Buckley are finally coming to pass. It was Smith who first viewed the academy as a business with students as customers and professors as employees. As such, Smith wrote, a professor's pay should be linked to the number of students who sign up for his courses. According to a science professor at Pennsylvania State University, administrators have begun allocating departmental funding on the basis of student enrollment in each department's introductory courses, pitting the proverbial "Rocks for Jocks" against "Physics for Poets." To keep their enrollment up, this professor's department was considering cutting out even the most basic math since it made students worry that, God forbid, they might actually learn something. Inflating grades was another option. If the student is a customer, even on multiple-choice tests, apparently, the customer is always right.

William F. Buckley took a more ideological stance than Adam Smith in his bomb-throwing first book, *God and Man at Yale: The Superstitions of "Academic Freedom."* Professors who did not toe the trustees' pro-corporate line should be fired and

told to look for work at colleges "interested in propagating socialism." As for Yale's left-wing economics professor John Smith,
he should be barred from teaching because "he is inculcating
values that the governing board at Yale considers to be against
the public welfare."

Although tenure was first created to protect professors who
took on the powers that be, in the increasingly tenure-free academic workplace such biting criticism is destined to become a
thing of the past. As Yeshiva University professor Ellen
Schrecker put it, the main casualty of the new corporate orientation is the liberal arts, "the area that produces most critical
thought on key social issues." Indeed, in the late 1990s, in order
to better serve the needs of northern Virginia's high-tech companies, the president of George Mason University barred undergraduates from majoring in French, German, or classics. The
move echoed a successful bid in the early 1990s at Washington
University in St. Louis and an unsuccessful one at Yale to eliminate the sociology departments. So much for conservatives as
the defenders of the "Great Books." Jennifer Washburn observed in her 2005 book *University, Inc.: The Corporate Corruption of American Higher Education* that earlier debates between
campus liberals and conservatives have been rendered quaint by
"the more pressing issue [of] whether undergraduates are taught
any meaningful literature or history at all."

In 1918, in the days before tenure or academic freedom had
been established, the radical Norwegian-American economist
Thorstein Veblen subtitled *The Higher Learning in America,* his
book on the academy, "A Memorandum on the Conduct of Universities by Businessmen." He had initially toyed with an alternate subtitle, "A Study in Total Depravity," but propriety won
out. Were he alive today, he would surely regret his decision.

At the Wake

In September 2005, as the new school year was beginning, I returned to my alma mater to attend a recruiting session for graduate students hosted by McKinsey & Company, the management consulting giant. As the academic job market has collapsed, banking and consulting firms have stepped up to recruit the highly credentialed surplus labor. The presentation and wine-and-cheese reception was held at the Quinnipiack Club, just off the scraggly New Haven Green. With its red brick facade, white-washed interior, and requisite oil paintings of landscapes and maritime scenes, it remains a throwback to a time of understated Yankee elegance.

McKinsey, though the launching pad for today's multicultural class of global movers and shakers, shares some of the Quinnipiack Club's Yankee sensibility. The recruiters subscribe to the rule made famous by Michael Lewis in *Liar's Poker*: they never mention money—or the hopeless academic job market that packs the hall.

Keith Lostaglio, a genuinely charming middle-aged consultant who dropped out of a Yale PhD program long ago, addressed the crowd in a jacket and open collar. His main purpose seemed to be to reassure the audience that just because they don't know anything about business, doesn't mean they can't work at the world's leading management consulting firm.

"You folks have the ability to solve complex problems," he flattered the crowd, assuring them that after McKinsey's three-week "mini-MBA" training program they would be able to handle the most complex problems corporate America could throw at them. Lostaglio was there to allay the fears that pervaded the room—that they had spent years preparing for jobs that didn't exist. Sure, it was true that no one was going to pay them to study Dante, but that didn't mean McKinsey wouldn't pay them more than they'd ever make studying Dante to do something 180 degrees removed from what they'd set out to do.

Lostaglio's backup crew gave examples of their work at the firm—analyzing why an IT company's revenues are stagnant; figuring out how to accelerate the clinical trials for a new drug— but the pitch for McKinsey remained strangely amorphous. "We do lots and lots of PowerPoint charts," said Michael Yoo, an MIT PhD turned McKinsey consultant. Yoo, like the others, had "the McKinsey look"—what you'd get if you put a gawky grad student through a *Queer Eye for the Straight Guy* makeover.

"We work reasonably hard," Yoo said. "My day, all told, is about an eleven-hour day. Now, if you're like me, that's considerably less time than I spent working in the lab on a given day." The implication was that people work hard at McKinsey, but no harder than graduate school students. That a graduate school project was something a person purposefully selected to devote a number of years to while McKinsey assignments were dictated by the random needs of the market was never addressed. Helen Merianos, a Philadelphia-based consultant who earned her Yale doctorate in 2004, talked through her day on a recent pharmaceutical industry assignment that brought her to Seattle. The workday started at 7 A.M.—"I'm an early riser," she explained— and ended at 8 P.M. when she "ate room service at my hotel." She tried to deliver the line with a modicum of upbeat gusto, which just made her existence sound all the more pitiable.

Lostaglio's pitch was more cryptic. "Why would you come to McKinsey?" he asked rhetorically in front of his latest PowerPoint slide. "Essentially you would come to grow faster and achieve more," he said, adding that McKinsey is "probably the best career accelerator." The key, he told the crowd, is that you will "develop your 'personal capital'"—apologizing a moment later for "fitting right into the urban legend that [McKinsey consultants] use jargon all the time." But the problem with the phrase was not that it was abstruse but that it was perverse. "Personal capital" bespeaks a degraded notion of what a human being is, tantamount to calling Yosemite National Park "lumber." But the phrase, so eerily reminiscent of Bob Dylan's sneering description of people who do what they do just "to be nothing more than something they invest in," was particularly dispiriting when addressed to a group of PhD candidates, not MBAs. These were people who had rebelled against the prevailing notion that they should just maximize their earning potential, seeking other goals, only to end up silently nodding at McKinsey PowerPoint slides.

While there are no sit-ins to protest corporate recruiting on campus as there were during the Vietnam War when weapons manufacturers came calling, there are strains of anticorporate feeling. On campus, the name McKinsey has become synonymous with selling out. At my commencement in 2000, the gag graduation song, set to the tune of "American Pie," included the verse:

> And on Wall Street i-bankers lurk,
> To steal our souls, put us to work.
> We'll sell our youthful whimsy.
> We'll all work for McKinsey.

During the recruiting session, a conspicuously under-dressed student waited until the question-and-answer session to ask why, if McKinsey was such a great company to work for, their turnover was so high. The consultants replied that the opportunities opened up by a job with the company were just so good they couldn't keep people. The gadfly replied that the company's working conditions sounded like something out of North Korea.

Hyperbole? Yes. But work-life balance at McKinsey (or the lack thereof) is a serious problem for the company and makes recruiting and retaining women of childbearing age almost impossible. In an era when medical and law school student bodies are now half female, McKinsey struggles to attract even a token female presence despite recruiting beyond the still-male-dominated business schools. In North America, only 22 percent of McKinsey consultants are women. Shockingly, the minimum recruiting goal is just 30 percent. Yet it is not only women for whom the incessant working hours take a toll. Yoo advertised that he leaves the office each evening between 6:00 and 8:30 to see his kids—before getting back to work.

As one male PhD turned McKinsey consultant told me, "There are almost no fifty-year-old McKinsey partners. They retire, they're done. They've worked really hard, they have enough money in the bank, and they're like, 'I don't want to do this anymore.'" This consultant didn't want to do it anymore after only two years. It's a far cry from the academy, where professors love their jobs so much, many work until the day they die, despite earning salaries below those of their twenty-something students who leave academe for consulting.

Though overt comparisons to the academy are avoided, the McKinsey pitch is that the work is meaningful, too. McKinsey's recruiting brochure opens with the line, "Do you want to make a difference?" as if it were the Peace Corps. Throughout Lostaglio's presentation, he kept casually mentioning McKinsey's work for nonprofits like the Bill and Melinda Gates Foundation as well as the "pro bono, like the work we did for the New York Fire Department in the fall of 2001." But only 5 percent of McKinsey's work is for nonprofits and governments. The remaining 95 percent is to help companies boost profits. But enriching the already rich is not something that captures the imaginations of the bright young people they need to recruit.

Exactly how you make a difference is something you only find out once you've been hired; the work McKinsey does for corporate America is generally kept confidential. A leaked internal memo published by the *New York Times* in 2005 gives a taste. In it, Wal-Mart's executive vice president for benefits, joined by a team of McKinsey consultants, devised ways to cut back the world's largest retailer's health-care and fringe benefits without adding to the public backlash against the company's abominable labor practices. The solution concocted to this complex problem: attract lower-cost, healthier employees. The report called for "all jobs to include some physical activity (e.g. all cashiers do some cart-gathering)" and suggested capping employee life insurance payments at $12,000 rather than the current level of a year's salary (Wal-Mart employees earn on average about $17,500 a year). Life insurance, the report said, was "a high-satisfaction, low-importance benefit, which suggests an opportunity to trim the offering without substantial impact on associate satisfaction." After all, they'll probably only notice the benefit cut once they're dead! You have to suspect it was one of McKinsey's guilt-ridden Ivy League liberals who leaked the memo.

Despite having an audience made up exclusively of graduate

students, Lostaglio never mentioned the work consulting firms do for universities. These firms played a significant role in bringing the New Economy Kool-Aid into university presidents' offices. A 1998 report by consulting firm Coopers and Lybrand (now PricewaterhouseCoopers) suggested universities save money by moving more university courses to the Internet. The report noted two areas of cost savings: "The first is the need for bricks and mortar; traditional campuses are not necessary. The second is full-time faculty. [Online] learning involves only a small number of professors, but has the potential to reach a huge market of students." As the students in the audience had by now surely realized, at the funeral for the academic life, it's better to be the gravedigger than the deceased.

Partisans Revue: The Rise
of the Right-Wing Think Tanks

While college teaching has been reduced to a part-time gig, in one area of the intellectual job market positions have been growing in recent years: think tanks. Centrist establishment foundations like the Brookings Institution and the Council on Foreign Relations have been around for nearly a century, but the boom in right-wing philanthropy since the 1970s has transformed the intellectual landscape. Conservative foundations now outspend liberal ones by a factor of more than ten to one. Today the conservative Heritage Foundation has a larger budget than Brookings and employs scores of policy wonks at salaries that often dwarf what comparable thinkers would earn in university sociology or political science departments. Unlike earlier think tanks,

Heritage, the American Enterprise Institute, and the Competitive Enterprise Institute make no pretense of the disinterested search for truth that used to mark intellectual life. They do not offer tenure. Outlandish statements are encouraged—especially to journalists—because they serve to shift the debate by transforming clear-cut issues into "he said–she said" controversies. As Heritage president Edwin Feulner divulged in 1995, "We're not here to be some kind of PhD committee giving equal time. Our role is to provide conservative public policymakers with arguments to bolster our side. . . . We don't just stress credibility. We stress timeliness. We stress an efficient, effective delivery system. Production is one side; marketing is equally important."

Even intellectually honest conservatives admit something has gone wrong. Fareed Zakaria laments that think-tank researchers are "chosen for their views, not their expertise. . . . They understand that they were not hired by these think tanks to be free-thinking intellectuals." And Zakaria is no liberal. This is a man who, doing his best Dark Lord of the Sith impersonation, argued in *The New Yorker* that America must "embrace [its] imperial destiny."

Dispensing with the academic practice of peer review, right-wing think tanks occasionally bypass even journalistic filters, beaming their misinformation directly down upon the public. In 1997, the Competitive Enterprise Institute, funded by conservative philanthropists and ExxonMobil, ran radio ads claiming "thousands of scientists agree there's no solid evidence of a global warming problem"—a statement that is simply not true. A 2004 review of the 928 scientific papers published on the subject between 1993 and 2003 found that all concluded global warming was occurring. As the executive editor-in-chief of the leading journal *Science* wrote in an editorial, "Consensus as strong as the one that has developed around this topic is rare in science."

The think tanks take a similar tack in thwarting broadly popular reforms. With polls showing overwhelming support for universal health insurance, millions of dollars are pouring into conservative think tanks working against reform. Defending the indefensible is an expensive proposition, but it seems money is no object. For self-interested corporations, this isn't charity, it's an investment (regardless of what the IRS thinks). In addition to the usual suspects—AEI, Cato, and Heritage—the Discovery Institute, the Seattle-based think tank best known for championing the teaching of "intelligent design" in public school science classes, has even jumped into the debate. Apparently, no one has told them that it's intellectually inconsistent to reject Darwinism while embracing Social Darwinism.

The Left has belatedly tried to respond to the rise of the right-wing think tanks, most recently with the founding of the Center for American Progress in 2003, but it is outgunned. Left-of-center think tanks can find themselves dependent on corporate funders for largesse, limiting their ability to take on the powers that be. The leading labor-funded think tank, the Economic Policy Institute, is no match for Heritage and company. EPI's budget is smaller and politicians are wary of adopting its positions, whatever their merits, since corporations outspend labor in political donations more than fifteen to one.

While conservatives fret that American college campuses remain bastions of the left, the financial advantages of the right have rendered this fact virtually irrelevant. The Left may be winning the war of ideas among budding intellectuals, but when it becomes time to give out the megaphones, the right-wingers regain the upper hand. For those who don't think the right thoughts—pun very much intended—the life of the mind is nearly impossible to sustain.

7

SAVE YOURSELF:
ACTIVISM IN THE CITY OF ST. FRANCIS

High Mass

San Francisco may be the only place in America where a grown man can spend an evening riding a purple 1970s-era one-speed bicycle and not receive a single skeptical glance. I had obtained the Raleigh with coaster brakes, the kind usually reserved for children's bikes, through the generosity of a friend of a friend of a friend in order to take part in the January 2006 Critical Mass ride, a monthly bike ride cum protest through the city's streets.

Around 5:30 P.M., cyclists began massing in the Ferry Building plaza at the base of Market Street for the 6 P.M. start. I was immediately welcomed by a middle-aged white man with a gigantic Jamaican-style joint. "It's almost Bob Marley's birthday," he told me by way of explanation.

At 6:00 California time (6:15 PST), the ride began. Cyclists rang their bells as the mass descended down Market Street, closing it off to vehicular traffic. The San Francisco Critical

Mass always begins on Market Street and then veers off wherever the lead cyclist decides, spontaneously taking a new route each month. The atmosphere was carnival-like, with one man providing music through a car battery–powered sound system, though there were also somber moments, as when the ride briefly became something akin to a funeral procession for Sarah Tucker, a twenty-six-year-old cyclist who had been killed two weeks earlier by a Honda SUV in a hit-and-run.

A number of bikes bore printed yellow signs reading BICYCLING—A QUIET STATEMENT AGAINST OIL WARS. When Critical Mass started in 1992, this may have been a radical claim. The day I rode, energy independence had been the crux of Thomas Friedman's *New York Times* column—as good a barometer as any of an idea gone mainstream. "We are in a war with a violent strain of Middle East Islam that is indirectly financed by our consumption of oil," Friedman wrote.

Today, Critical Mass itself is an idea gone mainstream. Rides have taken place on every continent save Antarctica. The protests have dramatized the number of cyclists in cities, a presence often overlooked as they solitarily whir by in traffic, and have helped push through reforms like adding bike lanes to major streets and letting cyclists bring their bikes on mass transit systems.

While the ride prides itself on being leaderless, the initial idea for it had to come from someone. Success has many fathers and one of them is Chris Carlsson, a forty-eight-year-old veteran activist who lives and works in the Mission District. Carlsson, with close-cropped gray hair, in jeans and a black sweater, looks like the mild-mannered father he is. Through a fluke low rent, Carlsson still enjoys the lifestyle of genteel poverty the Bay Area once doled out so generously—a palm tree out the window in the backyard and low-cost, high-quality produce and wine on the kitchen table.

In 1978, Carlsson moved to the Haight-Ashbury section of the city, paying $125 a month to share a two-bedroom with a roommate. Adjusted for inflation, that would be just $375 today. As Carlsson explained, it might as well have been another world. "Today, if you came here you'd look on Craigslist for a room in somebody's apartment and you'd be lucky to get something for $750," he estimated. "And you better make enough money to pay $750 a month plus food and every other thing you need, utilities. And you probably have to pay for your own health insurance. . . . The pressure on your cost of housing translates into tremendous pressure on what you can do with your time, because you have to make so much more money just to pay for housing just to be here."

Back then, Carlsson made more money than he needed for basic living expenses with a job as an environmental canvasser for Citizens for a Better Environment. Soon he established a typesetting business (now a desktop publishing business) to pay the bills so he could spend time on his activist and intellectual pursuits.

His first major indie creation was *Processed World,* a not-for-profit 'zine launched in 1981 as "the magazine with a bad attitude." Its purpose: to explore the "bifurcation of having to make some living doing some stupid-ass job, where at least they'll pay you, and then being a real human being that's engaging the world with your creative talents—whether you're a philosopher or a historian or an artist or a dancer or a photographer" in your spare time. Each issue of *Processed World* was distributed nationally through independent bookstores and in San Francisco's financial district, so-called Wall Street West, by Carlsson and

his costumed partners in crime (they would dress up as investment bankers and bow in unison at the stock ticker in front of
the Charles Schwab building). The downtown sales festivals
were where the magazine found most of its writers—alienated
number crunchers and memo drafters by day, social critics by
night.

"The most common response we would get is 'Oh my god,
I'm not insane. Thank you. I thought I was the only one who felt
this way,'" Carlsson recounted. "Most of the workforce downtown are people like us; they have to do whatever just to pay the
rent. What can you do for a living if you have a liberal arts education? You work for a corporation. You don't want to. You think
it's stupid while you're there. You're usually a lot smarter than
the people you're working for. But that's how you can get money
because you can't get money doing the interesting work you
want to do."

Subscribing to the cut-off-your-nose-to-spite-your-face strain
of radicalism, Carlsson dismisses any reforms to help people
balance work and life or limit corporate power—even union organizing or the expansion of free speech rights on the job—as
useless palliatives. "There's something fundamentally perverse
about buying and selling human time. We're selling our labor to
some agenda we don't have a say over," he railed. "There's no
democracy around work. You can't speak your mind; you don't
have any say over how it's done or why it's done or how it's
arranged or the ecological consequences." Better to figure out
how to order human society without wage labor than try to re-
strain the worst aspects of the current order.

Regardless of his ultimate goals, Carlsson's second project,
Critical Mass, has yielded reforms most people concerned about

the environment would hail even if Carlsson himself won't. Since it's an event that bills itself as leaderless, Carlsson only claims to be among a group of daily bicycle commuters and bike messengers that came up with the idea for Critical Mass, not the founding father. In August 1992, Carlsson went to a meeting of the Bike Coalition, a reform group working to make San Francisco more bicycle friendly, and proposed that all the downtown commuters ride home together once a month. "Everybody was dealing with a sense of isolation and danger that was imposed by how stupidly our streets are engineered and the cultural assumptions that go with that." Each cyclist had independently rejected the American car culture and its requisite paradox: "I hate driving but I need a car to get to work. And I hate my job, but I have to make car payments." By pooling these critics, who daily risked life and limb and endured the scorn of "normal" Americans, Carlsson created what he termed a critical mass.

The first ride attracted fifty riders. "We were shocked at how fun it was," Carlsson remembered. "Fifty bikes will fill up the road. That was the idea, to fill the street with bikes and displace cars. Little did we know how big it would become. We just figured, if we could get to a couple hundred it would be incredible." By January 1993, one hundred people showed up for the ride; by October of that year, one thousand. Only months after the first San Francisco ride, Carlsson heard of a Critical Mass in Poznan, Poland. When you create something captivating in a global city, it can become a global phenomenon.

For Carlsson, the ultimate goal of Critical Mass was to get people to question the wage labor system. As he put it, "Transportation is a means to an end. The question is, why are we in such a hurry? Our very presence is a protest against the stupidity of life. But you don't really need to emphasize that. It's much more fun and tricky and subversive to emphasize the pleasure side of it." While contemporary American urban planning only lets people congregate to buy things, be they sports tickets or consumer goods at the mall, Critical Mass offered a "rolling party in the streets" with no admission fee or gasoline required—no need to sell your labor to participate (especially if you have a friend of a friend of a friend with a purple Raleigh to lend you).

Compared with advertising, which promises pleasure through consumption, Carlsson explained, a Critical Mass ride produces pleasure through community. "There's clearly a hedonistic consumerist pleasure that drives marketing for almost every product, usually sex-related," he said. "We're a miserable society full of alienated, frustrated, isolated, lonely people. And so promising that stuff gets you to go out and buy something hoping it will solve that whole big empty space in your life. And guess what, that purchase didn't quite get there. Guess I'll have to find another purchase . . . to bring me that sense of community and that sense of love and contentment I just can't quite ever get to and I'm always rushing around trying to get there and I never get there. Meanwhile I'm spending an awful lot of my life doing things I don't give a shit about, but it gives me the money I need to go on with this endless pursuit of buying things. So there's this hopeless rat wheel that people are stuck on and pleasure is the driving motivation. But if you can actually create a space of real pleasure, real conviviality, where you connect with other human beings, you don't have to give them any money, you don't have to buy anything to be there, you just need to show up on your bicycle and be open-minded and openhearted and have a conversation and you feel great. It creates this amazing euphoria. I had no idea it would do that as much as it has."

Despite its failure to bring down the wage labor system, even Carlsson concedes, "It far exceeded my expectations."

501(c)(3) Nation

It seems reasonably safe to assume Critical Mass would never have come out of a nonprofit organization. Its brand of creativity springs from late nights at a dive bar or parties honoring Bob Marley's birthday, not ten o'clock meetings in a downtown conference room. How could anyone convince a board of funders to sign off on an unpermitted roving urban carnival, even if it might lead to real-world reforms? With the leaderless Critical Mass, there is no one to sue. With a nonprofit organization (a 501(c)(3) in IRS-speak), there is. But for today's activists, nonprofits are how activism has to be structured. There's simply no other way with health-care coverage more precarious than ever and Bay Area rents at a new post–dot-com normal. (As older activists point out, it's really the new new normal—the 1980s boom also left rents markedly higher post-bust than they were pre-boom.)

Mike Hudema tackles many of the same issues addressed by the ad hoc Critical Mass. A director of the Independence From Oil campaign at Global Exchange, a San Francisco–based nonprofit that works on a slew of social justice causes, Hudema walks to work and bikes everywhere else. He's even ridden with Critical Mass. But his activism, aimed at greening Ford, the least fuel-efficient among the Big Three automakers, is much more buttoned-down than the monthly bike protest. "Part of it is trying to change individual people's choices in terms of trying to get them to cycle more and trying to end our car culture," Hudema said in a conference room cum bike-storage area in Global Exchange's loftlike office. But most of the Independence From Oil campaign focuses on the nuts and bolts of getting Ford to produce more fuel-efficient cars. (Ford's current vehicles, Hudema noted, get worse gas mileage than the company's Model T did a century ago.) Hudema's Jumpstart Ford project relies on mundane tactics—writing letters to Ford's CEO and lobbying city and state governments to use fleets of fuel-efficient vehicles. The wackiest thing they've done to date is unfurl a huge banner—"Ford: Holding America Hostage to Oil" with a gas nozzle held up to Lady Liberty's head—at the Los Angeles Auto Show. "The theory behind a corporate campaign is to pick whoever the worst culprit is in the industry, target them, try and force them to come to a demand set and once they do, use their example to pressure the rest of the industry to do the same thing," Hudema said, sounding vaguely corporate himself.

Working on these issues in today's San Francisco means living with roommates and only dreaming of starting a family. Still, Hudema has it better than many; his educational debt is manageable because he grew up in Canada. An attorney—the only one at Global Exchange—his Canadian law school tuition came to just over $4,000 a year. Even in-state tuition at UC Berkeley's law school runs nearly $25,000 a year.

One of Hudema's Ivy League–educated colleagues at Global Exchange, Meredith Dearborn, is inspired by earlier, more free-form models of activism. The blond, blue-eyed Bay Arean breathlessly recounted the history of the Black Panthers from the 1960s and '70s. "If you look at the Black Panthers over in

Oakland, they were just like, 'Hmm, our kids are hungry. That's why they're doing badly in school, because they're starving. So let's have a free breakfast for kids program.' And the people of Oakland, through just a little bit of 'Hey, don't you want to do this one morning a week?'—they started feeding their kids." This, Dearborn noted, led to political organizing. Why, after all, in the richest nation in the world, were so many kids going to school hungry?

In Dearborn's view, the role of a grassroots organizer is to ask, "If you had a million dollars, what would you do right now?" and then figure out how to do that within the community—without the million dollars. But the role of a 501(c)(3) activist is different: win a grant for that million dollars, in turn often forfeiting control of the project to the funders, usually corporate entities with little interest in fundamental social change. While Global Exchange doesn't take corporate money and works hard not to kowtow to funders—it gives up potential Ford Foundation grants to run the Jumpstart Ford campaign—all nonprofits face a constant balancing act, deciding when to shake their cups and when to shake their fists. "When you're that dependent on outside sources of funding, you're always going to be a little bit beholden to people that occasionally you're not comfortable being beholden to," Dearborn said.

Valerie Orth of Global Exchange's Sweatshop-Free campaign put it bluntly: "The more radical you get, the less funding you're going to get." But the greater the concentration of wealth becomes, the more funding is needed to run a nonprofit in a major city like San Francisco. The more radical solutions become justified by the economic realities, the less likely they are to be proposed. One founder of a progressive nonprofit told me that liberals have to tread lightly in fighting inequality because of, well, inequality. With so much in the hands of so few, he explained, if you piss off a Bill Gates or a Warren Buffett and they start cutting their checks to the Heritage Foundation, the fight will be over for good.

Even with a relatively robust budget, the life of the 501(c)(3) activists at Global Exchange is hardly lavish. The nonprofit's employees all make between $24,000 and $50,000 a year, in a city where living alone in a rental apartment is a four-figure monthly proposition. As Orth put it, "Once I have kids, I don't think any of this is sustainable. I don't know how anyone at Global Exchange has kids." But as far as activist groups go, Global Exchange, with a steady paycheck and benefits, is a pretty sweet deal.

By contrast, the San Francisco Living Wage Coalition doesn't pay a living wage. In fact, it doesn't pay its staff anything at all. This irony seems lost on Karl Kramer, the stoic, goateed codirector. Strapped for cash, the organization, which is funded by labor, community, and religious groups, decided to make all its positions volunteer rather than hypocritically paying less than the wage they advocate.

"When we did pay wages, it was pegged at $15 an hour because, at the time, the wage surveys were showing that a single parent with one child required $14.50," Kramer explained. But with health care and rents on the rise, Kramer said, "the wage surveys are showing $29 an hour and we sure as hell wouldn't be able to afford to pay $29 an hour." So instead, Kramer and his fellow codirector take paid gigs on the side to make ends meet. (The $29-an-hour rate comes out to nearly $60,000 a year, which sounds like a lot. But when you do the math, spending 25 percent of pretax income on rent would only allow $1,250 a month to spend on housing—just enough for a basic living space for two people in the Bay Area.)

Hardly some quixotic grassroots organization, the San Francisco Living Wage Coalition is one of the most successful groups of its kind in the nation. Kramer and his fellow volunteer activists have proven themselves an able match against well-paid corporate lobbyists. Largely on account of the group's work, the San Francisco Board of Supervisors, as the local city council is known, voted in the highest minimum wage in America—$8.82 an hour in 2006 and pegged to the regional cost of living.

Despite its prominence, the group works out of a tiny office in the Redstone Building on Sixteenth Street in the Mission District. Built in 1913 by the San Francisco Labor Council and originally known as the Labor Temple, the building's five-hundred-seat auditorium was once used as a union meeting hall. Upstairs there were medical and dental offices to provide health care to workers. It was here that the 1934 San Francisco general strike was planned.

When most of the unions moved to greener suburban pastures in the late 1960s, the building became a home for nonprofit and grassroots groups. Threatened with eviction during the dot-com boom, the Redstone's activists wisely got the building certified as a historic site, protecting it from developers' wrecking balls. Thus, the Redstone, which resembles a rundown public high school, remains a hive of grassroots activity. A number of the groups in the building, including the San Francisco Living Wage Coalition, are fighting to win back the exact same things won by the building's union tenants during the Roosevelt years.

Without a living wage himself, Kramer lives in a boarding-house down the block from the Redstone, paying $625 a month for his room. It suits him, but he admits, "The way I'm living now would be very irresponsible if I had a family."

Today, more than ever, the City of Saint Francis lives up to its name—and not merely on account of the disproportionate number of residents who think they can communicate with animals. A magnet for those who choose a life of service over the life of comfort made possible by their educations, their lives echo Francis of Assisi, a religious figure very much like Buddha or Moses, who rejected the luxury into which he was born. "After acquiring a little knowledge of reading and writing, [Francis] was assigned to work in a lucrative merchant's business," wrote Bonaventure in his 1260 biography. But "God implanted in the heart of the youthful Francis a certain openhanded compassion for the poor" that ultimately led him to a life of poverty, chastity, and service. (While modern birth control removes the celibacy requirement, giving up the chance to have children is increasingly the price of public service.)

Troublingly, the sacrifices demanded of activists are most extreme in places where they are most needed—places like San Francisco, where inequality has risen to Third World levels. As activism has become mutually exclusive with a conventional family life, the activist community has become an assemblage of idealistic young people taking a few years off before professional school or a corporate job, a handful of liberal trust-funders, and a slew of eccentric nonconformists—the three groups that together form the easily mocked "sushi-eating . . . *New York Times*–reading . . . body-piercing . . . left-wing freak show" immortalized in the conservative Club for Growth's 2004 attack ad against Howard Dean. For the trust-fundless young grads who still choose it, a life of service and activism has become a life of asceticism. But as ascetics become the only people who can pursue activism, the work they do gets tainted in the public eye by the eccentricities of those who perform it. As the penchant for body piercing shows, when activism becomes synonymous with sainthood, even stigmata get trendy.

Social movements bring about social change. The suffragettes marched long before the Nineteenth Amendment passed; labor organizing preceded the New Deal; the civil rights movement preceded the Civil Rights Act. Government does not reform on its own, only when pushed by popular pressure. What is so frustrating about our current moment is that only a return to more egalitarian economic policies could free talented young people to fight for the social change so many of them believe in. But without such a change, a broad-based movement for reform is much harder to build. What is clear is that the current model of 501(c)(3) activism won't work. An America of entrenched wealth and widespread poverty cannot rely on saints to address its social ills. This has been tried before. It was called the Dark Ages and, despite the inspiring works of Saint Francis, it did not pan out so well.

Freedom Bound (and Gagged)

In the stairwell of the Stanford sociology department, a modern office cloaked within the Mediterranean monastery facade of the university's main quad, a hot-pink poster caught my eye. "Join the movement to end educational inequity," it exhorted. The fine print explained that the application deadline for Teach for America was rapidly approaching.

Since the program's launch in 1990, TFA has placed more than fourteen thousand recent graduates from elite colleges like Stanford in underfunded inner-city and rural public schools.

The program accepts only 20 percent of its applicants; 12 percent of Yale's class of 2005 applied for a job with the program—and half were rejected. The numbers are impressive, but upstairs the man I was here to see, Professor Doug McAdam, was hard at work on a study of Teach for America applicants—and he wasn't convinced TFA was much of a movement, despite the claims of its hot-pink recruitment posters.

He should know. McAdam is one of America's foremost scholars of social movements, best known for his book *Freedom Summer*, a groundbreaking study of the white northern civil rights volunteers who went to Mississippi in 1964 to register black voters and set up makeshift "Freedom Schools" for black children trapped in the Jim Crow educational system. McAdam told me about his work with TFA alumni: "In general, most of them feel like they're proud of the contribution they made, they're glad they did it. Their political attitudes remain liberal. They continue to espouse those values. They're going to be active citizens of a conventional sort, but they're not going to continue to engage in intensive activism or service."

This is in sharp contrast to what McAdam found when he studied an earlier generation of elite college students similarly drawn to the fight against inequality. By comparing the life paths of those who completed Freedom Summer in 1964 to those who backed out, he discovered the project had been far more than a summer stint—it had been a life-transforming event. Freedom Summer acted as a "kind of activist basic training," in McAdam's phrase. When the volunteers returned to their campuses, they went on to take leading roles in all the major social movements of the 1960s and '70s—the free speech movement, the women's movement, and the antiwar movement.

One might assume it was the intensity of the experience that transformed the young activists. The threat of violence was a fact of life for the Freedom Summer volunteers; just before most journeyed south, three civil rights workers, including two white northerners—Michael Schwerner and Andrew Goodman, both of New York—were lynched in the backwoods town of Philadelphia, Mississippi. But McAdam credits the outlook the volunteers brought to the program for its powerful effects. They grew up "at a time when there's sort of a generalized celebration of America. It was not just the most powerful country on the face of the earth but the most moral. And they more or less believed this." Raised in an America of broad-based prosperity, where, from their experiences, it seemed hard work would get a middle-class man a comfortable suburban home, and hard work would get his son or daughter a berth at Oberlin or Stanford, they were shocked to see the shotgun shacks and shotgun-toting sheriffs of the Deep South. When they got to Mississippi, "the gap between the ideal and the real was just extraordinary and they really struggled to make sense of that. For many of them, they couldn't. It just radicalized them."

Compared to the Freedom Summer participants, McAdam said, "Teach for America volunteers are idealists, but they're not as naive as the fifties and sixties kids. They already have a jaundiced view of America. And what they see in Teach for America is not really unexpected." Raised in an America that makes no pretense of trying to eliminate poverty or of providing even separate but equal schools for minority youth, "they understand that they're going into resource-poor schools and that racism is real and poverty is real. I'm not saying that it's not a powerful experience. I'm not saying that it doesn't change them in certain ways. But the idea that they're transformed, that they become different people because they've seen things they didn't expect is just not credible." Only 28 percent of Teach for America volunteers keep teaching after their two-year commitment is up. McAdam notes that the majority abandon the field of education altogether.

Contrast that with the experience of Freedom Summer volunteer Mario Savio. When Savio returned to the San Francisco Bay Area, he just couldn't dive back into his physics studies at UC Berkeley. He felt there were more pressing concerns for the nation, so he began giving speeches and soliciting donations for civil rights groups in the central campus courtyard in front of the university administration building, Sproul Hall. When administrators tried to stop him, arguing that he didn't have the right to grandstand on university property, he felt his free speech rights had been violated. Drawing on his "activist basic training" in Mississippi, Savio used protests and sit-ins to press the administration to change its position. When it refused, the protests grew, launching the free speech movement that forced universities across America to live up to their claims as bastions of open expression.

But the sight of students occupying buildings instead of attending lectures in them also produced a backlash. In 1966, while running for governor of California, Ronald Reagan frequently mocked the campus radicals in speeches to conservative audiences—red meat for the red-baiter crowd. If elected, Reagan vowed, he would appoint former CIA director John McCone to "investigate charges of communism and blatant sexual misbehavior on the Berkeley campus." But after being voted in, Reagan never made good on the promise. Instead he focused his attention on a different higher education policy: instituting tuition for in-state students at the long-free University of California. The taxes that financed free rides at Berkeley were eroding the California Dream, Reagan argued. To save it, tax-and-spend liberalism had to go.

By instituting in-state tuition, Reagan overturned a hundred-year-old tradition at Berkeley that had, for generations, given California's best and brightest an Ivy League–caliber education at no cost. "The state should not subsidize intellectual curiosity," Reagan declared, defending his tuition policy. In practice this meant that a college education was no longer a right earned by the highest achievers; rather, it was a privilege for the rich and an investment for everyone else. Most students would go into debt to study a practical subject hoping that they would one day recoup the principal plus interest. As Milton Friedman put it in his writings a few years before Reagan enacted his tuition policy, "Individuals should bear the costs of investment in themselves and receive the rewards." In the end, tuition and other conservative economic policies did more to undermine student activism than any CIA-style investigation ever could.

A plaque now sits in the courtyard in front of Sproul Hall commemorating the Free Speech Movement. Every time I've visited Berkeley, I've had no trouble reading it, because no one was ever protesting, speaking, or soliciting money there to combat racial or economic injustice. A short walk from the plaque, there is another monument, the Free Speech Movement Cafe. Decorated with photographs of Savio and other 1960s protesters, the cafe provides a place for students to get their free speech out quietly, behind closed doors, but students mostly use it to caffeinate themselves before pulling all-nighters.

Berkeley today is known for its preprofessionalism, not its activism. In part it is ever-rising tuition that puts the screws on students. To this day, the Berkeley administration maintains the ruse that it is "tuition-free" by calling in-state tuition bills "student fees." But even more than the rising tuition, it is the experience of living in Berkeley—now the second most economically unequal city in America, that shapes students' attitudes. (Berkeley's inequality is topped only by Atlanta's, the largest city in the Deep South, the region whose inequities once stood out so starkly to the students of middle-class postwar California.) No longer a hippy-dippy college town of bumper sticker–covered VW Vanagons, Berkeley has divided into ultrarich and desperately poor. When students see the disparity between life up the hill from campus and down the hill in the flats near the Oakland city line, they get the message. Like their parents before them, these kids don't need a weatherman to know which way the wind blows. Forget saving America, students conclude, save yourself.

Under these circumstances, it is surprising so many young people are still drawn to Teach for America. A TFA brochure I picked up at a 2005 college job fair carried the catchphrase "Start Here" on the cover, underscoring the tacit understanding that you're not signing up for a lifetime of teaching, that after completing the program you can get back on the path to the lifestyle formerly known as middle class. Inside, the brochure touts Teach for America's "graduate school relationships," which allow participants to defer admission at places like Harvard Business School, Yale Law School, and Princeton's Woodrow Wilson School of Public and International Affairs. It does not mention any schools of education. Of the three featured alumni, one is still a teacher, another works for a human rights nonprofit in Washington, and a third is an investment banker at Goldman Sachs, one of several corporate firms that actively recruit TFA teachers at the end of their stints. The banker, who ultimately made the decision to pursue America's highest-paying career path, offers this sidesplitting observation: "Before I arrived at Teach for America's summer training institute, my perception was that money could solve all of our school's problems. Now I realize how wrong I was."

McAdam believes the recruiting materials are purposefully "designed to suggest that this is really a temporary detour from the main line you're on. I'm convinced they are quite conscious about how they are trying to frame this so as not to scare people off by suggesting you're making a lifetime commitment to something." But even asking for a two-year commitment to public service is a tough sell: "I was surprised when we did the interviews and the surveys with the Teach for America folks, how many of them said that their parents were really opposed to them doing this because they were risking throwing away their education. The idea that they, having gone to Princeton or Stanford, were now going to get tracked into teaching was deeply scary to their parents. The parental attitude was 'You're wasting your education because the returns to this particular occupational investment are not going to be good.'"

Somewhere Ronald Reagan is surely smiling. His vision of education as a personal capital investment is firmly entrenched, closing off the options of service and activism through the fiscal facts on the ground, even more than through parental pressure.

In the 1960s, activism was mainstream. The nation ultimately backed the civil rights demonstrators in their suits and ties, their bloodstained, starched collars. In that time, young meritocrats flocked to public service and activism after graduation. In an era of broadly shared prosperity and the flattest income distribution in the nation's history, young people could use college to expand their minds and question authority rather than gunning for a slot at Harvard Business School. After graduation, modest rents in major cities fueled a progressive milieu. Communities organized without having to sell out to corporate funders for a million-dollar grant that barely pays the bills.

Back then, it appeared Reagan had lost his battle with the student radicals at Berkeley. His pledge to sic the former CIA chief on them came to nothing. So did his threat of expulsion, that students must, as he put it, "obey the rules or get out." But the economic policies he enacted successfully stifled subsequent generations of would-be student activists, destroying the legacy of the civil rights martyrs Michael Schwerner and Andrew Goodman, as indeed he intended. In 1980, when Reagan announced his candidacy for president of the United States, he chose an unusual location. Not Sacramento or Hollywood or Washington, but a tiny southern town called Philadelphia, Mississippi.

8

WHAT YOUR COMPANY CAN DO FOR YOU: POLITICS AS A VOCATION

The Closing of the New Frontier

Ask not what your country can do for you—ask what you can do for your country," President John F. Kennedy famously intoned in his 1961 inaugural speech. Spurred by the youthful president, the New Frontier generation flocked to the Peace Corps and social justice movements. Yet it was not just the young who were moved by the speech. Charles Robertson, well into his fifties, also took the call personally.

Robertson had served in World War II, yet despite his military service he knew he had the capacity to do more for his country. Having married into the A&P supermarket fortune, he had millions at his disposal. Soon after hearing Kennedy's challenge, he approached his alma mater, Princeton University, to see how they might use his money to fund scholarships for non-wealthy but idealistic students to enable them to pursue public service. Later that year, Robertson donated $35 million in A&P stock to a foundation to train graduate students at the Woodrow

Wilson School of Public and International Affairs for posts in the federal government.

As America got further entrenched in an unpopular war in Vietnam, fewer and fewer Woodrow Wilson students were signing up to work for Uncle Sam. Robertson began to worry that too few of the students being trained with his money were pursuing government service. Were he alive today, he would still be worrying. The same problem still plagues the Woodrow Wilson School as its students pass up the public sector for lucrative fields like management consulting. As the school's dean, Shirley Tilghman, acknowledges, only 30 to 40 percent of her school's graduates go to work for the government.

The persistence of the problem seems odd, considering that students' values have swung back to the service orientation of the Kennedy era. Disenchantment with scandal-ridden corporate America and a post-9/11 reevaluation of priorities should have made public service work alluring once again. According to a 2005 survey of students at top universities, government and public service are the areas in which most graduates would ideally like to work. With federal staff incompetence a major factor in a trio of recent tragedies—9/11 (FBI), the Iraq War (CIA), and Hurricane Katrina (FEMA)—the need for sharper minds in government is clear. But the economic realities of a winner-take-all America have rendered New Frontier–style idealism another luxury few can afford.

This was not the way it was supposed to be. Citing the stated objective of the foundation that Charles Robertson established for the Woodrow Wilson School—"To strengthen the Government of the United States . . . by improving the facilities for the training and education of men and women for government service"—Charles's son, William, is suing Princeton to get his father's money back. If successful, William's suit would make the foundation independent of the university. "Working for McKinsey . . . is not strengthening the government of the United States," William said, explaining the rationale for his lawsuit, the most expensive in Princeton's history. "We have been mugged, and we want justice."

While the foundation fracas is peculiar to Princeton, the troubling trend of idealistic students going to public policy school only to end up working in the private sector is not. Even at Harvard's School of Government, named (ironically, in hindsight) for President Kennedy, most students aren't asking what they can do for their country. In 1997, only 34 percent of the Kennedy School's graduates entered the public sector, a level the dean called "a crisis." A program to make public service more attractive, begun in 1999, has shown modest results. The school successfully lobbied the federal government to raise the salary for its prestigious two-year Presidential Management Fellows Program to $36,000 and created a $10,000 loan forgiveness package for graduates pursuing public service. But there's only so much the school can do. The salary gap between the public and private sector continues to grow unabated. Even with these efforts, in 2004, only 46 percent of the school's graduates were taking government jobs. The cultural shift toward service hasn't been enough to overcome the economic realities. Starting a family in the nation's capital even on the recently raised salary of $36,000 a year doesn't cut it. It's not anywhere near enough to live in a D.C. suburb with good public schools or to pay for a private school in the city.

"Ask not what your country can do for you—ask what you can do for your country" remains a noble sentiment. But today, the country does so little for its people—not even providing free, high-quality public education in its capital city—that even those who ask what they can do for their country come up with few viable answers.

Capital [sic] Hill

The new math of public service skews politics further to the right. Chatting with students in the cafeteria at Patrick Henry College in Virginia, a conservative evangelical institution founded in 2000, *New Yorker* correspondent Hanna Rosin listened as students mulled over the salaries on Capitol Hill. A recent Patrick Henry graduate they knew was making $32,000 as a congressional aide. Fine, if you're single, they decided, but not enough to support a family—and being conservative Christians, most of them planned on doing that. As if to answer their career concerns, the Right, funded largely by the boom in corporate profits, has created an entire infrastructure of think-tank and lobbying jobs outside of government that pay a family wage, if not more. And the gravy train starts early.

While most Washington interns scrounge around for housing—during my summer there I shared a house with five roommates and lived in a tiny basement bedroom—Heritage Foundation interns enjoy a more gracious lifestyle. The far-right think tank recently opened a $12 million dormitory adjacent to its Capitol Hill headquarters. Interns are paid a stipend and enjoy subsidized accommodations in the dorm. Some rooms include balconies with views of the city. After graduation, right-wing Washington presents plentiful opportunities to its minions.

Even for those who attempt the public service route, taking

modestly paid jobs on the Hill, selling out has become a foregone conclusion. A 2006 *New York Times* article dubbed Capitol Hill staffers "lobbyists-in-training." The numbers are stark: young congressional aides are paid salaries in the $20K–$30K range; lobbyists make at least six figures. "The disparity in salaries," veteran Beltway observer Charlie Cook told the *New York Times,* "[has] gotten so enormous that you could be a medium-high-level congressional staffer, and you go downtown and the first day be making more money than your boss, the senator, made." The connections formed on the Hill make congressional aides highly marketable in the corporate lobbying suites on K Street. The sector is hiring with a vengeance. During the George W. Bush administration, the number of lobbyists more than doubled, to over 34,750—and the price they charged for their services doubled as well.

Although K Street may seem a corridor of political power as natural as Pennsylvania Avenue itself, it is a relatively recent creation. In 1968, there were only sixty-two registered lobbyists in Washington. Lobbyists began proliferating in the late 1970s, spurred by right-wing intellectuals like Irving Kristol (City College's answer to Yale's William F. Buckley), who successfully urged the business community to mount a counteroffensive against the liberal consensus that had governed the country since Roosevelt. Business political action committees (PACs)—pots of money that fund favored candidates' campaigns—grew from 89 in 1974 to 1,206 in 1980. Business bosses hoped to renegotiate the New Deal, getting themselves off the hook for public expenditures so they could keep more for themselves. With Reagan's election, they got their wish. Government embarked on a deregulatory free-for-all. As long as businesses were there to ask for favors, they got them. But to be at the table, they needed lobbyists.

Between 1981 and 1985, the number of registered lobbyists in D.C. quadrupled.

At first, the rise of lobbying was about greed, pure and simple—not just for the corporate clients, but for the lobbyists themselves. The classic example is that of Henry Kissinger, who, after retiring as secretary of state, shunned the traditional role of elder statesman for the lucrative role of corporate consigliere. He formed Kissinger Associates and sold his connections to the highest bidders.

As in any game where the rules are abandoned, those with the fewest scruples win. A moral race to the bottom quickly ensued. When selling out was an anomaly, there was little pressure to do it. Today, selling out is so rampant it has reshaped the Washington economy, making it all but mandatory. Selling out is no longer just for dark, twisted Kissinger types. These days, people who'd never dream of secretly bombing Cambodian civilians are joining up.

With tens of thousands of six- and seven-figure lobbyists bidding up the prices of real estate and private school tuitions in the area, people can no longer live a middle-class life on a middle-class government salary. The capital region is now home to five of the seven richest counties in the nation. It is not uncommon for federal workers to commute from West Virginia. Idealistic young parents, faced with the unsavory choice between a two-hour commute they'd hate or a job they can barely stomach, generally go for the job—and then assuage their guilt by sending their kids to a Quaker school.

Of late, it isn't enough for liberal sellouts to send the kids off to Sidwell Friends, hold their noses, and go to work. In a new twist, the cherished firewall between public and private persona is being eroded; corporations don't just want to lease your mind, they demand to own your soul. Lobbyists are now expected to personally tithe, giving away their own money to congressional candidates who back their clients' interests. The going rate is $25,000 to $50,000 per lobbyist per election cycle—about the same as the annual salary for a young staffer on Capitol Hill.

Both conservatives and liberals have flocked to K Street, but the growth of lobbying is not politically neutral. It benefits the Right. While Democratic staffers routinely sell out, crossing ideological lines to work for well-paying conservative corporate clients—civil rights movement veteran Andrew Young took a job shilling for Wal-Mart—it is almost unheard of for Republicans to lobby for liberal groups like the National Resources Defense Council or the AFL-CIO. Journalist Nicholas Confessore observed in *The Washington Monthly*, "The lobbying industry doesn't just breed cynicism and bad government. It creates a systematic, partisan imbalance—against liberal and progressive interests represented by voters, and in favor of traditional conservative and corporate interests represented by money." When wonks are sold to the highest bidder, public policy is, too. Even when voters gave Congress back to the Democrats in the 2006 elections, no one could say whether substantive policy changes would result. The only thing Washington pundits knew for sure was that the reward for Democrats willing to sell out had just gone up. Before the Democratic sweep, the going rate on K Street for a top staffer from a midlevel House Democrat's office was $180,000; after the election, it was $400,000.

Through lobbying and PACs, the rise of corporate power threatens democracy itself. Ralph Reed, the Christian Coalition leader who was reborn as a K Street lobbyist, explained in his 2000 pitch letter to Enron that "in public policy, it matters less who has the best arguments and more who gets heard—and by whom." This is the great truth of contemporary Washington. The age-old promise of democracy—that public policy could be based on reasoned deliberation and majority rule—is being subverted by plutocracy, a system in which self-interested elites buy the policies they want, regardless of the virtues of their arguments or the level of popular support. In 2002, a Bush administration aide openly mocked those who still rely on Enlightenment rationality to weigh the merits of various policy options, calling them "the reality-based community." With entrenched wealth calling the shots, official Washington has become a status quo maintenance machine, perpetually privileging what *is* over what *might be*.

The Millionaires' Club Once More

The Heritage Foundation interns aren't the only people who live in dorms on Capitol Hill. Congressmen do, too. In a city overstuffed with six-figure lobbyists, even congressmen and senators, paid annual salaries of over $165,000 to maintain a residence in their district and in Washington, are relative paupers in the capital's housing market. According to a 2005 *New York Times Magazine* cover story, Pennsylvania senator Rick Santorum commuted two hours a day from Leesburg, Virginia, because it was "as close to Washington as [the Santorums] could afford a home big enough for their family."

Senators Charles Schumer and Richard Durbin bunk up with Congressmen George Miller and Bill Delahunt in a two-bedroom Capitol Hill town house purchased by Miller in the 1970s, when congressmen could still afford to buy homes near their offices. Miller declined my request to discuss his congressional boardinghouse. Perhaps he'd learned to be cautious, since previous articles had cited peeling blue paint on the facade, Cheez Doodles in the couch, a beer shelf in the fridge, and rats the size of cocker spaniels. When multimillionaire Jon Corzine was elected to the Senate, Schumer half-seriously invited him to join them. Corzine declined—and reportedly paid $4.7 million for a home in the Cleveland Park section of the city.

On a deeper level, this sitcom-worthy situation is no laughing matter. Lifelong public servants like Schumer—the son of a Brooklyn exterminator and a 1974 Harvard Law graduate who worked as a lawyer for a summer before quitting to run for the New York State Assembly as a grassroots Democrat—are a dying breed. The Senate is well on its way to reearning its Gilded Age nickname, the "millionaires' club." According to financial disclosure statements, at latest count, at least forty of the hundred senators are millionaires. But the disclosure statements do not count primary residences as assets. If they did, Schumer would be one, too, due to the tenfold appreciation on his Brooklyn apartment, purchased in 1983.

Can You Fix the System When the System's Fixed?

In an era in which selling out has become the norm, only the most over-the-top excesses of official Washington qualify as a scandal. Hillary Clinton's taking campaign contributions from credit card companies and then flip-flopping on bankruptcy legislation is business as usual; Representative Randy "Duke" Cunningham's giving weapons manufacturers a "bribe menu" written on official congressional stationery listing prices for his services is a scandal. Thousands of wealthy lobbyists displacing middle-class public servants in the greater D.C. area? Business as usual. Jack Abramoff associate Michael Scanlon displacing visiting royalty with his $17,000-a-month apartment at the Washington Ritz-Carlton? Scandal. Enron donating money to establish a research institute at Harvard to turn out propaganda for its deregulatory agenda? Business as usual. Jack Abramoff directing his clients to hire Brian Mann's *fake* think tank under the pretense of turning out similar propaganda? Scandal. (That Brian Mann is not a policy wonk but a yoga instructor is more than a scandal, it's a hoot.)

But even in this corruption-plagued climate, young people remain drawn to public service. A Kennedy School survey of American college students found that while 70 percent of students believe today's crop of elected officials are selfishly motivated, nine in ten students still feel that running for and holding elective office are honorable things to do. But getting to the point where one can run for office in an honorable way—without campaign finance whoredom—is another story.

With staggering education debt, taking the leap directly from school to public service is less of an option. A young grad hoping to follow in Senator Schumer's footsteps—straight from university to politics—would likely be saddled with six figures of educational debt and have to make hundreds of thousands more for a home before embarking on a career of public service. As Matt's story shows, this is exactly what some are doing.

"I'm probably one of the leading experts in the United States on the Medicare prescription drug law," Matt told me. Wonky, khaki-clad bravado to be sure—a veritable Georgetown pickup line—but probably true nonetheless. As a health-care specialist at a leading consulting firm, Matt has done scores of reports for major pharmaceutical companies on how to reap the highest profits from the 2003 law. It shouldn't be too hard. The pharmaceutical lobbyists who crafted the legislation ensured that the government would have to buy wholesale quantities of drugs at retail prices. As is plain to see, the American health-care system "is a huge mess," said Matt. And his job is to help "pharmaceutical companies take advantage of it."

You'd think a leading expert on health-care policy who calls the system "a huge mess" might be working to fix it, not game it. Indeed, Matt got his start in health-care policy hoping to do just that. Always a liberal politics junkie, as a high school student on Long Island he volunteered for Bill Clinton's 1992 presidential campaign. Then, after his freshman year at Yale, he interned at the U.S. Department of Health and Human Services just as Congress was debating Clinton's proposal for universal health care. "I was going to congressional hearings and reporting back to the assistant secretary for legislation, who reports to the secretary on what's going on day-to-day. It was a great time to be in Washington—sort of hopeful and excited about the possibilities."

When Clintoncare crashed and burned, Matt focused on other things. He majored in physics and earned a PhD in astronomy. Still, he couldn't shake the politics bug and worked on the Gore campaign in 2000. Even after deciding the life of a research scientist wasn't for him, politics didn't seem like a workable option, either. He had recently married a history graduate student, whose annual stipend was less than $20,000.

"Why am I not doing politics now?" he mused, repeating my question. "I actually did talk to people about it. And the truth is that it is actually economically unfeasible. There is no money. I looked into it and if I were working for a political consulting firm that also did some corporate work, sixty thousand dollars was good—that's the best. If you go and work on a campaign, those guys get paid like thirty grand."

So Matt went for management consulting instead, earning a six-figure paycheck. It was fine for a while, but as he and his wife contemplated having children, the grueling consulting schedule—leaving his apartment at 7 A.M., returning at 11 P.M.—was no longer tenable. "I started recognizing that I couldn't have a family with the traveling. If you're away four days a week—literally gone—that was not going to make me happy. People do it. But they have different priorities in life than I do." So now the plan is to work less, make more, and then, one day, jump back into politics. For Matt, this means hedge funds, investment vehicles that use complex mathematical modeling, often developed by PhD-holding scientists and mathematicians, to beat the market. This is high finance at the highest end; minimum investments are generally $1 million. If you're a regular investor saving for retirement, don't expect a hedge-fund manager to return your phone calls. Their move to hire PhDs like Matt is the purest expression of the trend toward turning the brightest members of the middle class into high-end servants for the superrich. A hedge fund manager's explicit mandate is to make the rich even richer.

Matt expects he will ultimately go back into politics. "One of the draws of being at the hedge fund is that the person who recruited me to do this is himself very interested in politics. He said, 'I go to fund-raisers now, I'm involved with folks and also I have enough money in the bank that when the right thing comes along, somebody I like, I'll volunteer for that campaign. I'll quit the job, it doesn't matter,'" Matt recalled. "That was a big inducement."

Maybe Matt is all talk. Saying you want to get rich in order to serve the public good sounds a lot nicer than saying you want to get rich in order to drive a Lamborghini. But whatever his intentions, the Schumer model of earning your diploma and diving right in is no longer viable. The Corzine model—do well, then do good—has become the only way to go into politics as your own man (or woman).

"People who do not have big money going in have a tendency to have lots of weird friends they don't like. You end up with whoever that McDougal guy was down in Arkansas, the Whitewater guy," Matt said, referring to one of Bill Clinton's sketchier donors. Weird friends aside, going into elective office without your own money means spending as much time fund-raising as legislating. It is not uncommon for congressmen to spend their mornings on legislation and their afternoons or evenings making fund-raising phone calls. Even worse, the fund-raising corrupts the legislating. Representatives end up so dependent on corporate largesse that they feel they can't take on powerful interests—pharmaceutical companies, for example—when powerful interests conflict with the common good.

"It's a problem," Matt fretted. "If you look at politics, there are a lot of wealthy people and that bothers me that we haven't found a way to make it work."

But if you can't beat 'em, join 'em.

9

HAZARD PAY FOR THE SOUL:
THE LEGAL PROFESSION

The View from Hogwarts

In Dean Harold Hongju Koh's office at Yale Law School, a cavernous gothic chamber that one student compared to Hogwarts Academy, sits a prominently displayed picture of the dean greeting the Dalai Lama. The photograph seems appropriate, and not merely because Koh is an international human rights lawyer. In his annual speech to new law students encouraging them to pursue public interest work, the middle-aged, charmingly chubby Koh endorses an almost Buddhist sense of nonattachment to the material world—something his students will surely need. By the beginning of their second year, the largest and most powerful corporate law firms in the world will dangle six-figure salaries before them, often for doing little more than glorified secretarial work. In 2005–2006, 144 corporate law firms flocked to campus to recruit 191 second-year (2L) students. (Two non–law firms came, too—Goldman Sachs and McKinsey.)

"What I say in the speech," Koh recounted, speaking to me

from behind his dean-sized desk, "is don't ever do anything for money. You start down that road and the question is not whether you could be bought, but what's the price." The law school's career development office Web site lists the going rate, informing students deadpan that "a graduate accepting a position in a large New York City law firm will earn approximately $140,000, while a graduate commencing work with a small public interest law firm in D.C. may earn anywhere from $30,000 to $45,000. A graduate starting work with the New York County District Attorney's office will earn $48,000." By steering students to consider less lucrative public interest work, Koh has had more success than most of his counterparts at the nation's top law schools. But even at Yale, which has a reputation for attracting students of an idealistic and intellectual bent, as 1L Steven Ruckman put it, "a vast majority come in saying they'll do public interest work and a vast minority goes out actually doing it." The flocking of elite law students to large corporate law firms clearly pains Koh. "My view is that the most privileged lawyers should not blindly serve the most privileged clients," he said. "I'm constantly amazed at why the most privileged are serving the most privileged."

What Koh is witnessing seems to go against not merely everything his students claim to stand for but against the grain of youth as it has been understood for centuries. Adam Smith wrote in 1776, "The contempt of risk and the presumptuous hope of success are in no period of life more active than at the age at which young people choose their professions." When I read the Adam Smith quote to Dean Koh, he looked at me incredulously and requested that I read it again. I did, and again he paused, gazing off toward the far end of his office. "It's not what I see at all," he finally responded. "I see some of the most successful students being quite risk-averse," going into high-paying corporate law jobs despite the often grueling and dispiriting work. Most of his students, he reasoned, don't take the jobs in the hopes of getting fabulously rich. They do it to avoid the risk of being poor.

As the rich have gotten richer and corporate profits have sky-rocketed, corporate law firms have seen their fortunes rise with them. This has allowed the firms to raise their salaries, which in turn has pushed up pay for law professors, who could theoretically defect to the private sector. Their raises are passed along to students in the form of steep tuition increases. Top law schools have instituted loan forgiveness programs to encourage students to pursue public interest work despite their tuition debts, but in America's most important cities, crammed with young cash-flushed corporate lawyers and a real estate market dominated by the high-rent "lawyer lofts" that cater to them, the cost of living has made taking a public interest job a financially perilous proposition. In the end, the ever-growing salary gap—and the prestige gap that goes with it—overwhelms most students.

For society at large, the issue is not what are talented young lawyers doing, but what are they not doing? A young prosecutor told me, on his last day on the job, that he loved the DA's office, even felt he had saved people's lives, but if he kept working there he could never pay off his tuition debts and support a family with his wife, a social worker. He was heading to a private firm. When I asked him what his advice to current law students would be, he replied simply, "Have no debt: marry money or be independently wealthy."

While Koh may suggest disregarding the financial implications of your career decisions—he claims to not remember his own salary—most people don't seem to operate that way. The dean tells incoming students that blaming debt load for a decision to go corporate is "an embarrassing excuse. I really urge you never to use that excuse in public." But at a certain point, the numbers matter, especially for students at schools that can't match Yale's loan forgiveness program. As David Stern, executive director of Equal Justice Works, formerly the National Association for Public Interest Law, now sees it, "The educational debt crisis is going to break the back of most nonprofit organizations in the next ten years. The numbers do not add up. You cannot take a public interest job without some other means of support." He explained, "Most of the people who make decisions about this—law school board members—come from the private sector," and they figure if they're paying their first-year associates six-figure salaries, students should be able to handle serious debt. But according to an Equal Justice Works survey, two-thirds of law students said law school debt prevented them from considering a public interest or government job. Not surprisingly, two-thirds of organizations that employ public interest lawyers reported retention and recruiting problems. With law school tuition having doubled in the past decade and showing no signs of slowing down, the average debt load of a law school graduate is now more than $84,000.

"The commitment, the energy for public interest work, for legal aid work, is as great as it's ever been," said Don Saunders, director of civil legal services at the National Legal Aid and Defender Association in Washington. But debt is deterring too many young lawyers after just a few years on the job. "People of my age—I'm in my midfifties—we started this work growing up in the sixties. Most of us have spent our careers doing it. We came out of law school largely debt free. There was a whole generation that was able to dedicate their lives to this work and they're getting older."

Public interest legal offices from coast to coast are describing the same gap. There are the lifers—1960s movement people nearing retirement—and idealistic young people, who move on after just a few years when they decide to start families, which leaves very few experienced attorneys in the prime of their careers in between. "My take is that poor people are not for practicing on before going on to a 'real career,' once you have some experience," Saunders said. But that seems to be exactly what is happening.

Among the Muggles

Gabrielle Prisco, a 2003 NYU Law grad, works at the ACLU as a First Amendment attorney. She loves her job, but deciding to become a lawyer took a lot of convincing. When, as a Staten Island high school student, she won a citywide moot court competition, her mentor, Jackie James, who worked at a Wall Street firm, discouraged her from becoming a lawyer. James had started out as a public interest attorney but, unable to pay her debts, switched to a corporate firm. Thoroughly disgruntled, James told Prisco that working with the moot court team was the most fulfilling part of her job. When the local *Staten Island Advance* interviewed Prisco for its article, "Verdict on Curtis Moot Court Team: Guilty of Success," the reporter, who surely thought he was feeding the champ a softball with "Do you want to be a lawyer when you grow up?" got an earful. She told him that though she was interested in environmental law, "you can't support yourself that way," unless you are independently wealthy, like Robert F. Kennedy Jr., an attorney with the Natural Resources Defense Council. "I don't go home to a house with monogrammed silverware," she added.

Prisco changed her mind during college at Vanderbilt while she was interning at a shelter for runaways and observed the inadequate legal representation the teenagers received. "I had a feeling that we could do so much as counselors, but there was this point at which our power ended and that the law has this immense power and I wanted to tap in to that," she told me over lunch at a restaurant near her office. (The ACLU staff shares a building with the corporate firm Sullivan and Cromwell but is prohibited from using the firm's cafeteria.) Prisco chose NYU in part for its reputation for public interest law. The school also boasts a loan forgiveness program, which offers full repayment of tuition debt for graduates making under $44,000 in public interest jobs and partial repayment for those earning up to $74,000. Prisco owes NYU $1,400 a month in debt payments; with a salary in the $50K range, the loan forgiveness program cuts her share to $800 a month. It's still a struggle. Despite a full scholarship for college, Prisco said she has to borrow money from her parents, retired schoolteachers, to get by. "There are times I don't have any money in my bank account and I'm waiting to get paid and I have to take my quarters to Commerce Bank and cash them in."

For her NYU classmate, Erik, public interest work wasn't an option. Raised in suburban St. Louis, the only "out" student in his two-thousand-student high school, Erik got into Stanford—a 1950s-style American Dream story for the son of a local union official and a supermarket checkout clerk, neither of whom had gone to college. After Stanford, Erik went to work for the Civil Rights Division of the U.S. Justice Department. Determined to become an attorney fighting for gay and lesbian civil rights, he entered NYU Law in 2001. While in school, he interned for the ACLU's Lesbian and Gay Rights Project.

When I met him in 2005, he wore "architect" glasses and a fashionable purple-flecked dress shirt. But despite his hip taste and progressive politics, he was not exactly manning the barricades. Under the weight of tuition debt and lacking a parental safety net, Erik took a job as an associate at a Manhattan law firm famed for its top-ranked union-busting department. "We represent NYU when it busts its unions," he told me, with a sardonic smile. The only luxuries afforded by Erik's six-figure salary are his ability to cover his debt payments and live roommate-free in a one-bedroom apartment in Brooklyn. "When you sit down and look at the numbers, it's really horrible," he said, explaining his decision to go corporate over coffee at one of the three Starbucks outlets within a one-block radius of his Midtown office. "I think it's an abysmal situation."

Though his lifestyle is hardly lavish, Erik's cost of living is considerable. A generation ago, my mother could live a block from Central Park as medical resident. Today, corporate law associates commute from Brooklyn. And it's not just New York. Ralph Nader, who has been employing public interest lawyers for decades through groups like his Center for Study of Responsive Law, cited the rising cost of living in Washington, D.C., as one of the top problems he faces in keeping his best young attorneys. (One of those wayward attorneys was Brendan, the Harvard Law grad who left for a firm so he and his wife, Johanna, could buy a home, as discussed in chapter 2.) "The squeeze is on in many directions," Nader told me. While loan forgiveness may make living on a public interest salary feasible in a smaller city or rural area, in the centers of government and business where it is most crucial, it no longer cuts it. "There are people who'll go on food stamps but those are a very, very small number," Nader said. "Most of them have to have some kind of economic security so they can just pay their bills."

And many young people bump up against the rising cost of living before they even finish school. As college towns from Cambridge to Austin to Palo Alto have gone from quirky, low-priced hippie enclaves to overpriced knowledge-industry hubs, the cost of living for students has soared. Don Saunders, who graduated from the University of North Carolina law school at Chapel Hill in the 1970s, explains, "When I went there it was very affordable but now it costs a fortune." No longer a sleepy southern college town, Chapel Hill is now a corner of the so-called Research Triangle, home to multinationals like pharmaceutical giant GlaxoSmithKline and the high-end professionals they employ.

Diane Downs, associate dean of career planning at the University of Pennsylvania Law School, says that even a generous loan forgiveness program like Penn's "doesn't turn a $40,000-a-year job into a $125,000-a-year job. It turns a $40,000-a-year job into a $40,000-a-year job." And in metropolitan America, $40,000 doesn't buy what it did a generation ago. Loan forgiveness can't address the salary gap and it can't address the regional inequalities that have made the cost of living in America's financial, cultural, and political centers so much higher than in less influential regions of the country.

From Seller's Market to Sellout Market

Despite the numerous barriers to pursuing public interest careers, the conventional wisdom outside the legal academy is that law students are simply conservative careerists, eager to become what one critic calls "servants of the power elite." In truth, law students have long been inclined to service, often on the front lines of reform. Since the merit-based admissions policies of the 1960s transformed elite universities, welcoming students of an intellectual bent regardless of race, religion, or gender, incoming students at top law schools have been an overwhelmingly left-leaning bunch. Even in the reactionary Reagan years, political conservatives were vastly outnumbered by liberals and leftists on elite law school campuses. The Federalist Society, the influential association of conservative lawyers, was founded in 1980 by Yale Law student Steven Calabresi after he was shocked to find he was one of only two students in a ninety-student lecture course who had voted for Reagan. A 1986 poll showed 70 percent of Harvard 1Ls expressed an interest in practicing public interest law after graduation. As 1989 Harvard Law graduate Richard Kahlenberg pondered in his law school memoir *Broken Contract*, "How is it that so many students can enter law school determined to use law to promote liberal ideals and leave three years later to counsel the least socially progressive elements of our society?"

Today's incoming students are no different. Yale's Dean Koh said that "when someone decides to become a lawyer, they should do so for a reason. And the reason is that they want to somehow make the world better. That's certainly what I read in their admissions essays." At Yale Law, the halls are covered with posters for progressive activities and events—a petition urging the Bush administration to stop the genocide in Darfur, organizational meetings for clinics offering free legal advice to immigrant workers and low-income tenants, even a speech by Al Franken.

Despite the politics of their students, the elite law schools are rightly considered factories for corporate law firm associates. When we speak of "entrenched" wealth and power, these are the grunts who dig and man the trenches, the shock troops of the status quo. In 2001, two-thirds of Harvard's class went directly into private practice, with more following after brief stints as judicial clerks. Only 5 percent went into public interest and government work combined. At NYU Law, widely considered one of the top training centers for public interest lawyers, 10 percent of its 2004 graduates pursued public interest law, 4 percent went into government, 19 percent went on to judicial clerkships, and 67 percent went to private law firms.

This has not always been the case. In the 1960s, the flood of resumés flowing to corporate firms dried up. In 1964, only 54 percent of Harvard Law grads went into private practice; by 1968, that number had dropped to 41 percent. Progressive students opted to serve the poor at public defender and legal aid offices, or the public good through government service.

Corporate law firms, whose prestige and power has always come from their ability to rope in the best young legal talent, knew they had a problem on their hands. Sensing the mood, the savviest firms dressed up as liberal institutions, adding pro bono (literally "for the good" in Latin) divisions to take on cases for the vast majority of people and institutions that could never afford their hourly rates. At the time, the executive committee of the Washington-based firm Hogan and Hartson circulated an internal memo, cynical even by the standards of the profession, noting "a tendency among younger lawyers, particularly those with the highest academic qualifications, to seek out public service–oriented legal careers as an alternative to practice in the larger metropolitan law firms." The committee suggested that expanding their pro bono work could have "a favorable impact upon recruitment."

Starting in the late 1960s, Hogan and Hartson and other large corporate firms began to rebrand themselves as progressive institutions. Another major D.C. firm, Wilmer, Cutler, and Pickering, provided free legal services to African-Americans arrested during the riots that erupted following the assassination of Martin Luther King Jr. in 1968. But there were limits to what the firms were willing to do; their work could never conflict with the interests of their paying customers. While Wilmer associates were giving free legal advice to blacks in the ghettos of D.C., partner Lloyd Cutler was busy stalling auto safety legislation to require the Big Three automakers to equip their vehicles with airbags. In the time the firm successfully delayed the bill, more than 100,000 Americans died in car accidents in which their lives would have been saved by airbags. To put the figure in perspective, 58,000 Americans died in the Vietnam War.

As top students turned away from corporate law, an observer at the time noted, "starting salaries began to reflect the emergence of a seller's market." In 1967, the Wall Street megafirm Cravath, Swaine and Moore pushed its starting salary up to the then unheard of sum of $15,000 a year. Many top firms matched it. Soon the large firms had opened up a modest salary gap with the public and nonprofit sectors: by 1972, starting salaries at Manhattan firms were up to $16,000 while the federal government offered its newly minted lawyers $13,300 and Legal Aid of New York paid $12,500. Since then, the salary gap has widened, accelerating most rapidly in the 1980s and '90s. Today, it is not uncommon for top law firms to pay recent grads $100,000 more than public interest employers pay theirs.

Surprisingly, few scholars have examined how such a dramatic change in starting law salaries could occur during a period of time in which the wages of most Americans have been flat. The perverse truth of the matter is that corporate law salaries— like those of the corporate elite generally—have risen in large part because the wages of most Americans have not. According to a 2006 report by economists at Goldman Sachs, the wage stagnation of recent years is the key reason for the corporate profit boom. As corporations and the superrich have gotten richer, so have the firms that service them. Since the mid-1980s, when *The American Lawyer* began its annual survey, profits at the nation's hundred top law firms have more than quadrupled. As SUNY-Stony Brook economics professor Michael Zweig explained to me, corporate firms "through their legal work are arranging for these corporations to make tens of billions of dollars and they fashion legislative agendas that are worth hundreds of millions of dollars to these industrial entities, so they're paid accordingly." If there were simply an overall imbalance in supply and demand for attorneys, all lawyers would have seen similar increases in their pay. Yet, as Zweig notes, those attorneys serving average Americans, like legal aid lawyers and public defenders, have seen their salaries stagnate.

But growing profits at elite law firms only mean that the firms can pay higher salaries, they don't ensure they will. The salary gap has increased because only enormous salaries can win over bright young lawyers who went to law school to take on the powers that be, not serve them. What was true in the 1960s—that all things being equal most top students will not work in corporate law—remains true. And that is why all things are *not* equal— indeed, that is why they have been growing ever more unequal ever since. The extra cash is hazard pay for the soul.

Firms with a liberal reputation excel in winning over progressive law students. One major New York firm offers vegan options in its cafeteria for all the fervent environmentalists on staff; it also represents ExxonMobil and Monsanto. Lawyers at the nation's top-grossing corporate law firm, Skadden, Arps, were the leading contributors to John Kerry's presidential campaign. While critics at Common Cause, the campaign-finance reform group, argued that the firm was trying to buy influence for its clients who were pushing a media deregulation agenda, a more likely explanation was that many of the attorneys were trying to buy back their own mortgaged souls. After working all year lining the pockets of Bush's corporate cronies, there's nothing to help a guilty liberal sleep at night quite like cutting a fat check to the Democrats.

The idea, of course, that any amount of tofu or pro bono work could transform a corporate law firm into a progressive institution is patently absurd. A 2005 *New Yorker* cartoon pithily summed matters up: as two corporate attorneys walk down the steps of a courthouse, the older lawyer says to the younger one, "Remember, we can only afford to do all this pro bono because of how much anti bono pays." Current trends in the legal profession may render even this equation obsolete. In recent years, even as elite law firm profits have soared to new heights, the firms' pro bono work has been scaled back. While the top-grossing hundred firms' lawyers averaged fifty-two hours of pro bono work a year in 1993, by 2002 the number had fallen to thirty-nine hours. In 2004, more than two-thirds of the top hundred firms failed to meet their own professional organization's minimum standards for pro bono work—the American Bar Association's recommendation of fifty hours per lawyer per year.

The Banality of Evil

One of the puzzling things about law school is that students who are eager from day one to join corporate law firms are often derided as "corporate tools," and those who struggle with the decision but invariably sell out are regarded as people of moral substance. While signing up with a corporate law firm would be natural for students of a Social Darwinist or libertarian bent, or for those singularly driven to maximize their earning potential, most of the students who end up working as corporate associates are liberals, ostensibly committed to the goal of building a more equal America. It might be comforting to imagine that it was the hard-core libertarian lawyers, who believe that the market should be entirely self-regulating, who lobbied against auto safety legislation, but Wilmer, Cutler, and Pickering is an overwhelmingly liberal firm, and chief lobbyist Lloyd Cutler was a Democrat.

Yale's Dean Koh frets about the intellectual dishonesty of it all. "I think the students who want to choose jobs because they're being paid more money should simply say 'I'm choosing the job because I'm being paid more money and because money matters to me more than other things.' They should just say it."

In explaining the transformation of public interest–seeking 1Ls into six-figure-salary-seeking 3Ls, critics often blame the method of instruction, which they see as tantamount to a moral lobotomy. As students are taught to argue both sides of any case, the theory goes, they lose track of their own beliefs about right and wrong. Needless to say, some professors teach the law as if it were a game or a sport, not a discipline requiring moral judgments. As one Harvard professor told his class, "It is your client who defines what is right." But for every professor in that mold there is another, like Dean Koh, who teaches that lawyers have a "duty to assess what they are ready to do and not just what the client wants them to do." And law school is rarely the first time students realize that intellectual arguments can be made on both sides of an issue. In high school debate—a common activity for future law students of America—positions are often determined by the toss of a coin. In their experience as undergraduates studying the humanities, most law students have probably come across a few good arguments for bad things, say, Aristotle's defense of slavery. Despite the intellectual rigor of his argument— it's Aristotle, by Jove!—few students come away from Book I of *Politics* converted. But then, no one is offering them six-figure salaries to defend slavery.

Well, almost no one. In 2004, California-based oil giant Unocal was sued for allegedly using slaves to build its pipeline in Burma in cooperation with that country's Communist junta, the State Law and Order Restoration Council (later renamed the State Peace and Development Council—apparently the original name wasn't quite Orwellian enough). Unocal faced trial in a Los Angeles courtroom for complicity in using slave labor as well as in committing other human rights violations including rape, torture, and murder. Defended by a number of law firms including the California corporate firm of Munger, Tolles, and Olson, Unocal ultimately settled out of court.

That same year, Yale Law graduate Rohit Khanna, class of 2001, mounted a primary challenge to incumbent congressman Tom Lantos, a Bay Area Democrat. When an article in the alternative *San Francisco Weekly* tarred the twenty-seven-year-old

Khanna for working at Munger, Tolles, and Olson, which in addition to defending Unocal offered the usual array of corporate law firm services—defending companies that bust unions, pollute the environment, and discriminate against women and minorities—Khanna fired back a letter to the editor. Protesting what he saw as guilt by association, Khanna wrote, "I worked on none of these types of cases while at Munger, Tolles, & Olson. Munger has a reputation for public service and pro bono work; partner Ronald Olson was a trustee of President Clinton's legal defense fund." Like so many of his fellow law school classmates, he had ended up at a corporate law firm, convincing himself that it was morally acceptable as long as he could avoid certain assignments.

Mildly ironic, considering his corporate law job, Khanna was challenging twelve-term incumbent Tom Lantos, a supporter of the Iraq war, from the left flank. Painfully ironic, considering his firm's work, Khanna was out to unseat the only member of Congress who had at one time been a slave. Congressman Lantos, a Hungarian-born Jew, spent World War II in a forced labor camp.

Life at Kafka, Camus, and Weber LLP

In addition to compensating students for the psychological costs of having to work for institutions that defend union busters and sexual harassers, if not always clients that are literally slave drivers, law firm associate salaries have risen in inverse proportion to plummeting working conditions. It is an open secret on law school campuses that being an associate at a large corporate firm is a bad job in every respect except pay. While firms have gotten recruiting down to a science—plying students with light working hours and luxurious liquid lunches over the summer—it's impossible to cover up the true nature of the job. A recent Harvard Law graduate recounted how one recruiter tried to tout his firm's humanity by assuring him that his love of reading for pleasure would be "tolerated" by the firm. "You can have one outside interest," the attorney explained—reading, for example, or a dog, or a wife, but not, say, a dog *and* a wife. That would be pushing it. That summer, at a different firm—the "tolerance" pitch hadn't won him over—he told an associate about the weekend plans he'd arranged with his friends. "Friends?" the associate replied. "Yeah, I used to have friends."

The sacrifice of a social life might be understandable if the work opportunities were unparalleled, but most young corporate attorneys are as likely to see the inside of a courtroom as they are the inside of a rocket ship. For many, this brings on the dispiriting feeling that years of preparation for serious, meaningful work have been all for naught. As Dean Koh noted in his public interest–pushing speech to incoming students, "I can tell you from my own experience that there is nothing more depressing than realizing that you are fungible with others." As wealth and power have become so concentrated at the top, this archetypal experience of workplace alienation, long common in jobs further down the socioeconomic scale, has crept into fields like law, once set apart as a "learned profession." At Covington and Burling, the large D.C. firm where Koh worked following his Supreme Court clerkship, partners referred to associates as "bodies." Finding themselves understaffed on a particular case, they would scream, "Get me another body!" While pulling an all-nighter on a case in which two giant companies were suing each other, Koh could no longer remember which side he was representing. Even worse, he realized he didn't care. He concluded he had to seek other work. "I didn't care who got the money," he tells his students. "I *want* to care about who wins."

Koh also tells current students about the young alums who often call him with their tales of being stuck in a big law firm with a job they hate but a salary they have become dependent on. "I hate my job but I can't move," Koh quotes a former student as saying. "If you ever find yourself saying that, something went desperately wrong. Desperately wrong."

With the rise in salaries, there has been a dramatic rise in working hours expected from young lawyers. In the 1960s, corporate associates were expected to bill 1,450 hours a year; today, 2,000. Studies show that to honestly bill two hours of work, an attorney needs to spend about three hours in the office; thus billing 2,000 hours a year means leaving work only to sleep. One associate described the pressure to bill hours as being "like a pie-eating contest where the first prize is all the pie you can eat."

Such dark humor is common among attorneys. At one major New York firm, associates engage in an informal competition over who has been given the most Kafkaesque assignment. The current leader, when one associate told me of the contest, was Greg, a tall, goateed young litigator who was given twenty-five hours of audiotapes in which a group of accountants described a reinsurance transaction. The Kafkaesque element that appealed to the associates was the concept of meta-boredom: one might imagine nothing could be more boring than being an accountant and having to discuss a reinsurance transaction for twenty-five hours—nothing more boring, that is, except being the lawyer charged with listening to and writing memos based on those tapes. Soon after winning the Kafka contest (perhaps the prize was all-you-can-eat pie?), Greg decided it was time to apply for a federal government job. He kept the tapes on his desk to steel his nerves for the near-six-figure pay cut. "No matter how good the money is, these tapes remind me of how horrible this can be," he said.

Not all assignments rise to these heights of complexity. One Harvard Law student, as a summer associate at a major Wall Street firm, was presented with two giant boxes of papers. Each paper had a number on it; his job was to put the pages in number order. For the work, the summer associate was paid roughly $60 an hour; the client was billed somewhere around $200 an hour. Sure, this young man was maximizing his earning potential doing this work, and the firm was, in turn, maximizing its profits—but what a colossal waste of human talent. Perhaps when we have conquered war, poverty, and environmental degradation, we could afford to have our brightest young people pour out their efforts by stacking sheets of paper in number order. But we're not there yet—in part because we've created a system in which our best and brightest pour out their youthful energies on inane assignments like this for the likes of Halliburton, Wal-Mart, and Unocal.

The Metamorphosis

How do so many top law students end up doing work 180 degrees removed from what they set out to do? Greg explained his transformation on his lunch hour in a coffee shop a safe distance from his office. "If you told me five years ago I'd be working at a firm, I would have just laughed. I would have been amazed. There's no way I would have believed you. There's no way."

After graduating from a liberal arts college, Greg toyed with applying to law school, but put off the decision for a year and took a job as a VISTA volunteer on the Lower East Side of Manhattan. In the mid-1990s, the neighborhood where he worked was littered with crack vials.

Greg worked in the neighborhood with residents who were struggling with psychiatric problems in addition to poverty. He came to feel that all too often "people with disabilities are treated as criminals rather than people who need care and services." He was infuriated by the obliviousness of most Americans to the problems his clients faced in the heart of the nation's financial and media capital. Unlike most idealists in his position, addressing these inequities through law and public policy was not his first impulse; in his view, a change of attitude had to precede a change of policy. Rather than attend law school, Greg decided to pursue an MFA in creative writing, with a plan to write a novel based on his experiences in the mold of John Steinbeck and Upton Sinclair. "I thought if I could portray those stories in a fictional setting, maybe that would help. When people read stories they get connected to the characters," he said. But after falling for a poetry student in graduate school, his creativity, which had largely been fueled by loneliness, dried up. He finished the program, married the poetess, and took a job as an inner-city social worker, before finally deciding to go to law school. Despite acceptances from two Ivy League schools, the New Jersey native opted to attend an in-state law school to keep his debt load, already swollen from undergraduate studies and the MFA, from getting out of control.

When he arrived on campus, Greg recalled, he was "extremely committed" to practicing public interest law. At the end of his first year, he won a prestigious fellowship, awarded to the top public interest law prospects in the class. But the doors the award opened were not to environmental or poverty law, but to corporate firms. It was easy. Two previous fellowship winners had gone to the same elite Wall Street firm with a reputation for attracting liberal associates and a dedication to pro bono work. With the ease of on-campus interviews and two alumni connections, Greg ended up spending a summer at their corporate firm.

"It's pretty sick," he admitted to me. As soon as he saw the kind of money on offer, he began to internalize the idea that he was entitled to it. When a New Jersey firm tried to recruit him by dangling a more livable work schedule than the firms across the river, Greg asked what they paid. Five thousand dollars a month, he was told—half the going rate on Wall Street. "I felt my face turn red. I was like, that's all? I couldn't believe that that was my reaction," he recalled. "I couldn't believe this was me." When he received his first firm paycheck that summer, the amount deducted in taxes alone was greater than any paycheck he'd ever received in his life.

His first few days at the firm were a crash course in class privilege. "The first thing I remember—it was the second day, and this was all pretty foreign to me—this guy comes around asking you if you want your shoes shined," Greg said, recounting a scene more New Delhi than New York. "The attorneys would take off their shoes and the guy would be in the hall just scrubbing their shoes. And then people would give him like five bucks or whatever the going tip rate was."

The culture shock never quite wore off. At a farewell dinner for summer associates that he attended with his wife, she mentioned at the table that they had briefly lived on a commune in New England. "I thought I was going to have a heart attack right at that moment," Greg remembered, noting how a partner he was close with quickly riffed on New England, steering the conversation safely away from any implicit criticisms of the corporate law lifestyle. Still, his coworkers "were really frightened. I think if there were children there, they would have removed their children from the table."

And this firm was hardly conservative by the standards of the industry. In fact, Greg had also chosen the firm because they offered their summer associates the opportunity to spend two weeks working for a public interest institution while receiving the same $2,500-a-week salary. Midway through the summer, Greg headed to Legal Services for New York City, which served his old Lower East Side neighborhood. "The way they work in there, it's just incredible," he said of the independent poverty law center funded largely with federal tax money through the Legal Services Corporation. "The computers never work. They're so slow, even trying to get access to WestLaw [the indispensable online search engine for court decisions] is just so slow it's painful. It's extremely frustrating."

When the summer associates rotated back to the firm from their two weeks in the public interest world, all anyone could talk about was the discrepancy in resources. Noting how similar the Legal Services office was to his social-work days, Greg mused, "If you came into that originally, you might be a little frustrated that things don't work well, but you sort of accept it and adapt." But the contrast—wondering if there'll be a striped sea bass entrée at lunch versus wondering if there'll be paper in the printer—was striking. In his darker moments, Greg entertained the notion that the firm used the program in a cynical attempt to boost their retention rates by giving summer associates a small taste of the saint's life. Whatever the intent of the firm, the discrepancy in resources and pay is no accident. As part of the Right's continuing effort to defund the Left, in 1995 the Gingrich Congress cut the Legal Services Corporation budget by a third. By starving legal aid offices of resources, Republicans deprived would-be public servants of opportunities to serve and, more importantly, deprived needy clients of the chance to receive top-notch legal representation. The funding has yet to be fully restored.

Even more perverse, Greg said, was that firm lawyers were the ones who garnered the prestige of community service. The nonprofit "had these legal services awards and [the recipient] was always a partner at a big firm. So you had these people who work every day for part of their career, and there's no recognition. But if you're a partner at a big firm and you get a first-year associate to work on a pro bono case for you, you get these crazy awards for commitment to pro bono and public service."

While Greg was plotting his escape from the firm, he finally understood why people like him sometimes put on the golden handcuffs for life. Having served as a summer intern at Ralph Nader's group Public Citizen, Greg first read about corporate law in Nader's 1996 book *No Contest: Corporate Lawyers and the Perversion of Justice in America*. "I just remember thinking, 'Those guys are sick. What are they doing? What happened? What did they lose?' Obviously I'm not that extreme, but I've lost a lot." Part of it, he admitted, is the carrot of working in a functional office and earning big money, but another factor is the stick of family finances and debt. "It's sort of like a horrible excuse. I used to rail at my friends who would use debt as an excuse because I do believe there are ways to work around it. But it's tough." Greg's wife, an adjunct professor at a small public university in New Jersey, earns just $2,000 a course—closer in pay to the shoeshine guy than to the law students he bows and scrapes for. "I think that the reality is with children, depending on what the financial situation is, I think it would be really difficult to pursue public interest law. But five years ago I would have definitely done it. I wouldn't have cared. I would have said the sacrifices don't matter to me. But now, now they do. So I've pretty much sold out."

10

RELEASING THE TRAP

How to Rebuild the Middle-Class Democracy

As Franklin Roosevelt took office in March 1933, decades of lax business regulation, tax cuts at the top, and government-abetted union busting had yielded a dramatically unequal nation. America was intended to be a middle-class democracy—a consciously crafted alternative to the class-bound aristocracies of Europe—but in the years between Reconstruction and the Great Depression, that vision had been turned on its head. "Economic royalists," as Roosevelt called them, had amassed unprecedented power while one-third of the nation was mired in poverty. Insecurity plagued all but the wealthiest of the wealthy.

Roosevelt's program for rebuilding the middle class was simple: bring up the bottom and hold down the top. To bring up the bottom, he offered government protection to the right of workers to organize and created America's first minimum wage—25 cents an hour—in 1938. To hold down the top, he proposed, first in 1936 and again in 1942, capping annual incomes by instituting a 100 percent income tax bracket. His 1942 proposal suggested it kick in at $25,000—about $300,000 today. Congress found this proposal too radical but met him halfway, instituting a 94 percent tax on income over $200,000 (a couple million dollars in today's money). After the war, the top rate was lowered to 91 percent. With these policies in place, when the postwar boom came, it turned America back into a middle-class society. America had no more millionaires after the 1950s than it had had during the Roaring Twenties; instead, it had a greatly expanded middle class. By contrast, the economic gains of recent years have shot the number of millionaires (and billionaires) through the roof, dramatically raising the price of the American Dream. Meanwhile, most Americans have seen no benefit at all; in five of the last six years, the nation's median income has actually dropped.

Although FDR was the first president to implement these egalitarian policies, he was hardly the first political leader to understand the benefits of progressive taxation and a middle-class society. Ancient Athens, the world's first democracy, was also the world's first society to institute a progressive tax system. (In its earlier tyrannical period, the Athenians had lived under an imposed flat tax.) Consequently, democratic Athens became the world's first society to fully unleash its most talented citizens. Among the free male population at least, Athenians were free to pursue their full range of talents, writing plays and philosophical texts, not merely making money, the great preoccupation of both underdeveloped societies and dramatically unequal societies like our own. By shifting the burden of supporting the government to those who could best shoulder it, the prosperous polis began to enjoy the fruits of civilization that its wealth made possible.

One of Athens' greatest unleashed talents, the philosopher Aristotle, discerned a connection between a society dominated by the middle class and political stability and justice. The rich and poor, he noted, were prone to criminality (think Enron and the Crips), while the middle class obeyed the laws. He concluded that a just and well-run state must be controlled by a middle-class majority.

In the East, too, thinkers gleaned a connection between egalitarian distributions of wealth and social well-being. Confucius wrote, "Where wealth is centralized, the people are dispersed. Where wealth is distributed, people are brought together."

In the United States, with its plentiful land, open frontier, and constitutional ban on hereditary titles of nobility, it was not until the Gilded Age that the forces of plutocracy gained the upper hand. Yet decades earlier, Thomas Jefferson had written that it was theoretically possible for "the laws of property [to be] so far extended as to violate natural right." Under such conditions, he endorsed progressive taxation as the best method of addressing the inequities. A "means of silently lessening the inequality of property," Jefferson wrote, "is to exempt all from taxation below a certain point, and to tax the higher portions of property in geometrical progression as they rise." Late in life, he began to grow worried. "I hope we shall crush in its birth the aristocracy of our monied corporations which dare already to challenge our government," he wrote in 1816.

By Roosevelt's time, the measures Jefferson envisioned were long overdue. The Gilded Age had put American egalitarianism in danger. The British visitor Lord Bryce observed in 1888, "Sixty years ago, there were no great fortunes in America, few large fortunes, no poverty. Now there is some poverty . . . many large fortunes, and a greater number of gigantic fortunes than in any other country in the world." Roosevelt's aim was not to remake the United States from scratch, but to restore the original promise of America, a land where the vast class differences that plagued Europe would not permanently take root. His goal, as Langston Hughes put it in a 1938 poem, was to "let America be America again."

Today, we are a nation with millions of millionaires and millions of working poor that has largely given up on lifting up the bottom and holding down the top. As the lid has come off, public goods like education have gotten so expensive that millions are priced out and millions more contort their working lives to stay afloat. Dyed-in-the-wool Republicans have long been wary of an egalitarian America. As onetime Republican campaign strategist Kevin Phillips put it, "The concentration of wealth [is] what the Republican party is all about." But what was once the reactionary fantasy of a handful of archconservatives is now embraced by the entire Republican Party, by much of the Democratic Party establishment, and, through diversity-in-lieu-of-equality ideology, by many Americans who consider themselves "liberals." Even as the insecurity that has long plagued working-class Americans has worked its way up the socioeconomic ladder—consider Google's college-educated temps with no health care or job security—there has been no serious political effort to counteract these trends.

In recent decades, cozying up to business and the political donor class has become an explicit strategy among New Democrats affiliated with the conservative Democratic Leadership Council. The DLC think tank, the misnamed Progressive Policy Institute, used its very first policy paper to oppose raising the minimum wage. Reactionary positions like this one may win corporate donations—Philip Morris, Merck, and, before its implosion,

Enron, all cut checks to the DLC—but they have eaten away at the party's popular appeal. A 2006 Pew survey found 86 percent of Americans support raising the minimum wage. Thomas Frank was being downright polite when he called the Democrats' strategy of running away from economic populism rather than running on it "criminally stupid."

At the other end of the economic spectrum, the Republican tax-cutting rampage, with its misguided belief that progressive taxation tethers the talented by punishing success, shows no signs of abating. Despite myriad studies demonstrating that the Bush tax cuts have only accelerated the upward redistribution of wealth, the president continues to argue that they should be made permanent. While even Andrew Mellon, the tax-slashing Treasury secretary of the 1920s, conceded that "the fairness of taxing more lightly incomes from wages [than] from investments is beyond question," Bush has lowered the top tax rate on investments to 15 percent—below the rate on wage and salary income paid by middle-class Americans. And Bush has championed the permanent elimination of the estate tax, a sure route to creating a hereditary aristocracy (a form of polity against which his very existence ought to serve as a stern warning).

Sadly, the contemporary Democratic Party has also abandoned a taxation strategy that would rebuild the middle class. Instead, it has shifted the tax burden to the middle class to pay for tax cuts for the rich. Democrats have repeatedly raised the Social Security tax, a payroll tax on only the first $94,200 of earned income that disproportionately hits the middle class. When Democrats first agreed to this policy to help cover Reagan's budget deficits, Senator Daniel Patrick Moynihan rightly called it "thievery." Yet the thievery continues. In 1970, the maximum Social Security tax was $327. Today it is nearly $6,000.

More and more, the parties disagree only on social issues, both agreeing that progressive taxation and regulation of business should be kept to a minimum.

Despite living in the least heavily taxed society in the Western world, a generation of unanswered Republican antitax rhetoric and an unfair distribution of the tax burden has convinced most Americans that taxes are still too high. In nations where there remains an active debate on taxation, government services, and economic inequality, all but conservatives support higher taxes. Sixty-two percent of Britons told pollsters in 2001 that taxes were too low. Only 1 percent of Americans agreed.

But with the tax system we have, it is no wonder Americans are so dissatisfied. As *New York Times* tax beat reporter David Cay Johnston has exposed, when you add up all the taxes Americans pay—income, payroll, consumption—we essentially have a flat tax. Americans making $50,000 to $75,000 pay the same percentage of their incomes in taxes as the four hundred highest-income families in the country. And despite paying this de facto flat tax, what do Americans get for it? The Britons who told pollsters taxes were too low presumably understood that higher taxes meant better health care and higher education. In the United States, higher taxes mean *less* money for health care and higher education. It's no surprise we're such antitax zealots.

But the United States could adopt the British strategy—using progressive taxation to fund health care and higher education. This would not merely trim the wealth of the wealthy, it would ensure that a person does not have to become wealthy just to provide for one's family. In doing so, it would free America's most talented to pursue all their ambitions, just as it did in ancient Athens. Those Americans who hoped to become rich as Croesus could still pursue their dream, but so could those best suited to become philosophers like Aristotle, playwrights like Euripides, or politicians like Pericles.

Freedom Through Free Higher Education

The cost of a single year at a top private college is now equal to the nation's median household income. Not surprisingly, college administrators are failing to woo students from low- and moderate-income families, casualties of sticker shock, fear of debt, and the sorely underfunded high schools that many low-income children attend without gaining a preparation for college. In the 1960s, federally supported student aid, combined with modest tuition and merit-based admissions, helped elite colleges to diversify. Today, the trends have been reversed. In the decades after World War II, the proportion of students from upper-income families on elite campuses fell. Today, it is rising again.

More than just limiting who can attend a top college, the tuition spiral means career options for those who do are hemmed in by debt. Two-thirds of students now graduate in the red. Average debt loads have doubled in the past decade, as has the percentage of college students graduating with debt. Almost no one is immune: nearly half of children from six-figure-earning families now take out loans for college. While only 5 percent of young people currently start their professional lives with educational debt loads that place them six figures in the hole, as tuitions continue to outpace inflation, this percentage is growing rapidly. And the most indebted are generally the most talented and ambitious—those who don't come from wealthy families, but pursued elite higher education regardless. As journalist

Brendan Koerner put it in the *Village Voice,* educational debt constitutes an "ambition tax." Diverting these people away from public service and creativity is already taking its toll. And it will only get worse.

Debt-ridden graduates' choices are further constricted by the understanding that unless the system is changed their children's tuition will be even higher. According to current estimates, *public* college tuition for a child born today will be $150,000. Private college tuition is estimated to be at least double that. Back when public colleges were largely free, private college tuitions were modest, and the nation's wealth more broadly shared, America's unusual system of higher education financing was defensible. Today, it is not.

A simple reform, endorsed by economist and former Cornell budget director Ronald Ehrenberg, would allow elite private colleges to peg their tuitions to inflation or inflation plus 1 percent per year. This would effectively call a truce in the educational spending arms race, which has now spiraled beyond useful improvements like computer clusters to superfluous things like cushy dorms. The proposal has been stalled because it requires that colleges be given an antitrust exemption by Congress to allow them to collectively coordinate their prices. Yet it is hard to argue that the current system of "free market" pricing, which has resulted in annual tuitions equal to annual household incomes, is serving the public good. Ehrenberg also suggests that Congress close the loophole that lets universities keep their tax-exempt status even if, unlike other nonprofits, they fail to spend 5 percent of their endowments every year. This would force universities to spend rather than hoard their billions. For many top schools, we're talking real money. Five percent of Harvard's endowment comes out to over $1 billion a year.

While these reforms are practical and achievable, they do not get to the heart of the problem: financing education through debt is doing it backwards. A more reasonable way to fund education, embraced in the rest of the developed world, is through progressive taxation. Let students earn a free berth at a top university through talent and hard work. Then let them do what they want with their lives, taking any number of available jobs or striking out on their own as entrepreneurs. Undoubtedly, a healthy number will want nothing more than to become as rich as possible. Through progressive taxation, those who go into high-paying fields will bear a larger burden of supporting the education system that gave them their ticket to riches. But those who seek to give back to society in other ways—through teaching, the arts, or government service—could do that, too, free from worries about debt or their children's tuitions.

How would we create such a system? We used to have one. Many of our public universities were once tuition-free. When they were, they served as ladders of social mobility. My grandparents, for example, the children of immigrants, attended the City University of New York, which, in their day, was both excellent and free. Today it is neither.

And the situation keeps getting worse. As the low-tax vision of freedom continues to go unchallenged, state education funding lags, and public university tuitions grow higher and higher. Embarrassingly, at the University of Virginia, founded explicitly to provide education at public expense to those with talent but without wealthy parents, only 8 percent of the 2005 budget came from taxpayer dollars—and, as mentioned earlier, only 8 percent of students came from the bottom half of the income distribution. Top public institutions, like the law school at UC

Berkeley, have begun instituting tuitions nearly as high as their private peers. Rather than serving as beacons of freedom for students hoping to go into public service, public universities have become sellout factories, virtually indistinguishable from their private rivals. Using taxes rather than tuition to fund public universities is fiscally feasible. Nations far less wealthy than our own manage to do it. It is simply a matter of political will.

But private universities should not be let off the hook. While most developed nations have few, if any, private colleges, Britain is an exception. In the United Kingdom, they have used a hybrid model of privately run universities funded largely with public money.

After World War II, Britain's flagship university, Oxford, was transformed into a state-funded institution. A generation into the experiment, the university had made great strides in going from blue blood to blue collar, boasting five times as many undergraduates from working-class backgrounds as Harvard. In 1962, Parliament passed a law to provide full tuition for all British undergraduates and stipends for those from modest backgrounds. This voucher system is still in place, though it is now supplemented by modest tuition. Oxford gets a $10,000 annual grant per student and a state-capped tuition fee of up to $6,000 based on ability to pay. Endowment funds and outside grants make up the rest of the budget. While British aristocrats grouse that Oxford isn't what it used to be—and indeed some top professors have defected to American universities, with their sky-high pay (funded by sky-high tuition) for academic superstars—Britain's top universities have been able to maintain excellence and a large degree of local control. The latest rankings put Oxford, along with the similarly funded Cambridge, among the top five universities in the world. The U.S. Supreme Court's 2002 ruling that Cleveland's primary and secondary school voucher program was constitutional suggests that a publicly financed voucher system for higher education modeled on the British system would be constitutional as well, despite the religious affiliations of many private colleges.

Because of the retreat of government support, private dollars make up a larger proportion of higher-education funding than public dollars for the first time in decades. Our privately funded educational system speaks to our mixed-up priorities, not our inability to make publicly funded higher education a reality once again. Because of the opposite trajectories of our higher education policies, Britain has made strides in dismantling its inherited class system while America has been building one.

Quality Public Schools as a Right, Not a Privilege

In his 1991 jeremiad *Savage Inequalities,* Jonathan Kozol details the funding discrepancies between city and suburban public schools and tallies the cost in lives. He concludes his discussion of the New York–area schools, where twice as much money is spent on a child in the well-to-do suburbs as in the city, with a simple statement: "In an ethical society, where money was apportioned in accord with need, these scalings would run almost in precise reverse." At the time, Kozol hoped to arouse compassion in his readers for the children of the poor. More than a decade after his book was written, those "savage inequalities," left unaddressed and coupled with rising economic inequality, have made the failings of America's primary and secondary educational system everyone's problem.

During his research, conducted from 1988 to 1990, inner-city teachers and principals at school after school sheepishly confessed to Kozol that they sent their own children to top-notch private or suburban schools. In many of America's major metropolitan areas today, teachers and principals no longer have that luxury. The escape routes professional parents traditionally used have been closed off. In cities, gentrification has made magnet school admissions more competitive than ever. The upward redistribution of wealth has ratcheted up private school tuitions and home prices in suburbs with good public schools. Equalizing school funding is no longer just the right thing to do to ensure all children start life on a level playing field; it is necessary if we are to ensure parents' freedom to live adult lives typified by choice rather than economic compulsion.

The professional parents interviewed for Kozol's book often demonstrated a solipsistic, self-serving obliviousness to the plight of the poor. Now, fifteen years later, the fact that many of today's liberal arts graduates can't easily buy their way out of America's unabashedly unequal education system may seem just desserts. But vengeance is not a constructive response— even if it is a common one, particularly on the Left, where many dismiss parents' desires for good schools as a sign of internalized "privilege." That progressives often buy into the conservative notion that our wealthy nation is not wealthy enough to provide good schools for all its children shows how overwhelming the conservative consensus has become. The consensus should be just the opposite: ensuring that every public school district has the funds it needs to offer high-quality education should be beyond debate in any rich nation that calls itself a democracy.

The Overworked American

As the class divide has widened, it has increased the desperation of educated people to stay on the right side of it. As a result, professionals are now working harder than ever to keep themselves and their families from falling into the abyss. CNN reported in 2001, "You're not imagining it. . . . The United Nations International Labor Organization has the proof: 'Workers in the United States are putting in more hours than anyone else in the industrialized world.'"

This statistic should be surprising. In general, as nations grow wealthier and their workers more productive, they work shorter hours. For decades, America followed this pattern, but over the last generation the trend has been reversed. While the British work 7 percent less than they did a generation ago, we work 20 percent more.

As the CNN report suggests, many Americans don't fully understand how bizarre we are. We are so busy working, we rely on stereotypes—for example, that the Japanese are harder workers—because we have no time to see the rest of the world. While today it is within the economic reach of a middle-class American to go to Japan—round-trip fares sometimes dip below $500—few do. Jet lag precludes a long weekend, increasingly the only kind of vacation working Americans can take. (In reality, the Japanese now work on average a hundred fewer hours a year than Americans do.)

U.S. workers have no government-mandated paid vacation—a benefit that exists in every other industrialized country and even some developing nations (six weeks in Brazil, three in Saudi Arabia). Even in those professional jobs that offer three or four weeks of paid vacation—enviable amounts in America—those who take them are often seen as slackers, liable to be passed over for promotion or even fired. No wonder only 20 percent of Americans even bother to get a passport.

But why do we work so much? Not out of greed but out of something approaching its opposite: the new inequality has rendered the standards of living of all but the wealthy so precarious that overwork has become the price of standing still on a moving treadmill. As income inequality has returned to Gatsby-era levels, so have working hours. Americans are literally working as many hours now as they did during the 1920s.

It's easy to see how this phenomenon works at the bottom of the economic spectrum. The rise in corporate power and the decline of unions means low-skilled workers have less leverage to negotiate their working hours and time off. A working-class job in a unionized Ford plant included paid vacation; a working-class job at a nonunion fast-food joint likely does not.

The rise in hours among professionals has the same roots. As rising inequality has pushed up the sticker price on the American Dream, a new generation seeking the same homeownership and quality schools that were widely available to professionals a generation ago must work that much harder to attain the same things. High marginal tax rates that once discouraged workaholism have been repealed. When top tax rates were higher, only professionals who enjoyed their jobs or were seeking a promotion put in tons of hours. If Uncle Sam was going to get 70 percent of your $10,000 bonus, why put in the extra time? If it wasn't your true calling, it made more sense to clock out at five and get some exercise, play catch with your kids, read the newspaper, or volunteer on a political campaign. (It's called *"free time"* for a reason.) But today, the top tax rate of 33 percent sends the message that greed is good, and with ever more cash needed to attain the basics, most offices have enough people burning the midnight oil that those who clock out at five do so at their peril.

When Ronald Reagan slashed tax rates, inducing work was on his mind. After all, it was as an actor in 1940s Hollywood, when millionaire movie stars faced a 91 percent tax rate, that Ronald Reagan became a conservative. After shooting a few pictures, Reagan saw no incentive to work, so he didn't. (Screen a few Reagan flicks and you'll quickly see why he was unable to fathom that some actors might view their work as an art form with value in itself, not merely a way to get rich quick.) Renowned for his complete lack of a traditional American work ethic—he famously quipped, "They say hard work never killed anybody, but I figure why take the chance?"—it seemed to Reagan that people could only be made to work through compulsion or greed. His push to slash welfare at the bottom and taxes at the top flowed from this cynical view of humanity. But economic incentives alone can't account for why today's Hollywood stars continue to make movies or today's CEOs continue to show up for work. After a certain point, they become so rich that adding another zero to their bank accounts has no impact on their lifestyles. If they didn't get some noneconomic satisfaction out of what they were doing, they wouldn't be doing it.

Thus, it is the nonwealthy—those who have to work—who are hurt by the policies Reagan enacted. His policies didn't just push the poor off the dole, they pushed professionals' noses to the grindstone. Because of the peculiarities of American labor law, professionals are more vulnerable to "speed-up"—a term coined for overwork back in the days when bosses could literally speed up the rate of movement on the assembly line—than less skilled workers. Salaried professionals aren't eligible for overtime pay when they work more than forty hours a week. Managers, an overly broad category that encompasses anyone who directs an underling's work regardless of whether they're paid a salary or own the company, have no legal right to unionize. This creates perverse incentives for employers to overwork their professional staff. Professional overtime is literally free labor. In the industries packed with ambitious, debt-soaked young graduates—corporate law and management consulting—salaries have soared while working conditions have plummeted. In these industries, the forty-hour workweek no longer exists, and even the weekend and the lunch break are no longer taken for granted. Among tech professionals, a majority report working more than forty hours a week; 37 percent regularly work over fifty hours.

It may be comforting to know that these employees are well paid, but that doesn't mean overwork has no consequences. An hour at work is an hour you can't spend with your family, an hour you can't devote to your community, an hour you can't use for your own personal development. As the nineteenth-century labor movement slogan said: "Eight hours work, eight hours rest, eight hours what we will." The final eight have been swallowed by work and its requirements in contemporary America, and the result is our impoverished civic and family lives. The average American two-income couple talks just twelve minutes a day; American parents play with their children on average forty minutes a week.

An hour is an hour is an hour whether spent in a coal mine or a cubicle. You may not get black lung working in an office park, but you're kidding yourself if you think overwork isn't detrimental to your health. While the forty-year-old businessman's massive heart attack is so common it has become a cliché, the full health effects of overwork are still being uncovered. A UC Davis study of female lawyers found that those who worked long hours were three times more likely to suffer a miscarriage than those who worked a traditional 9-to-5 schedule with a lunch hour or those who worked part-time. (Of course, these are not the "unborn children" conservatives get all worked up about.)

For the good of American workers at all levels on the wage scale, we have to slow down the treadmill.

Addressing the Salary Gap

In the aftermath of the Enron scandal, the Senate Finance Committee issued a sixteen-hundred-page report. One of the key reasons Enron didn't get caught until it collapsed, the report concluded, was that its shelters were so complicated the IRS couldn't understand them. The accountants and tax lawyers Enron had hired to create its tax shelters were better than the IRS agents hired to police them. Today, many of the top tax shelter advisers are former IRS employees. It should be expected when you consider the yawning gap in salaries between the public and private sectors. For the brightest agents, switching sides has become the normal career path. According to whistle-blowers, IRS agents routinely treat clients represented by top firms with kid gloves because they're gunning for lucrative job offers at those very firms.

That the government pays its professionals below-market rates is no accident. Reagan's assistant federal workforce direc-

tor wrote in a 1986 *Wall Street Journal* op-ed that doing so channels the most talented young people into corporate America—
exactly where, in his opinion, they ought to be. The recent
corporate crime wave is an understandable side effect of living
in the nation Reagan made.

But the rising salary gap between the public and private sectors can be addressed. Enacting truly progressive taxation would
do a lot to pull after-tax incomes closer together. Look at how
the current tax system treats the $50,000-a-year government
prosecutor and the $150,000-a-year corporate lawyer working op-
posite sides of the same white-collar crime case. The income tax
rate on the last dollar earned by the prosecutor is 25 percent,
while the last dollar for the corporate lawyer is taxed at 33 percent. However, when Social Security taxes are factored in, the
tax differential disappears. The prosecutor pays a 6.2 percent
flat tax on her whole salary, but the corporate lawyer only pays
the tax on her first $94,200; she gets the equivalent of a 6.2 per-
cent raise on the remaining $55,800. In the end, the system is
anything but progressive.

The second way to address the gap is even simpler: the public sector should pay its professionals more. It need not match
the preposterous executive salaries of the private sector, but it
must compete for professional talent. The geography of the new
inequality necessitates paying higher salaries to public sector
workers in the more expensive regions of the country. The majority of today's top college graduates tell pollsters that they want
to work in government and public service. If they could do so
and be assured a life of homeownership and good schools for
their children, far more would surely act on these desires. This
would not only help them, it would help us all.

Healing Our Health-Care System

The American health-care system has accomplished the seemingly impossible feat of spending more money and getting worse results than the system of any other developed nation. Of late, our average life expectancy has fallen not just below those of our peer countries, but those of poorer nations like Greece and Martinique. A recent study of the U.S. and British health systems found that the richest third of Americans are sicker than the poorest third of Britons. This statistic is particularly shocking considering the United Kingdom spends less than half as much on health care per person as the United States and its system has worse outcomes than the more egalitarian health-care systems of continental Europe. It is also shocking because the British are among the only people in the world who rival Americans when it comes to overindulgence in food and drink.

In America, the working poor and the self-employed are up a creek. Even seemingly secure professionals are just a divorce or a downsizing away from losing coverage. And those with coverage remain in danger because of insurance companies' aversion to paying for preventive care.

The best way to ensure lower costs and better outcomes in the American health-care system would be to reform it—no shocker here—along the lines of the numerous nations with lower costs and better outcomes. A universal, publicly funded system would ensure that all Americans have health-care coverage and would eliminate the outrageous overhead costs that insurance companies waste on screening out those with preexisting conditions and rationing care to their policyholders.

While Americans overwhelmingly believe in universal coverage, reform has been stymied in Washington by the companies that profit from the system that makes Americans sick. Today doctors, long wedded to the money and status they derived from the status quo, are losing faith. In part, the change in opinion is generational: the American Medical Student Association backs a single-payer system while the American Medical Association does not. But practicing doctors are being won over even if their official representatives at the AMA keep their heads in the sand. In a 2006 Fox News story on the problems in American emergency rooms, the correspondent had to admit, "The doctors interviewed . . . unanimously decried the deterioration of emergency room care and see a single-payer universal health plan as the answer." If reactionary Fox News couldn't scrounge up a doctor against single-payer health care, it surely wasn't for lack of effort.

The End of Compassionate Conservatism (and Compassionate Liberalism, Too)

When America created its own particular variety of social safety net after World War II, it made sense. Major employers were offering jobs for life. Widespread union membership ensured health care and rising wages for most workers. The GI Bill meant a generation of Americans could graduate from college debt-free. One income could support a middle-class family.

None of these things are true today. And this necessitates a new role for government.

What holds us back is an outdated view of the social safety

net as a form of charity for those too poor or old or infirm to get what they need on their own (think George W. Bush's "compassionate conservatism"). In other developed countries, social insurance is based on an understanding that modern society requires that we pool our resources for certain necessities. Nearly all of us, at some time in our lives, face enormous expenses. Rather than having each member of society face this cost on his or her own, we should pool the risk and share the cost. If we don't, all but the superrich will end up scrounging for basics like child care, health care, and education.

Consider raising children. This is a terribly expensive endeavor—in fact, reproducing is now the number-one risk factor that an American will end up filing for bankruptcy. The official government estimate for upper-middle-class families is that they will ultimately spend $270,000 raising a child to age seventeen—a number that doesn't include higher education. And it's a low-ball estimate. It tallies up the annual child-care and education bill for a four-year-old at a preposterously low $2,750.

Despite the staggering expenses, statistics show most of us will raise children. For a woman, biological necessity dictates that this will happen early in her adult life, likely before she has hit the prime of her career and has saved the requisite money. Hence the current twin epidemics of relying on parents for money well into adulthood, what the *New York Times* dubbed the "Bank of Mom and Dad," and that retro-hip Victorian pastime, frog-kissing. Understanding economic realities and biological facts, most developed nations provide universal child care subsidized through tax dollars. Everyone pays into the system before, during, and after they have small children. When they have their children, they take advantage of the child-care benefits. To an extent, these programs help fund themselves by allowing more mothers to remain in the workforce, continuing to pay taxes into the system even as they use day care for their children. More important, they increase people's freedom, allowing them to marry for love, reproduce based on their emotional readiness rather than financial considerations, and balance work and family as they see fit.

Without such a program, fewer and fewer educated young women are having children at all, a phenomenon one journalist named "The Baby Boycott." Fully one-third of American women in their late thirties with graduate degrees are childless. In 2003, *The New York Times Magazine* published a cover story on what it called "The Opt-Out Revolution"—well-educated women taking time off from professional careers to raise children. But it missed the forest for the trees. Statistics show the real "opt-out revolution" is educated women opting out of having children altogether.

If childbearing comes early in life, higher education comes even earlier. Even the most industrious young person couldn't possibly foot the bill for college through her own initiative. These days, it's hard to know whether to laugh or cry at the jar marked "tips for college" at your local scoop shop. No number of lemonade stands and paper routes can raise $150,000 by age eighteen. Thus we end up relying on parents to foot the bill and then feign surprise when we see that our top universities are filled with the children of wealthy parents.

The spiraling costs of health care and education mean even the comfortably upper middle class is no longer that comfortable. Children from upper-middle-class families routinely go into debt to go to college. In terms of health care, professionals, not just low-end service workers, can find themselves uninsured. In 2005, only 63 percent of college graduates in entry-level jobs had company-provided health-care coverage, down from 70 percent in 2000. Even the elite professions are no longer immune. A physician colleague of my mother's was recently diagnosed with cancer, forcing her to leave her job. For eighteen months, she can keep her insurance through COBRA. Afterward, if she isn't healthy enough to return to work, she will find herself uninsured and unable to get affordable coverage. At that point, the only ways to get insurance will be to declare bankruptcy and go on Medicaid, have her husband, who had been covered through her plan, find a new job with insurance, or find a new husband (3 P.M.—radiation therapy; 6 P.M.—speed dating).

As stories like this become more common, the debate is changing. On health care, universal coverage now has overwhelming majority support from the American people. It's just a matter of getting the political system to overcome the inertia of entrenched interests to enact it. As for education, as growing inequality pushes tuition higher and higher, more and more articulate college-educated people are feeling the squeeze. As American history has shown ever since the Stamp Act, this is not the demographic you want to piss off. Few will continue to accept an America in which health care, education, and child care—what are rightly considered human rights in the rest of the world—are sold to the highest bidder.

And it's not just health care and education that are targeted for reform. People under thirty-five are the only age group in which most say they would vote to join a union if offered the chance. Young people were the force behind the campaign of Howard Dean, the reformist Democrat insurgent in the last presidential election. In the general election, among voters under thirty, even Mississippi was a blue state. When we know doctors who may end up without health insurance and French majors from Vassar who are living in subsidized housing—hardly the image Reagan had in mind when he demonized the "welfare queen"—it's bound to change our outlook on the promise of America. So does our experience in the professional labor market, which gives the lie to conservative rationalizations for income inequality. It's not about education. The tremendous salary gaps within the legal profession are all among people who, by definition, have the same amount of formal education. It's not about hard work, either. Nobody believes six-figure lobbyists work harder than congressional staffers. And it's not about the work's value to society. By that standard, teachers would be earning more than the people marketing junk food to their students. It's about the work's value to corporate America. Professional pay is nothing but a measure of one's obeisance to the plutocrats.

To the rising generation, the need for a new New Deal is clear. The only question that remains is whether the overwhelming power of the status quo will thwart our reformist impulses by turning the most articulate among us into self-loathing corporate drones.

The Triumph of American Pragmatism Over American Exceptionalism

A key reason historians have always cited for America's lack of an adequate safety net is our belief in social mobility—our so-called American exceptionalism. No matter how wide the gulf between rich and poor, the thinking went, a rich kid could always end up poor and a poor kid could always end up rich. Talent mattered more than inherited wealth. While the myth was always larger than the reality—moving up was always easier for whites than for anyone else and moving down was rare—in the period after World War II, Americans really did enjoy tremendous social mobility. But with the dramatic rise in inequality over the last generation, and with it, a newly entrenched economic elite hostile to creating policies to ensure equality and freedom for all, America's social mobility is now on par with class-rigid Great Britain. Surprisingly, for observers on both the left and right, the most egalitarian societies—those of Scandinavia—exhibit the greatest degree of social mobility. The Right had long believed that a laissez-faire market system provided the greatest opportunities for people to move up, unburdened by government regulations or progressive taxation. The Left largely agreed with this proposition, but felt the goal of equality outweighed the need for increased dynamism. In today's knowledge-based economy, it is clear that egalitarian policies that guarantee higher education, health care, and child care—the sorts of policies that release talented individuals from dependence on employers, spouses, and accident of birth—are in fact best for ensuring social mobility and unleashing creativity.

The vast majority of Americans have always wanted a society in which individuals can define their own fate. The system that once allowed for this has broken down, so we must build a new one. American pragmatism must trump American exceptionalism. As FDR said, "To some generations much is given. Of other generations much is expected. This generation of Americans has a rendezvous with destiny."

BEYOND "WHAT SHOULD I DO WITH MY LIFE?"
TO "WHAT SHOULD WE DO WITH OUR COUNTRY?"

Countless times when I gave people the cocktail party sketch of this book, they replied, "Oh, so it's sort of like that Po Bronson book, *What Should I Do With My Life?*"

"Not exactly," I would offer.

Bronson's 2002 bestseller tells the inspiring stories of people who found meaning in their lives by overcoming "the seduction of money." Researched in the brave new world "after Enron," when "we were losing our respect for corporate leaders," Bronson found "dozens of people who were morally troubled by their work. They felt they were screwing society, not improving it."

One such screwer is the man Bronson calls "Bryce." With a geology degree from the University of Texas in Austin, Bryce landed a job with an environmental consulting firm. It sounded like a great gig—getting paid to clean up the environment. But as he soon found out, the firm had been set up by a major oil company to provide "independent" analysis of its often leaky underground storage tanks. Bryce's bonuses would be linked to his reports that the tanks were not leaking gas or toxic benzene into the groundwater. After some time in the moral wilderness, Bryce switched sides, going to work for the county bureau that polices the oil companies. Despite having a government pay-check amounting to less than half of what he had made at the consulting firm, the story has a happy ending, as Bronson tells it. Bryce regained his moral compass and even got the girl (his rediscovered integrity wins the heart of his old high school sweetheart).

Considering the Hollywood ending, Bronson remains puzzled. "For all those who were morally troubled by their work, it surprised me how few considered simply switching sides." He does not speculate on why it is so rare, choosing not to raise questions such as, if Bryce had already been married with a few kids, could he really afford to switch sides? Would he be able to afford to send them to college at the ever-rising rates? Through his stories, Bronson inspires us to live better lives within the rules of society, but he does not challenge us to change those rules. Of course the county pays its watchdogs less than half of what the oil companies pay their consultants; of course the oil companies get away with hiring "independent" consultants from firms they secretly fund. The only thing we need to change is our attitude.

People like Bryce, or the saints profiled in this book, prove there are still those willing to make the ever greater sacrifices required to live lives in harmony with their values. But even if all the guilt-ridden sellouts pulled a Bryce, overcoming their guilt by becoming saints, it would not extricate us from our predicament. New sellouts would just step up to take the jobs they'd left. The saints' own children would ultimately face greater pressures to sell out as they emerged into adulthood buried in debt. To extricate ourselves, our resistance must be political. We must build a society that does not force these wrenching choices onto us all—a society in which supporting yourself and your family does not require selling your soul.

◆

To understand the futility of individual sainthood, consider the first time American society was overflowing with guilt-ridden sellouts. In the years after the Revolution, the United States was brimming with slaveholders who didn't believe in slavery, sitting atop a social order they knew to be unjust and out of character with the new nation.

"Abolitionist slaveholder," like "Lehman Brothers leftist," may sound like a contradiction in terms. Yet such people were common in late-eighteenth- and early-nineteenth-century America. The Revolution that embodied the egalitarian values of the Enlightenment made self-loathing hypocrites of many slaveholders who knew the slave system was morally wrong and had to be abolished, yet whose economic livelihoods came from it. The Marquis de Chastellux noted on his visit to Virginia just after the Revolution that the slaveholders were "constantly talking of abolishing slavery." While the young meritocrats of contemporary America are conflicted about their place near the top of our deeply unequal social order, their inner turmoil is nothing compared to what haunted the abolitionist slaveholders.

The abolitionist slaveholder par excellence was Thomas Jefferson. The man who famously declared that "all men are created equal" called slavery a "blot" and "stain" upon America. He drafted over a dozen pieces of legislation to abolish slavery in his home state of Virginia. As president, he tried to block slavery's expansion into the new states of the West. And yet Jefferson owned over two hundred human beings and had a penchant for giving them away as wedding presents. Dying in debt and knowing that his slaves were his family's best hope for financial security, the only slaves Jefferson freed in his will were Madison and Eston Hemmings—people we now know to have been his own enslaved children.

Jefferson was no saint. When the rules of society are unjust, saints follow their own set of rules; they answer to a higher authority. A Saint Thomas surely would have freed his slaves, martyring himself in the cause of equality, impoverishing himself and his family in order to do what was right. But Thomas Jefferson was unwilling to unilaterally free his slaves because it would put him and his family at an economic disadvantage relative to his contemporaries who would not free theirs. Instead, he endorsed changing the rules so that no one could own slaves, setting a baseline of ethical behavior beneath which no one could slip, no matter how alluring the profits. If everyone were forced to give up their slaves, Jefferson could do the right thing without martyring himself or dooming his offspring to poverty. Only by enacting decent rules, Jefferson understood, can we create a society in which the vast majority of us—neither saint nor criminal, neither so good we will go above and beyond what the rules require nor so evil we will break whatever rules are set—can live decent lives.

Rejecting Jefferson's wisdom, contemporary conservatives promised that a lack of rules (what they termed "deregulation," a neologism coined in 1965) would set us free. But the opposite is true. As James Madison put it in *The Federalist Papers*, "If men were angels, no government would be necessary." We don't need to become angels, we need to become reformers.

As in the time of slavery, our society does not need more saints, it needs better rules. The hypercompetitive and intensely

unequal system under which we now live is a product of the re-
moval of rules. Today, as we compete ever more fiercely to buy
our human rights—good educations, decent housing, and adequate health care—at the ever higher prices demanded by the
market, only those who stifle their altruistic urges can claim
these things; those who do not must forfeit them. Only by
changing the rules to rebuild the middle class and provide health
care and quality education for all can we create a society in
which you need not be a saint to live in harmony with your values should you happen to dissent from the reigning order.

◆

While conservatives have long feared that enacting more egalitarian policies would lead to sloth—Goldwater's "lazy dole-
happy people" and Reagan's "welfare queens"—the American
people must be trusted with the freedom such policies would
provide. The energy and creativity evident in the entrepreneurs
and professionals in this book should reassure us all. It is an energy and creativity that has typified Americans from the start—
the exceptional "mores" that Alexis de Tocqueville observed and
the "democratic style" that German social theorist Werner Sombart noted. It is the "style" of which Saul Bellow wrote when he
began his *Adventures of Augie March,* "I am an American,
Chicago-born—Chicago that somber city—and go at things as I
have taught myself, free-style." A more egalitarian America
would unleash our nation's talent. We could truly become the
"Creative Society" Reagan promised but his policies crushed.
We could reclaim our right to pursue happiness in myriad ways,
not merely the narrow pursuit of material wealth enshrined by
corporate conservatives and imposed by the system they have
created.

For an example of a talent unleashed to pursue happiness in his own unique way, one need look no further than Thomas Jefferson, the man who edited out of the Declaration of Independence John Locke's myopic "right to property" and replaced it with a more broad-minded, American concept: "the pursuit of happiness." Born an aristocrat, Jefferson could have lived a life of sloth, but as an American, he was far too ambitious for that. In his life, Jefferson made significant contributions to numerous fields whose principal rewards are nonmonetary—science, architecture, education, and politics. Jefferson understood that his aristocratic birth and private education had given him the ability to pursue his talents. Cognizant of his good fortune, he understood that a just and dynamic society would afford this opportunity to all, that a society should not leave the flowering of talent to chance. The gifted, not merely the high-born, must be able to contribute, both for their own sake and for the sake of society and humanity. For those as talented but not as privileged as he, a full flowering of talent would be impossible without egalitarian policies and institutions.

Jefferson's aim in crafting the modern world's first post-aristocratic society was motivated by a sense that so much talent was going to waste. As our society has grown more unequal, this same squandering of talent has begun to plague us again. Too many, trapped in poverty, are not given an adequate chance to develop their talents. Others reach their educational potential only to find themselves corralled, by debt and the financial burden of raising a family without a safety net, into an ever narrower set of career paths.

These problems, attributable to accident of birth, have no place in a post-aristocratic republic. Today, in a modern, prosperous America, we can afford to give free rein to all the talented, public-spirited, potential Jeffersons among us—rich or poor, white or black, male or female—and reclaim the pursuit of happiness. But to do so, we must overthrow the failed policies of recent decades and see through their mirage of false freedom.

Introduction

3. *"Moloch whose blood"*: Allen Ginsberg, "Howl and Other Poems" (San Francisco: City Lights Books, 1959).

7. *"fat man eating quails"*: Mickey Kaus, *The End of Equality* (New York: TNR Books/Basic Books, 1992), 14–15.

8. *poor and rich neighborhoods*: Jason C. Booza, Jackie Cutsinger, and George Galster, "Where Did They Go?: The Decline of Middle-Income Neighborhoods in Metropolitan America" (Washington, D.C.: Brookings Institution, June 2006), 11.

8. *only 41 percent*: Ibid., 4.

8. *smallest share*: Sam Roberts, "Study Shows a Dwindling Middle Class," *New York Times,* June 22, 2006.

8. *only 28 percent*: Booza, Cutsinger, and Galster, "Where Did They Go?" 7–8.

8. *nearly half of children*: Anya Kamenetz, *Generation Debt: Why Now Is a Terrible Time to Be Young* (New York: Riverhead, 2006), 7.

9. *decline in social mobility*: Janny Scott and David Leonhardt, "Shadowy Lines That Still Divide," *New York Times,* May 15, 2005.

9. *Nader outpolled*: Kelly Rohrs, "Nader Defeats Bush in Ward 1," *Yale Daily News,* November 8, 2000.

9. *opinion surveys*: Miranda Green, "Accountancy Moves Higher Up in Students' Jobs Wishlist," *Financial Times,* October 12, 2005. Despite

accounting firms' rise in the rankings, that sector remained behind public service.

10. *starting teachers:* Matt Miller, *The 2 Percent Solution* (New York: PublicAffairs Books, 2003), 121.

10. *priced out of the region's:* National Association of Home Builders, "Where Is Workforce Housing Located?: A Study of the Geography of Housing Affordability" (Washington, D.C., 2004). According to the report, teacher-headed households have been priced out of 92.4 percent of the New York area's census tracts.

11. *support universal health care:* Lee Walczac, Richard Dunham, Mike McNamee, and Ann Therese Palmer, "'I Want My Safety Net': Why Americans Aren't Buying In to Bush's Ownership Society," *BusinessWeek,* May 16, 2005.

12. *"We can have a democracy":* Louis Brandeis, quoted in Lewis Lapham, "Class Act," *Harper's,* July 7, 2006.

12. *Even executives' pay:* Malcolm Gladwell, "The Risk Pool," *The New Yorker,* August 28, 2006, 30.

13. *Harvard tuition ran $400:* Michael Bennett, *When Dreams Came True: The GI Bill and the Making of Modern America* (Washington, D.C.: Brassey's, 1996), 18.

13. *"athwart history":* William F. Buckley Jr., quoted in John Micklethwait and Adrian Wooldridge, *The Right Nation: Conservative Power in America* (New York: Penguin Press, 2004), 15.

15. *"No Arts; no Letters":* Thomas Hobbes, *Leviathan* (New York: Penguin Classics, 1651; 1985 edition), 186.

16. *voted for the same bill:* Elizabeth Warren and Amelia Warren Tyagi, *The Two-Income Trap: Why Middle-Class Mothers and Fathers Are Going Broke* (New York: Basic Books, 2003), 123–26.

16. *"The financial services industry":* Elizabeth Warren interview, "The Secret History of the Credit Card," *Frontline,* WGBH Boston, 2004, http://www.pbs.org/wgbh/pages/frontline/shows/credit/interviews/warren.html.

17. *"One of the most salient features":* Harry Frankfurt, *On Bullshit* (Princeton, N.J.: Princeton University Press, 2005), 1, 22.

17. *"act affirmatively":* Duncan Kennedy, "Legal Education as Training for Hierarchy," in *The Politics of Law: A Progressive Critique,* ed. David Kairys (New York: Basic Books, 1998), 54.

18. *"I have some notion":* William F. Buckley Jr., *God and Man at Yale: The Superstitions of "Academic Freedom"* (Chicago: Henry Regnery Company, 1951), xvi.

1. The Rising Sticker Price on the American Dream

20. *teachers have been priced out*: National Association of Home Builders, "Where Is Workforce Housing Located?: A Study of the Geography of Housing Affordability" (Washington, D.C., 2004), 5, 11.

21. *"Banana Republic economy"*: David Callahan, *The Cheating Culture: Why More Americans Are Doing Wrong to Get Ahead* (Orlando, Fla.: Harcourt, 2004), 67.

21. *African nation of Namibia*: Sam Roberts, "In Manhattan Poor Make 2 Cents for Each Dollar to the Rich," *New York Times*, September 4, 2005.

21. *most unequal country*: UN Human Development Report (New York: United Nations Development Programme, 2005), 38, 272.

21. *Berkeley, California*: Roberts, "In Manhattan Poor Make 2 Cents for Each Dollar."

22. *Republican Party donor*: Joel Bakan, "Corporations Unbound," in *Inequality Matters: The Growing Economic Divide in America and Its Poisonous Consequences,* ed. James Lardner and David Smith (New York: New Press, 2005), 192.

22. *top 5 percent own*: Edward Wolff, "The Rich Get Richer," *The American Prospect,* February 12, 2001.

22. *63 percent higher than*: Chamber of Commerce Researchers Association, ACCRA Cost of Living Index (Indianapolis, Ind.), Second Quarter, 1984; American Chamber of Commerce Researchers Association, ACCRA Cost of Living Index (Arlington, Va.), Second Quarter, 2004.

22. *median home price*: Reuters, "Home Prices in San Francisco Hit New High," September 14, 2005, http://money.cnn.com/2005/09/14/real_estate/homes_bayarea.reut/.

22. *percentage of income a household*: David Leonhardt and Motoko Rich, "Twenty Years Later, Buying a House Is Less of a Bite," *New York Times,* December 29, 2005.

23. *rents rose 76 percent*: Tamara Draut, *Strapped: Why America's 20- and 30-Somethings Can't Get Ahead* (New York: Doubleday, 2006), 13.

23. *"Surreal Estate"*: Column by Carol Lloyd, http://sfgate.com/columnists/lloyd/.

25. *While Google, which generated $3.6 billion*: Sam Gustin, "Google: The New Port Authority," *The Village Voice,* September 12, 2006.

28. *average sale price:* Dean E. Murphy, "Cut-Rate Homes for Middle-Class Are Catching On," *New York Times,* September 29, 2005.

28. *savage in California:* Jonathan Kozol, *Savage Inequalities: Children in America's Schools* (New York: Crown, 1991), 220.

28. *"local education foundations":* Eilene Zimmerman, "Class Participation: How Local Fund-raising Promotes School Inequality," *Harper's,* October 2005.

29. *"Funding to Novato Public Schools":* http://www.novatoschoolfuel.org/breakingnews.htm.

29. *priced out of 99.7 percent:* National Association of Home Builders, "Where Is Workforce Housing Located?: A Study of the Geography of Housing Affordability" (Washington, D.C.: 2004), 11.

31. *mayors of San Carlos and Cupertino:* Maria L. LaGanga, "Priced Out of Public Service," *Los Angeles Times,* March 29, 2005.

31. *projects for the upper middle class:* Murphy, "Cut-Rate Homes for Middle Class Are Catching On."

31. *"New York has always attracted":* Charles Bagli and Janny Scott, "110-Building Site in N.Y. Is Put Up for Sale," *New York Times,* August 30, 2006.

32. *"I'm shocked":* Guy Trebay, "Fashion Diary: The Prices! Rising Fast and Still Finding Buyers," *New York Times,* September 12, 2005.

32. *"triumph of upper America":* Kevin Phillips, *The Politics of Rich and Poor: Wealth and the American Electorate in the Reagan Aftermath* (New York: Random House, 1990), xvii.

33. *"fueled their demand":* Charles T. Clotfelter, *Buying the Best: Cost Escalation in Elite Higher Education* (Princeton, N.J.: Princeton University Press, 1996), 61.

33. *Dartmouth's tuition:* U.S. News and World Report, "America's Best Colleges 2006" issue.

33. *"can't understand why":* Matthew Quirk, "The Best Class Money Can Buy," *The Atlantic,* November 2005, 132.

33. *Though these trends were ameliorated:* David Leonhardt, "Climbing Up, and Losing Ground," *New York Times,* January 8, 2006.

34. *reduced federal student aid:* Clotfelter, *Buying the Best,* 69; Ronald Ehrenberg, *Tuition Rising: Why College Costs So Much* (Cambridge, Mass.: Harvard University Press, 2000), 83, 270.

34. *3 percent of students:* Jennifer Washburn, *University, Inc.: The Corporate Corruption of American Higher Education* (New York: Basic Books, 2005), 208.

34. *8 percent of students:* David Leonhardt, "The College Dropout Boom," in *Class Matters* (New York: Times Books, 2005), 93.

34. *"whose parents are"*: Thomas Jefferson, letter to M. Correa de Serra, quoted in "Jefferson on Politics and Government: Publicly Supported Education," http://etext.virginia.edu/jefferson/quotations/jeff1370.htm.

34. *better investment*: Ehrenberg, *Tuition Rising*, 9.

34. *now look nationally*: Robert Frank and Philip Cook, *The Winner-Take-All Society: Why the Few at the Top Get So Much More Than the Rest of Us* (New York: Free Press, 1995), 157.

36. *$38,851*: Agreement between the Board of Education of the City of Chicago and the Chicago Teachers Union, 1979 and 2003.

36. *most American college students now graduate in the red*: Mary Beth Pinto and Phylis M. Mansfield, "Financially At-Risk College Students: An Exploratory Investigation of Student Loan Debt and Prioritization of Debt Repayment," *The NASFAA Journal of Student Aid.* 35:2(2006),22.

37. *world's largest financial institution*: Michael Hudson, "Banking on Poverty," *Mother Jones,* July/August 2003.

37. *"For a guaranteed return"*: Citigroup Advertising Showcase, http://www.citi.com/citigroup/showcase/liverichly.htm.

38. *"Be independently happy"*: Joseph Lamport, "Wake Up and Smell the Subterfuge," Slate.com, February 4, 2002.

2. Home and Hearth

39. *"If you marry"*: Søren Kierkegaard, quoted in John Updike, "Incommensurability," *The New Yorker,* March 28, 2005.

45. *$29,000 a year*: http://www.dalton.org/information/admission/aid.asp.

46. *only 1,640 units*: Joseph Berger, "Homes Too Rich for Firefighters Who Save Them," *New York Times,* April 4, 2006.

46. *"Economics are the method"*: Margaret Thatcher, quoted in David Harvey, *A Brief History of Neoliberalism* (New York: Oxford University Press, 2005), 23.

49. *found more attractive*: Guenter Hitsch, Ali Hortacsu, and Dan Arieli, "What Makes You Click?: An Empirical Analysis of Online Dating," University of California at Santa Cruz, Economics Department Seminar (2004), figures 5.2 and 5.6.

49. *men in the teaching profession*: Alison Lobron, "Subtraction Problem," *The Boston Globe,* August 28, 2005.

49. *"predator-nurturer" marriage*: David Brooks, *Bobos in Paradise* (New York: Simon and Schuster, 2000), 16.

49. *consciously model it*: Cheryl Mendelson, *Morningside Heights* (New York: Random House, 2003), jacket copy, 136, 278, 326.

51. *$40 teapot*: Bryan Curtis, "Target: Discount Retail Goes to *The New Yorker*," Slate.com, August 17, 2005.

52. *unprecedented ad buy*: Stuart Elliott, "In a *New Yorker* First, Target to Be Sole Advertiser," *New York Times*, August 12, 2005.

52. *"burnish the image"*: Ibid.

52. *"then if I buy"*: Curtis, "Target: Discount Retail Goes to *The New Yorker*."

52. *million-dollar ad buy*: Elliott, "In a *New Yorker* First, Target to Be Sole Advertiser."

53. *four easy payments*: Business reply cards, *The New Yorker*, June 12, 2006.

54. *"epicurean selfishness"*: Samuel Coleridge, in Russell Jacoby, *The End of Utopia* (New York: Basic Books, 1999), xiii.

55. *"commodity fetishism"*: Karl Marx, in *The Marx-Engels Reader*, ed. Robert Tucker (New York: W.W. Norton, 1978), 319–21.

55. *"a golden age"*: Milton Friedman and Rose Friedman, *Free to Choose* (New York: Harcourt Brace Jovanovich, 1979), 3.

3. The Road to Microserfdom

56. *"America stands at the crossroads"*: Quoted in John A. Andrew, *The Other Side of the Sixties* (New Brunswick, N.J.: Rutgers University Press, 1997), 55.

56. *sunny Saturday*: Ibid., 56.

56. *state's largest elm tree*: Gregory Schneider, *Cadres for Conservatism: Young Americans for Freedom and the Rise of the Contemporary Right* (New York: New York University Press, 1999), 30, 31.

57. *C-word had become*: John Micklethwait and Adrian Wooldridge, *The Right Nation: Conservative Power in America* (New York: Penguin, 2004), 8.

57. *capture "democracy"*: Andrew, *The Other Side of the Sixties*, 56, 57.

57. *unleash individual talent*: Schneider, *Cadres for Conservatism*, 18.

57. *top marginal tax rate*: Kevin Phillips, *The Politics of Rich and Poor: Wealth and the American Electorate in the Reagan Aftermath* (New York: Random House, 1990), 77–78.

58. *oil and real estate*: Schneider, *Cadres for Conservatism*, 12, 31; Micklethwait and Wooldridge, *The Right Nation*, 51.

58. *Few of the students*: Schneider, *Cadres for Conservatism*, 33.

58. *tactics they often cribbed:* Rick Perlstein, *Before the Storm: Barry Goldwater and the Unmaking of the American Consensus* (New York: Hill and Wang/FSG, 2001), 410–11.

58. *YAF became known:* Schneider, *Cadres for Conservatism*, 17, 66–68, 74, 97, 98.

58. *attracting tens of thousands of applications:* Elizabeth Cobbs Hoffman, *All You Need Is Love: The Peace Corps and the Spirit of the 1960s* (Cambridge, Mass.: Harvard University Press, 1998), "Appropriations, Volunteers and Trainees, and Applications," Appendix.

59. *right-to-work laws:* Perlstein, *Before the Storm*, 28.

59. *"I would rather have":* Ibid., 37.

59. *equality of the postwar period:* Paul Krugman, "Losing Our Country," *New York Times*, June 10, 2005.

59. *"Government has a right":* Barry Goldwater, quoted in Perlstein, *Before the Storm*, 64, 269.

59. *put up signs:* Ibid., 342.

60. *"what kind of freedom":* Walter Cronkite, quoted in Schneider, *Cadres for Conservatism*, 80.

60. *"It is quite possible":* Theodore White, quoted in Perlstein, *Before the Storm*, 444.

60. *forty times:* Perlstein, *Before the Storm*, 391.

61. *lead to totalitarianism:* Friedrich August von Hayek, *The Road to Serfdom* (Chicago: University of Chicago Press, 1944).

61. *"opened new frontiers":* Milton Friedman, *Capitalism and Freedom* (Chicago: University of Chicago Press, 1962), 3–4, 15.

61. *heavily annotated volume:* Micklethwait and Wooldridge, *The Right Nation*, 48.

62. *"One of the traditional ways":* Ronald Reagan, quoted in Robert Dallek, *The Right Moment* (New York: Free Press, 2000), 39.

62. *nationally televised speech:* Perlstein, *Before the Storm*, 501.

62. *"tousled boyish haircut":* Kiron K. Skinner, Annelise Anderson, and Martin Anderson, eds. *Reagan: A Life in Letters* (New York: Free Press, 2003), 705.

62. *"near hemophiliac liberal":* Micklethwait and Wooldridge, *The Right Nation*, 90.

62. *"There is no such thing":* Perlstein, *Before the Storm*, 502.

62. *his own "Creative Society":* Ronald Reagan, *The Creative Society* (New York: Devin-Adair, 1968).

63. *"The point of the present occasion":* William F. Buckley Jr., quoted in Schneider, *Cadres for Conservatism*, 86.

63. *flocked to Ralph Nader's:* Nicholas Lemann, "The Kids in the Conference Room," *The New Yorker,* October 18, 1999.

64. *"effete snobs":* Richard Nixon, quoted in Phillips, *The Politics of Rich and Poor,* 38.

64. *minimum annual income:* Micklethwait and Wooldridge, *The Right Nation,* 70.

64. *"about as nutty as":* Richard Nixon, quoted in Schneider, *Cadres for Conservatism,* 121.

64. *five-thousand-word:* Lewis Lapham, "Tentacles of Rage," *Harper's,* September 2004.

64. *"the time had come":* Lewis Powell, quoted in David Harvey, *A Brief History of Neoliberalism* (New York: Oxford University Press, 2005), 43.

64. *"stampede to support":* Lewis Powell, quoted in John B. Judis, *The Paradox of American Democracy: Elites, Special Interests, and the Betrayal of the Public Trust* (New York: Pantheon, 2000), 117.

64. *"lies in organization":* Lewis Powell, quoted in Harvey, *A Brief History of Neoliberalism,* 43.

64. *the Business Roundtable:* Ibid.

65. *nearly half of Americans:* Micklethwait and Wooldridge, *The Right Nation,* 89.

65. *"Of course they remember":* Quoted in Perlstein, *Before the Storm,* 487.

65. *capital gains tax:* Phillips, *The Politics of Rich and Poor,* 49.

65. *favor the rich:* Micklethwait and Wooldridge, *The Right Nation,* 89.

65. *"Does the federal government":* Terry Culler, "Most Federal Workers Need Only Be Competent," *Wall Street Journal,* May 21, 1986.

66. *a higher ratio:* Lewis Lapham, "Editor's Notebook," *Harper's,* April 2005. The current ratio in France is 15:1; in Sweden it is 13:1; in the United States it is 475:1.

66. *"What I want to see":* Ronald Reagan, quoted in Phillips, *The Politics of Rich and Poor,* 52. The quote is from 1983.

66. *"The party of the little man":* Ibid., xi.

66. *"The Reagan Revolution":* David Stockman, quoted in Robert Perrucci and Earl Wysong, *The New Class Society: Goodbye American Dream?* (Lanham, Md.: Rowman and Littlefield, 1999), 71.

66. *Reagan ended the policy:* Phillips, *The Politics of Rich and Poor,* 67, 78, 80, 88, 111.

67. *minimum wage to fall below the poverty line:* Harvey, *A Brief History of Neoliberalism,* p. 25.

67. *"a successful economy":* George Gilder, quoted in Phillips, *The Politics of Rich and Poor,* 62.

67. *billionaires quadrupled:* Ibid., 24, 157, 179.

67. *no one had thought to count them:* "Reagan and the Homeless Epidemic in America," Democracy Now!, Pacifica radio program transcript, June 17, 2004; Kenneth L. Kusmer, *Down and Out, On the Road: The Homeless in American History* (New York: Oxford University Press, 2003), 239; Peter Rossi, *Down and Out in America: The Origins of Homelessness* (Chicago: University of Chicago Press, 1989), 44. Before the 1980s, Americans lacking adequate housing often lived in single-room occupancy hotels (SROs); "on-the-street" homelessness was virtually unknown.

67. *"Cutting government spending":* Ronald Reagan, quoted in Schneider, *Cadres for Conservatism,* 170.

68. *group was dwindling:* Schneider, *Cadres for Conservatism,* 160.

68. *Surveys showed:* Hendrik Hertzberg, "The Short Happy Life of the American Yuppie," *Esquire,* February 1988, 107.

68. *"defund the Left":* Thomas Frank, "Defunders of Liberty," *New York Times,* August 29, 2006.

68. *applied for the same entry-level:* Robert Frank and Philip Cook, *The Winner-Take-All Society* (New York: Free Press, 1995), 147.

68. *starting salary for new associates:* Phillips, *The Politics of Rich and Poor,* 169, 175.

68. *"the big questions":* Hertzberg, "The Short Happy Life," 101, caption.

69. *"most aged yuppie":* Ibid., 101.

69. *survey found 82 percent:* Phillips, *The Politics of Rich and Poor,* 213.

69. *campaign on social issues:* Thomas Frank, *One Market Under God: Extreme Capitalism, Market Populism, and the End of Economic Democracy* (New York: Doubleday, 2000) 27.

69. *single tax increase:* Micklethwait and Wooldridge, *The Right Nation,* 97.

69. *better-packaged platform:* Michael Graetz, *The Decline (and Fall?) of the Income Tax* (New York: W. W. Norton, 1997), 163.

70. *"Good Buildings":* Tom Wolfe, quoted in Paul Krugman, "The Rich, the Right, and the Facts," *The American Prospect,* September 1, 1992.

70. *tried to discredit it:* Ibid.

70. *"new industrial dictatorship":* Franklin D. Roosevelt, quoted in Cass Sunstein, *The Second Bill of Rights: FDR's Unfinished Revolution and Why We Need It More Than Ever* (New York: Basic Books, 2004), 76.

70. *"marginally less addicted":* Micklethwait and Wooldridge, *The Right Nation,* 366.

71. *most Americans thought:* Graetz, *The Decline (and Fall?) of the Income Tax,* 170–74.

71. *Clinton threw in the towel:* Frank, *One Market Under God,* 94, 314.

71. *rising inequality:* Louis Uchitelle, "College Degree Still Pays But It's Leveling Off," *New York Times,* January 13, 2005.

71. *deregulation:* Reuters, "Clinton Signs Legislation Overhauling Banking Laws," November 13, 1999; "Business Digest," *New York Times,* February 2, 1996.

71. *Microsoft or Cisco Systems:* David Cay Johnston, "Study Finds That Many Large Companies Pay No Taxes," *New York Times,* October 20, 2000.

71. *"The opposition":* Frank, *One Market Under God,* 17.

71. *"The libertarian view":* Jaron Lanier, quoted in ibid.

71. *working more:* Clara Jeffery, "The Road to Nowhere," *Mother Jones,* July/August 2005, 27.

72. *world's leading suicide location:* Tad Friend, "Jumpers," *The New Yorker,* October 13, 2003.

72. *the rising generation:* Martha Irvine, "Big Voter Turnout Seen Among Young Adults," *USA Today,* November 8, 2004; Neil Howe and William Strauss, *Millennials Rising: The Next Great Generation* (New York: Vintage, 2000), 214–17, 229–33.

73. *largest reductions:* Paul Krugman, *Fuzzy Math: The Essential Guide to the Bush Tax Plan* (New York: W. W. Norton, 2001), 90.

73. *only 2 percent of estates:* Paul Krugman, *The Great Unraveling: Losing Our Way in the New Century* (New York: W. W. Norton, 2003), 149.

73. *most stock is owned:* Edward Wolff, "The Rich Get Richer," *The American Prospect,* February 12, 2001.

73. *vast majority of the cuts:* Jonathan Weissman, "Congress Passes $350 Billion Tax Cut Bill," *Washington Post,* May 24, 2003.

73. *count on a windfall:* Krugman, *Fuzzy Math,* 105–7.

73. *didn't connect the proposed tax cuts:* Larry Bartels, "Homer Gets a Tax Cut: Inequality and Public Policy in the American Mind," *Perspectives on Politics* 3:1 (March 2005), 15–31.

74. *controls more wealth:* David Callahan, *The Cheating Culture: Why More Americans Are Doing Wrong to Get Ahead* (Orlando, Fla.: Harcourt, 2004), 67.

74. *taxes are too low:* Micklethwait and Wooldridge, *The Right Nation,* 303.

74. *the power to choose:* Hayek, *The Road to Serfdom,* 100.

74. *"it's your hurricane"*: Thomas Friedman, "Osama and Katrina," *New York Times*, September 7, 2005.

74. *no higher than in Great Britain*: Janny Scott and David Leonhardt, "Shadowy Lines That Still Divide," *New York Times*, May 15, 2005.

75. *Microserf*: Douglas Coupland, *Microserfs* (New York: ReganBooks, 1995).

4. Selling the Body Politic

76. *nation's most oft-struck employer*: Steven Greenhouse, "In Ivy League, Yale Is Leader in Labor Unrest," *New York Times*, April 4, 1996. In terms of number of strikes, no single workplace tops Yale, though industrial giants like Caterpillar and General Motors with dozens of factories have incurred more strikes in total.

76. *father was a union-busting corporate lawyer*: "An Appealing Magic," *Guardian*, May 17, 2003.

79. *"multicultural caste system"*: Garret Keizer, "Left, Right, and Wrong," *Mother Jones*, March/April 2005 (cover story).

79. *"Multiculturalism [went] from"*: Walter Benn Michaels, "Class Fictions," *Boston Globe*, October 9, 2005.

80. *1979 leadership change*: Lee Lescaze, "Change at Ford Foundation," *Washington Post*, January 30, 1979.

80. *replaced by Franklin Thomas*: John B. Judis, *The Paradox of American Democracy: Elites, Special Interests, and the Betrayal of the Public Trust* (New York: Pantheon, 2000), 163.

80. *rebounding record*: John Kifner, "From Brooklyn Restoration to Ford Foundation," *New York Times*, January 30, 1979.

80. *Bundy grew up*: Geoffrey Kabaservice, *The Guardians: Kingman Brewster, His Circle, and the Rise of the Liberal Establishment* (New York: Henry Holt, 2004), 6, 26.

80. *broadcast reruns*: Ibid., 276.

81. *create the emerging field*: Ibid., 431.

81. *resigned from the board*: Lesley Oelsner, "Ford Foundation Seeks a Skipper for Future Course," *New York Times*, January 3, 1979.

81. *"The Foundation exists"*: Henry Ford II, quoted in Judis, *The Paradox of American Democracy*, 163.

81. *front page*: Larry Kramer, "Ford Foundation to Stop Aid to 'Public Interest' Law Firms," *Washington Post*, September 14, 1979.

81. *effectively complied*: Judis, *The Paradox of American Democracy*, 164.

81. *profits rise:* Steven Greenhouse and David Leonhardt, "Real Wages Fail to Match a Rise in Productivity," *New York Times,* August 28, 2006.

83. *only 30 percent of American jobs:* Stuart Tannock, "Higher Education, Inequality, and the Public Good," *Dissent,* Spring 2006, 45.

83. *"for an American autoworker":* Mickey Kaus, *The End of Equality* (New York: Basic Books, 1992), 38.

83. *"You want to reverse":* Bill Clinton, quoted in Kaus, *The End of Equality,* x. Preface to the 1995 paperback edition.

83. *compared to college grads:* Louis Uchitelle, "College Degree Still Pays But It's Leveling Off," *New York Times,* January 13, 2005.

83. *"If college education becomes universal":* Michael Zweig, *The Working Class Majority: America's Best Kept Secret* (Ithaca, N.Y.: ILR Press, 2000), 45.

84. *giving out more lottery tickets:* James K. Galbraith, *Created Unequal: The Crisis in American Pay* (New York: A Twentieth-Century Fund Book/Free Press, 1998), 264–65.

84. *right to organize:* Human Rights Watch, "Unfair Advantage: Workers' Freedom of Association in the United States Under International Human Rights Standards" (2000), http://www.hrw.org/reports/2000/uslabor/.

84. *invaluable solidarity:* For a discussion of labor organizing among autoworkers during the depths of the Depression, see David Farber, *Sloan Rules: Alfred P. Sloan and the Triumph of General Motors* (Chicago: University of Chicago Press, 2002), 193–206.

84. *Anglo-American capitalism:* Thomas Friedman, "We're All French Now?" *New York Times,* June 24, 2005.

84. *minimum wage nearly twice:* BBC News, "Minimum Wage Increased to £5.05," February 25, 2005, http://news.bbc.co.uk/1/hi/uk_politics/4296097.stm.

84. *one in twenty:* John Micklethwait and Adrian Wooldridge, *The Right Nation: Conservative Power in America* (New York: Penguin, 2004), 7.

84. *higher than our own:* "A Taxing Question," *The Economist,* June 16, 2001.

85. *used it only once:* John Kerry, DNC acceptance speech, July 31, 2004: "We can and must finish the march toward full equality for women in this country."

85. *Bush outdiversified even Clinton:* Susan Page, "Bush Is Opening Doors with a Diverse Cabinet," *USA Today,* December 9, 2004.

85. *Linda Chavez:* Steven Greenhouse, "Senate Panel Gives Warm Welcome to New Labor Nominee" *New York Times,* January 25, 2001.

85. *"Welcome, Mr. Kaus"*: Aaron Wildavsky, "Cultural Identity Crisis," *National Review*, September 14, 1992, 56.

86. *"a magical world"*: Barbara Ehrenreich, *Nickel and Dimed: On (Not) Getting By in America* (New York: Metropolitan Books, 2001), 221.

86. *"Wherever they have settled"*: David Brooks, *Bobos in Paradise* (New York: Simon and Schuster, 2000), 269.

86. *"best of all possible worlds"*: Voltaire, *Candide*, trans. Robert M. Adams (New York: W. W. Norton, 1991 [1759]), 2.

87. *because they want to*: Richard Florida, *The Rise of the Creative Class: And How It's Transforming Work, Leisure, Community, and Everyday Life* (New York: Basic Books, 2002), 110.

87. *"Sometimes I'm asked"*: Lee Clow, quoted in Brooks, *Bobos in Paradise*, 136.

87. *"The long trajectory"*: Florida, *The Rise of the Creative Class*, 122.

88. *often twelve hours long*: Irving Bernstein, *The Lean Years: A History of the American Worker, 1920–1933* (Boston: Houghton Mifflin, 1960), 9.

88. *3.5 weeks more per year*: Florida, *The Rise of the Creative Class*, 145ff.

89. *"There is no corporation"*: Ibid., 115.

89. *vision of a "Creative Society"*: Ronald Reagan, *The Creative Society* (New York: Devin-Adair, 1968).

89. *"golden era of profitability"*: UBS report, quoted in Greenhouse and Leonhardt, "Real Wages Fail to Match a Rise in Productivity."

90. *"New ideas must use old buildings"*: Jane Jacobs, *The Death and Life of Great American Cities* (New York: Modern Library, 1993), 245. Originally published by Random House in 1961.

90. *"have never known a world"*: Brooks, *Bobos in Paradise*, 37.

90. *"Jacobs could not afford"*: Paul Goldberger, "Jane-Washing," *Metropolis*, July 2006, 92.

90. *"So many people"*: Jacobs, *The Death and Life of Great American Cities*, 325–26.

91. *"Creative Class people no longer"*: Florida, *The Rise of the Creative Class*, 78.

91. *"Super-Creative Core"*: Ibid., 69.

92. *"trivial, vulgar, and wasteful"*: Ibid., 325.

92. *"Writers are really people"*: Walter Benjamin, "Unpacking My Library," in *Illuminations*, ed. Hannah Arendt, trans. Harry Zohn (London: Fontana, 1992), 61.

93. *"While people can be hired"*: Florida, *The Rise of the Creative Class*, 5.

93. *72 percent of Americans*: Ibid., 27.

93. *"Karl Marx had it partly right"*: Ibid., 37.

93. *his famed focus groups:* Paul Maliszewski, "Flexibility and Its Discontents," *The Baffler*, no. 16 (2003), 77.

95. *"Part of Jefferson's genius"*: Joseph Ellis, in *Thomas Jefferson: A film by Ken Burns* (Walpole, NH: Florentine Films, 1997).

96. *"fatal and false dichotomy"*: James MacGregor Burns, quoted in Doris Kearns Goodwin, *No Ordinary Time: Franklin and Eleanor Roosevelt: The Home Front in World War II* (New York: Simon and Schuster, 1994), 485–86.

98. *"economic royalists"*: Franklin D. Roosevelt, quoted in Cass Sunstein, *The Second Bill of Rights* (New York: Basic Books, 2004), 76.

98. *"Property rights might so interfere"*: Roosevelt, in ibid., 26.

98. *"Roosevelt was asserting"*: Burns, quoted in Goodwin, *No Ordinary Time*, 486.

98. *"The American dream"*: Reagan, *The Creative Society*, 41.

99. *polls showed 58 percent:* Paul Glastris, "Bush's Ownership Society: Why No One's Buying," *Washington Monthly*, December 2005.

99. *"corresponding part of his personal freedom"*: Milton Friedman, *Capitalism and Freedom* (Chicago: University of Chicago Press, 1962), 8.

5. Start Up, Slip Down

108. *In California, insurance companies:* http://www.calhealth.net/.

109. *half of American bankruptcies:* Editorial, "No Easy Health-Care Fix," *San Francisco Chronicle*, February 7, 2005.

109. *28 percent of Americans:* Richard Carter, "EU Lags Behind US in Entrepreneurial Culture," *EU Observer*, January 18, 2005.

110. *14.7 percent of the European workforce:* European Commission, "Panorama of the European Union, Regions: Statistical Yearbook 2005," (Luxembourg: Office for Official Publications of the European Communities), 66.

110. *7.3 percent of Americans:* http://www.bls.gov/cps/cpsaat12.pdf, and phone interview with economist Mary Bowler, Labor Force Statistics Office, Bureau of Labor Statistics.

110. *lowest level in decades:* John Alexander Burton, "Putting the Spotlight on Small Business" (Washington, D.C.: Center for American Progress), July 2005.

110. *veteran failed entrepreneur:* Molly Ivins and Lou Dubose, *Shrub: The Short But Happy Political Life of George W. Bush* (New York: Random House, 2000), 19–33.

111. *"Berlin is an entrepreneurs' heaven"*: Bertrand Benoit, "Berlin Cool Comes in from the Cold," *Financial Times*, February 25, 2006.

111. *Its harshest provisions*: Louise Witt, "Small Business: When Entrepreneurs Risk It All and Lose," *New York Times*, July 7, 2005; Helen Huntley, "Bankruptcy Law Ensnares Businesses," *St. Petersburg Times*, July 10, 2005.

111. *65 percent of Americans*: Eric Alterman, "Corrupt, Incompetent, and Off Center," *The Nation*, November 7, 2005.

112. *leading industry for political donations*: Robert Pear, "Medicare Law Prompts a Rush for Lobbyists," *New York Times*, August 23, 2005.

114. *20 million Americans work*: Steven Greenhouse, "Labor Union, Redefined, for Freelance Workers," *New York Times*, January 27, 2007.

116. *nearly 200,000*: Irving Bernstein, *The Lean Years: A History of the American Worker, 1920–1933* (Boston: Houghton Mifflin, 1960), 335.

116. *$1,000 a year for individuals*: http://www.freelancersunion.org/health-insurance-a/.

117. *"The artist should be the freest"*: Bill T. Jones, quoted in Rose Eichenbaum and Clive Barnes, *Masters of Movement: Portraits of America's Great Choreographers* (Washington, D.C.: Smithsonian Books, 2004), 150. Courtesy of Smithsonian Books.

6. From *Partisan Review* to Partisans Revue

120. *"I used to think"*: Larry Ellison, quoted in Andrew Sullivan, "London Fog," *The New Republic*, June 14, 1999, 25.

120. *Abel lived briefly*: Russell Jacoby, *The Last Intellectuals: American Culture in the Age of Academe* (New York: Basic Books, 1987), 50.

120. *could support herself*: Ellen Willis, *Don't Think, Smile!: Notes on a Decade of Denial* (Boston: Beacon Press, 1999), 156.

120. *"Economic exigencies"*: Jacoby, *The Last Intellectuals*, 21.

121. *"SoBro"*: Joseph Berger, "Goodbye South Bronx Blight, Hello So-Bro," *New York Times*, June 24, 2005.

121. *"So many of the people"*: Marshall Berman, quoted in Rebecca Solnit and Susan Schwartzenberg, *Hollow City: The Siege of San Francisco and the Crisis of American Urbanism* (New York: Verso, 2000), cover blurb.

121. *"Each generation"*: Kyong Park, quoted in "The Dark Side of Architecture," *Metropolis*, January 26, 2006.

123. *"sommelier at a four-star restaurant"*: Dan Gross, "Don't Hate Them Because They're Rich: The Trickle-Down Effect of Ridiculous, Ostentatious Wealth," *New York*, April 18, 2005, 24.

123. *borough has a higher percentage:* Tim Henderson, Samuel Nitze, and Lisa Arthur, "Housing Costs Strain Budgets," *Miami Herald,* August 31, 2005.

123. *gentrification has become inadequate:* Solnit and Schwartzenberg, *Hollow City,* 21.

123. *Sunday real estate section:* Dennis Hevesi, "Yes, There Are Apartments Out There for $1,000," *New York Times,* March 13, 2005.

124. *number of college professors:* Jacoby, *The Last Intellectuals,* 14.

125. *flocked to liberal arts courses:* Solnit and Schwartzenberg, *Hollow City,* 96.

125. *hardly a PhD thesis:* Jacoby, *The Last Intellectuals,* 19.

125. *"No one who has a live sense":* Irving Howe, quoted in ibid., 82.

125. *took a job at Brandeis:* Ibid., 83.

125. *defund the Left:* Thomas Frank, "Defunders of Liberty," *New York Times,* August 29, 2006.

125. *"people who in a better time":* David Bromwich, "Literary Radicalism in America," in Nicolaus Mills, ed., *Legacy of Dissent: Forty Years of Writing from Dissent Magazine* (New York: Simon and Schuster, 1994), 195. Essay originally published in 1985.

125. *"tenured radicals":* Roger Kimball, *Tenured Radicals: How Politics Has Corrupted Higher Education* (New York: HarperCollins, 1990).

126. *number of college freshmen:* Derek Bok, *The Cost of Talent: How Executives and Professionals Are Paid and How It Affects America* (New York: Free Press, 1993), 21.

126. *polled higher:* UCLA Higher Education Research Institute, *The American Freshman Survey,* http://www.gseis.ucla.edu/heri/03_norms_charts.pdf.

126. *increased more than fifteenfold:* http://www.kaplan.com/AboutKaplan/.

126. *Elmo Picture Quiz:* David Brooks, "The Organization Kid," *The Atlantic,* April 2001, 44.

126. *"Future Workaholics of America":* Ibid., 40, 41.

127. *"We used to sit for hours arguing":* Betty Friedan, *The Feminine Mystique* (New York: W. W. Norton, 1964), 152–53.

127. *top field is business:* U.S. Department of Education, National Center for Education Statistics.

127. *majority of undergrads pursue:* Jennifer Washburn, *University, Inc.: The Corporate Corruption of American Higher Education* (New York: Basic Books, 2005), 217.

127. *pressures of the market:* Thomas Frank, *One Market Under God: Extreme Capitalism, Market Populism, and the End of Economic Democracy* (New York: Doubleday, 2000), 278.

128. *"make money, study money, or attract money":* Harvard Magazine, quoted in Washburn, *University, Inc.*, xiv.

128. *usually less than $3,000:* Modern Language Association, "Summary of Data from Surveys by the Coalition on the Academic Workforce," 1999, http://www.mla.org/documents/survey_coalition/repview_coalition.

128. *22 percent of college faculty:* Linda Ray Pratt, "Disposable Faculty: Part-Time Exploitation as Management Strategy," in Caryl Nelson, ed., *Will Teach for Food: Academic Labor in Crisis* (Minneapolis: University of Minnesota Press, 1997), 265.

128. *Tenured faculty has dropped:* John W. Curtis, "Trends in Faculty Status, 1975–2003" (Washington, D.C.: American Association of University Professors Research Office), May 26, 2005. In 2003, 46.3 percent of faculty were part-time.

128. *25 percent chance:* Anya Kamenetz, *Generation Debt: Why Now Is a Terrible Time to Be Young* (New York: Riverhead Books, 2006), 49–50.

129. *$10,000 to $18,000 a year:* Karen W. Arenson, "NYU Graduate Students Say They'll Strike to Unionize," *New York Times,* November 1, 2005; Scott Sherman, "Bitter Winter at NYU," *The Nation,* December 20, 2005.

129. *Harvard Electricity Policy Group:* Washburn, *University, Inc.,* 81–83.

130. *more than twice as much:* Ronald Ehrenberg, "Don't Blame Faculty for High Tuition: The Annual Report on the Economic Status of the Profession, 2003–2004," *Academe* 90:2 (March/April 2004), figure 2.

130. *bonus of 50 percent:* Ibid., table D.

130. *near-seven-figure pay:* Washburn, *University, Inc.,* 200, 205.

130. *pay should be linked:* Adam Smith, *The Wealth of Nations* (New York: Modern Library, 2000), 820–21. (Orig. pub. 1776.) See also Robert Reich's introduction, xvi.

131. *"interested in propagating socialism":* William F. Buckley Jr., *God and Man at Yale: The Superstitions of "Academic Freedom"* (Chicago: Henry Regnery Company, 1951), 189.

131. *"he is inculcating values":* Ibid., 186.

131. *tenure was first created:* Washburn, *University, Inc.,* 205.

131. *"area that produces":* Ellen Schrecker, "Will Technology Make Academic Freedom Obsolete?" in Nelson, *Will Teach for Food,* 296.

131. *George Mason University barred undergraduates:* Washburn, *University, Inc.,* 213.

131. *eliminate the sociology departments:* Liz McMillen, "Faculty Panel Asks Yale to Reconsider the Scope of Its Restructuring Plan," *Chronicle of Higher Education,* 1992; Anthony DePalma, "Bad Times Force Universities to Rethink What They Are," *New York Times,* February 3, 1992.

131. *"the more pressing issue":* Washburn, *University, Inc.,* 218.

131. *toyed with an alternate subtitle:* Robert L. Heilbroner, *The Worldly Philosophers: The Lives, Times, and Ideas of the Great Economic Thinkers* (New York: Simon and Schuster, 1953), 242.

132. *they never mention money:* Michael Lewis, *Liar's Poker: Rising Through the Wreckage on Wall Street* (New York: Penguin, 1989), 18.

134. *"nothing more than something":* Bob Dylan, "It's Alright Ma (I'm Only Bleeding)." *Bringing It All Back Home,* Columbia Records, 1965.

134. *"And on Wall Street":* Yale Banner 2000 (yearbook), 391.

135. *half female:* Jonathan Glater, "Women Are Close to Being Majority of Law Students," *New York Times,* March 26, 2001; Association of American Medical Colleges, "Medical School Applications Increase," http://www.aamc.org/newsroom/reporter/deco3/medicalapps.htm.

136. *"all jobs to include":* Memo quoted in Steven Greenhouse and Michael Barbaro, "Wal-Mart Memo Suggests Ways to Cut Employee Benefit Costs," *New York Times,* October 26, 2005.

137. *"The first is the need":* Report quoted in Washburn, *University, Inc.,* 220.

137. *boom in right-wing philanthropy:* Lewis Lapham, "Tentacles of Rage," *Harper's,* September 2004.

137. *ten to one:* Eric Alterman, *What Liberal Media?: The Truth about Bias and the News* (New York: Basic Books, 2003), 82.

137. *larger budget:* John B. Judis, *The Paradox of American Democracy: Elites, Special Interests, and the Betrayal of Public Trust* (New York: Pantheon, 2000), 124.

137. *often dwarf:* Alterman, *What Liberal Media?,* 89.

138. *"We're not here":* Feulner, quoted in ibid., 83.

138. *"chosen for their views":* Fareed Zakaria, *The Future of Freedom: Illiberal Democracy at Home and Abroad* (New York: W. W. Norton, 2003), 230.

138. *"embrace [its] imperial destiny":* Fareed Zakaria, "Our Way," *The New Yorker,* October 14–21, 2002.

138. *funded by conservative:* Chris Mooney, *The Republican War on Science* (New York: Basic Books, 2005), 82.

138. *thousands of scientists:* Judis, *The Paradox of American Democracy,* 240–41.

138. *928 scientific papers:* Mooney, *The Republican War on Science,* 81.

139. *"Consensus as strong":* Quoted in ibid., 80.

139. *polls showing overwhelming support:* Eric Alterman, "Corrupt, Incompetent, and Off Center," *The Nation,* November 7, 2005, 12.

139. *millions of dollars are pouring in:* "Right-wing 'Think' Tanks and Health Policy," Physicians for a National Health Program Newsletter, Summer 2005, 38–39.

139. *more than fifteen to one:* Robert Perrucci and Earl Wysong, *The New Class Society* (Lanham, Md.: Rowman and Littlefield, 1999), 71.

7. Save Yourself

142. *hit-and-run:* Jaxon Van Derbeken, "Hit-and-Run Driver Kills Bicyclist, 26," *San Francisco Chronicle,* January 13, 2006.

142. *"We are in a war":* Thomas Friedman, "State of the Union," *New York Times,* January 27, 2006.

143. *Adjusted for inflation:* Bureau of Labor Statistics inflation calculator, http://www.bls.gov/bls/inflation.htm.

151. *$8.82 an hour:* Office of Labor Standards Enforcement, San Francisco, http://www.sfgov.org/site/olse_index.asp?id=27605.

152. *"openhanded compassion for the poor":* Bonaventure, *The Life of St. Francis* (San Francisco: HarperSanFrancisco, 2005), 7–8.

154. *20 percent of its applicants:* Avi Zenilman, "Now That's Classy," *Washington Monthly,* September 2006.

154. *12 percent of Yale's class of 2005:* Tamar Lewin, "Options Open, Top Graduates Line Up to Teach the Poor," *New York Times,* October 2, 2005.

156. *only 28 percent:* Zenilman, "Now That's Classy."

156. *"investigate charges of communism":* Lou Cannon, *Governor Reagan: His Rise to Power* (New York: PublicAffairs Books, 2003), 278.

156. *instituting tuition:* Ibid., 273.

157. *hundred-year-old tradition:* Verne Stadtman, *The University of California, 1868–1968* (New York: McGraw-Hill, 1970), 110.

157. *"The state should not subsidize":* Ronald Reagan, quoted in Anya Kamenetz, *Generation Debt: Why Now Is a Terrible Time to Be Young* (New York: Riverhead Books, 2006), 31.

157. *"Individuals should bear the costs":* Milton Friedman, *Capitalism and Freedom* (Chicago: University of Chicago Press, 1962), 105.

158. *second most economically unequal:* Sam Roberts, "In Manhattan Poor Make 2 Cents for Each Dollar to the Rich," *New York Times,* September 4, 2005.

158. *disparity between life:* Jason C. Booza, Jackie Cutsinger, and George Galster, "Where Did They Go?: The Decline of Middle-Income Neighborhoods in Metropolitan America" (Washington, D.C.: Brookings Institution, 2006), 8. The report showed that the loss of middle-class neighborhoods and the growth of low- and high-income neighborhoods in the Oakland metropolitan area between 1970 and 2000 was even more extreme than in most American regions.

158. *one of several corporate firms:* Zenilman, "Now That's Classy."

159. *"Before I arrived":* Teach for America "Start Here" brochure.

160. *"obey the rules or get out":* Ronald Reagan, quoted in Cannon, *Governor Reagan,* 272.

160. *town called Philadelphia, Mississippi:* William Raspberry, "Reagan's Race Legacy," *Washington Post,* June 14, 2004.

8. What Your Company Can Do for You

162. *posts in the federal government:* John Hechinger and Daniel Golden, "Fight at Princeton Escalates Over Use of a Family Gift," *Wall Street Journal,* February 7, 2006.

162. *30 to 40 percent:* Maria Newman, "Princeton University Is Sued Over Control of Foundation," *New York Times,* July 18, 2002.

162. *ideally like to work:* Miranda Green, "Accountancy Moves Higher Up in Students' Jobs Wishlist," *Financial Times,* October 12, 2005.

163. *most expensive in Princeton's history:* Anna Mulrine, "Is Private Good Enough?" *U.S. News & World Report,* April 12, 2004.

163. *"We have been mugged":* William Robertson quoted in Hechinger and Golden, "Fight at Princeton Escalates Over Use of a Family Gift."

163. *dean called "a crisis":* Mulrine, "Is Private Good Enough?"

164. *$32,000 as a congressional aide:* Hanna Rosin, "God and Country," *The New Yorker,* June 27, 2005.

165. *"lobbyists-in-training":* Anne E. Kornblut, "Once Just an Aide, Now a King of K Street," *New York Times,* February 5, 2006.

165. *salaries in the $20K–$30K range:* Ibid.

165. *"The disparity in salaries":* Charlie Cook, quoted in ibid.

165. *doubled as well:* Jeffrey H. Birnbaum, "The Road to Riches Called K Street," *Washington Post,* June 22, 2005.

165. *only sixty-two registered lobbyists:* Chuck Lewis, on *Now with Bill Moyers,* PBS, October 18, 2002.

165. *spurred by right-wing intellectuals:* Nicholas Confessore, "Welcome to the Machine," *Washington Monthly,* July–August 2003.

165. *grew from 89 in 1974:* Robert Perrucci and Earl Wysong, *The New Class Society* (Lanham, Md.: Rowman and Littlefield, 1999), 70.

166. *lobbyists in D.C. quadrupled:* Confessore, "Welcome to the Machine."

166. *formed Kissinger Associates:* John B. Judis, *The Paradox of American Democracy* (New York: Pantheon, 2000), 177.

166. *five of the seven richest counties:* Thomas Frank, "Rendezvous with Oblivion," *New York Times,* September 1, 2006.

167. *$25,000 to $50,000 per lobbyist:* Robert Pear, "Medicare Law Prompts a Rush for Lobbyists," *New York Times,* August 23, 2005.

167. *Andrew Young took a job:* Larry Copeland, "Wal-Mart's Hired Advocate Takes Flak," *USA Today,* March 15, 2006.

167. *"The lobbying industry":* Confessore, "Welcome to the Machine."

167. *after the election, it was $400,000:* Thomas Edsall, "The Purse Changes Hands," *New York Times,* December 2, 2006.

167. *"in public policy":* Ralph Reed, quoted in David Cay Johnston, *Perfectly Legal: The Covert Campaign to Rig Our Tax System to Benefit the Super Rich—and Cheat Everybody Else* (New York: Portfolio, 2003), 305.

168. *"reality-based community":* Ron Suskind, "Without a Doubt," *The New York Times Magazine,* October 17, 2004.

168. *"as close to Washington":* Michael Sokolove, "The Believer," *The New York Times Magazine,* May 22, 2005.

168. *bunk up with:* Katherine Marsh, "Chuck's Place," *New York Times,* March 3, 2002.

168. *purchased by Miller in the 1970s:* Todd Purdum, "For 4 Collegial Congressmen, Life Looks a Lot Like College," *New York Times,* May 30, 1994.

169. *peeling blue paint:* Marsh, "Chuck's Place."

169. *paid $4.7 million:* Betsy Schiffman, "Who's Living in Corzine's House," Forbes.com, http://www.forbes.com/2002/04/26/0426movers .html.

169. *son of a Brooklyn exterminator:* Chuck Schumer's official Senate bio, http://schumer.senate.gov.

169. *forty of the hundred senators:* Sean Loughlin and Robert Yoon, "Millionaires Populate U.S. Senate," CNN, June 13, 2003.

169. *purchased in 1983*: Marsh, "Chuck's Place."

169. *listing prices for his services*: Brian Ross, "From Cash to Yachts: Congressman's Bribe Menu," ABCNews.com, February 27, 2006, http://abcnews.go.com/Politics/story?id=1667009&page=1.

170. *$17,000-a-month apartment*: Brody Mullins, "Behind Unraveling of DeLay's Team, a Jilted Fiancee," *Wall Street Journal*, March 31, 2006.

170. *70 percent of students*: Harvard University, press release, "Like Most Americans, College Students Rate President Bush Near Historic Lows, Harvard Poll Finds," November 16, 2005.

9. Hazard Pay for the Soul

175. *"a graduate accepting a position"*: Yale Law School Career Development Office, Web site, http://www.law.yale.edu/outside/html/Career_Development/cdo-faq.htm.

175. *"The contempt of risk"*: Adam Smith, quoted in Robert Frank and Philip Cook, *The Winner-Take-All Society* (New York: Free Press, 1995), 104.

176. *As the rich have gotten richer*: Steven Greenhouse and David Leonhardt, "Real Wages Fail to Match a Rise in Productivity," *New York Times*, August 28, 2006.

177. *two-thirds of organizations*: "From Paper Chase to Money Chase: Law School Debt Diverts Road to Public Service" (Washington, D.C.: Equal Justice Works, NALP, and Partnership for Public Service), November 2002, 6.

177. *average debt load*: Ibid., 5.

178. *"you can't support yourself"*: Don Gross, "Verdict on Curtis Moot Court Team: Guilty of Success," *Staten Island Advance*, December 6, 1992.

182. *"servants of the power elite"*: Robert Granfield, *Making Elite Lawyers: Visions of Law at Harvard and Beyond* (New York: Routledge, 1992), 15.

182. *long been inclined to public service*: For a discussion of elite law students as idealistic New Dealers, see John B. Judis, *The Paradox of American Democracy: Elites, Special Interests, and the Betrayal of the Public Trust* (New York: Pantheon, 2000), 54–55.

182. *vastly outnumbered by liberals*: Granfield, *Making Elite Lawyers*, 85.

182. *only two students in a ninety-student lecture*: Paige Austin, "The Elephant in the Room: How Yale Breeds the Conservative Superstars of

Tomorrow," *The New Journal* (undergraduate publication), September 2005.

182. *70 percent of Harvard 1Ls:* Granfield, *Making Elite Lawyers,* 44.

182. *"How is it that so many students":* Richard Kahlenberg, *Broken Contract: A Memoir of Harvard Law School* (Amherst: University of Massachusetts Press, 1999), 5.

183. *two-thirds of Harvard's class:* Harvard Law School Office of Career Services, http://www.law.harvard.edu/ocs/prospective_students/Graduate_Employment_Statistics.htm.

183. *67 percent went to private law firms:* NYU School of Law, Office of Career Services, http://www.law.nyu.edu/depts/careerservices/stats/jobtype/.

183. *only 54 percent:* Ralph Nader, "Law Schools and Law Firms," *The New Republic,* October 11, 1969, 23.

183. *"a tendency among younger lawyers":* Memo quoted in ibid.

184. *free legal services to African-Americans:* Ralph Nader and Wesley J. Smith, *No Contest: Corporate Lawyers and the Perversion of Justice in America* (New York: Random House, 1996), 4.

184. *more than 100,000 Americans died:* Ibid., 9.

184. *"starting salaries":* Nader, "Law Schools and Law Firms," 22.

184. *firms were up to $16,000:* Granfield, *Making Elite Lawyers,* 6.

185. *wage stagnation:* Greenhouse and Leonhardt, "Real Wages Fail to Match a Rise in Productivity."

185. *more than quadrupled:* Emily Barker, "Keeping Score," *The American Lawyer,* May 2004, 53.

186. *trying to buy influence:* Common Cause, "Bush and Kerry Fundraisers: What Have They Gotten and What Do They Want?" http://www.commoncause.org/site/pp.asp?c=dkLNK1MQIwG&b=196565.

186. *"Remember, we can only afford":* Pat Byrnes, cartoon, *The New Yorker,* January 3, 2005.

186. *two-thirds of the top hundred:* Barker, "Keeping Score," 56.

187. *students who are eager:* Granfield, *Making Elite Lawyers,* 149.

187. *lose track of their own beliefs:* Ibid., 59.

188. *"It is your client":* Quoted in ibid., 59.

188. *defense of slavery:* Aristotle, *Politics, Books I and II,* trans. Trevor J. Saunders (Oxford, Eng.: Clarendon Press, 1995), 6–7.

188. *Unocal was sued:* Kathy George, "Oil-Gas Giant Faces Landmark Trial over Slavery in Myanmar," *Seattle Post-Intelligencer,* December 1, 2003.

188. *settled out of court:* Marc Lifsher, "Unocal Settles Human Rights Lawsuit," *Los Angeles Times,* March 22, 2005.

189. *"I worked on none"*: Rohit Khanna, quoted on *San Francisco Weekly* Web site, March 2004, http://www.sfweekly.com/special/response.html.

189. *forced labor camp*: Congressman Lantos's official bio, House of Representatives Web site, http://lantos.house.gov/HoR/CA12/About +Tom/A+Holocaust+Survivor/A+Holocaust+Survivor.htm.

191. *1,450 hours a year*: Nader and Smith, *No Contest*, 331.

191. *needs to spend about three hours*: Niki Kuckes, "The Hours," *Legal Affairs*, September/October 2002.

191. *"like a pie-eating contest"*: Ibid.

196. *Gingrich Congress cut*: Anthony Lewis, "The New Priorities," *New York Times*, August 7, 1995.

10. Releasing the Trap

198. *25 cents an hour*: U.S. Department of Labor, "History of Minimum Wage Rates," http://www.dol.gov/esa/minwage/chart.htm.

198. *first in 1936*: Kevin Phillips, *The Politics of Rich and Poor: Wealth and the American Electorate in the Reagan Aftermath* (New York: Random House, 1990), 107.

199. *his 1942 proposal*: Sam Pizzigati, *Greed and Good: Understanding and Overcoming the Inequality That Limits Our Lives* (New York: Apex, 2004), xxvi.

199. *greatly expanded middle class*: Phillips, *The Politics of Rich and Poor*, 10, 160.

199. *nation's median income*: Dennis Cauchon, "Increase in Workers Drives Household Median Income Higher," *USA Today*, August 29, 2006.

199. *first society to institute*: David Cay Johnston, "The Great Tax Shift," in *Inequality Matters: The Growing Economic Divide in America and Its Poisonous Consequences*, ed. James Lardner and David Smith (New York: New Press, 2005), 165.

199. *imposed flat tax*: Maureen Cavanaugh, "Democracy, Equality, and Taxes," *University of Alabama Law Review* (Winter 2003), 479.

200. *just and well-run state*: Aristotle, *Politics, Books III and IV*, trans. Richard Robertson (Oxford, Eng.: Clarendon Press, 1995), 95–99.

200. *"Where wealth is centralized"*: Confucius, quoted in Pizzigati, *Greed and Good*, 358.

200. *"means of silently lessening"*: Thomas Jefferson, quoted in Cass Sunstein, *The Second Bill of Rights: FDR's Unfinished Revolution and Why We Need It More Than Ever* (New York: Basic Books, 2004), 117.

200. *"aristocracy of our monied corporations"*: Thomas Jefferson, quoted in David Sirota, *Hostile Takeover: How Big Money and Corruption Conquered Our Government and How We Take It Back* (New York: Crown, 2006), vi.

200. *"Sixty years ago"*: Lord Bryce, quoted in Phillips, *The Politics of Rich and Poor,* 158.

201. *"The concentration of wealth"*: Ibid., 34.

201. *first policy paper:* John Micklethwait and Adrian Wooldridge, *The Right Nation: Conservative Power in America* (New York: Penguin, 2004), 103.

202. *cut checks to the DLC:* Robert Dreyfuss, "How the DLC Does It," *The American Prospect,* April 23, 2001.

202. *A 2006 Pew survey:* Michael Dimock, "Maximum Support for Raising the Minimum Wage," Pew Research Center, April 19, 2006. Available online at http://pewresearch.org/obdeck/?ObDeckID=18.

202. *"criminally stupid"*: Thomas Frank, *What's the Matter with Kansas?* (New York: Metropolitan Books, 2004), 243.

202. *"the fairness of taxing"*: Andrew Mellon, quoted in Steven Weisman, *The Great Tax Wars* (New York: Simon and Schuster, 2002), 351.

202. *top tax rate on investments to 15 percent:* David Cay Johnston, "Big Gain for Rich Seen in Tax Cut for Investments," *New York Times,* April 5, 2006.

202. *nearly $6,000:* Social Security Administration Fact Sheet, http://www.ssa.gov/pubs/10003.html.

203. *least heavily taxed society:* Paul Krugman, "The Spiral of Inequality," *Mother Jones,* November/December 1996.

203. *Only 1 percent of Americans:* Micklethwait and Wooldridge, *The Right Nation,* 303.

203. *essentially have a flat tax:* David Cay Johnston interview, on motherjones.com, http://www.motherjones.com/interview/2006/04/david_cay_johnston.html.

203. *as the four hundred highest-income families:* David Cay Johnston, "Richest Are Leaving Even the Rich Far Behind," *New York Times,* June 5, 2005.

204. *rising again:* "Minding About the Gap," *The Economist,* June 11, 2005, 32.

204. *two-thirds of students:* Mary Beth Pinto and Phylis M. Mansfield, "Financially At-Risk College Students: An Exploratory Investigation of Student Loan Debt and Prioritization of Debt Repayment," *The NASFAA Journal of Student Aid* 35:2 (2006), 22.

204. *debt loads have doubled:* State PIRGs Higher Education Project, "Paying Back, Not Giving Back: Student Debt's Negative Impact on Public Service Career Options," April 2006, 4.

204. *nearly half of children:* Anya Kamenetz, *Generation Debt: Why Now Is a Terrible Time to Be Young* (New York: Riverhead Books, 2006), 7.

204. *only 5 percent of young people:* "Poll: Inside the World of the Twixters," *Time,* January 16, 2005.

205. *"ambition tax":* Brendan Koerner, "The Ambition Tax," *Village Voice,* March 17–23, 2004.

205. *at least double:* Hagar Scher, "5 Things Every New Parent Must Do," *Redbook,* April 2005, 85; Hillary Chura, "Cracking the Books for Financial Aid to College," *New York Times,* January 27, 2007.

205. *peg their tuitions:* Ronald Ehrenberg, *Tuition Rising: Why College Costs So Much* (Cambridge, Mass.: Harvard University Press, 2000), 278.

205. *close the loophole:* Ibid., 269.

206. *only 8 percent of the 2005 budget:* Sam Dillon, "At Public Universities, Warnings of Privatization," *New York Times,* October 16, 2005.

206. *only 8 percent of students:* David Leonhardt, "The College Dropout Boom," in *Class Matters* (New York: Times Books, 2005), 93.

207. *five times as many undergraduates:* Joseph Soares, *The Decline of Privilege: The Modernization of Oxford University* (Palo Alto, Calif.: Stanford University Press, 1999), 7–8.

207. *$10,000 annual grant per student:* "Free Oxford University," *The Economist,* May 21, 2005.

207. *among the top five universities:* The Times Higher Education Supplement, http://www.thes.co.uk/statistics/international_comparisons/2005/top_unis.aspx?window_type=popup. Cambridge was ranked third, Oxford fourth.

208. *private dollars make up a larger proportion:* Anna Bernasek, "What's the Return on Education" (contains the graph "Who's Paying More for College") *New York Times,* December 11, 2005.

208. *"In an ethical society":* Jonathan Kozol, *Savage Inequalities* (New York: Crown, 1991), 123.

209. *conducted from 1988 to 1990:* Ibid., ix.

209. *admissions more competitive:* Susan Saulny, "In Middle Class, Signs of Anxiety on School Efforts," *New York Times,* December 27, 2005.

209. *professional parents:* Kozol, *Savage Inequalities,* 178.

210. *"You're not imagining it"*: CNN.com, "Study: U.S. Employees Put In Most Hours," August 31, 2001, http://archives.cnn.com/2001/CAREER/trends/08/30/ilo.study/.

210. *we work 20 percent more*: Clara Jeffery, "The Road to Nowhere," *Mother Jones,* July/August 2005, 27.

210. *average a hundred fewer hours*: Porter Anderson, "Study: U.S. Employees Put In Most Hours," *CNN Career,* August 31, 2001.

210. *six weeks in Brazil*: Jeffery, "The Road to Nowhere," 27.

211. *working as many hours now*: Jill Andresky Frasier, *White-Collar Sweatshop: The Deterioration of Work and Its Rewards in Corporate America* (New York: W. W. Norton, 2001), 20.

212. *Reagan became a conservative*: Phillips, *The Politics of Rich and Poor,* 78.

213. *37 percent regularly work*: Ed Frauenheim, "Labor Group: Techies Less Optimistic," *New York Times,* September 1, 2005.

213. *average American two-income couple*: PBS *Affluenza* Web site, http://www.pbs.org/kcts/affluenza/diag/what.html.

214. *three times more likely*: Jane Brody, "Health Watch: Women Under Stress," *New York Times,* June 11, 1997.

214. *IRS couldn't understand*: David Cay Johnston, interview on motherjones.com, http://www.motherjones.com/interview/2006/04/david_cay_johnston.html.

214. *gunning for lucrative job offers*: David Cay Johnston, *Perfectly Legal: The Covert Campaign to Rig Our Tax System to Benefit the Super Rich—and Cheat Everybody Else* (New York: Portfolios, 2003), 215.

215. *they ought to be*: Terry Culler, "Most Federal Workers Need Only Be Competent," *Wall Street Journal,* May 21, 1986.

215. *majority of today's top college graduates*: Miranda Green, "Accountancy Moves Higher Up in Students' Jobs Wishlist," *Financial Times,* October 12, 2005.

216. *life expectancy has fallen*: David Williams and James Lardner, "Cold Truths about Class, Race, and Health," in *Inequality Matters,* ed. Lardner and Smith (New York: New Press, 2005), 103.

216. *richest third of Americans*: Paul Krugman, "Our Sick Society," *New York Times,* May 5, 2006.

216. *outrageous overhead*: Arnold Relman, "The Health of Nations," *The New Republic,* March 7, 2005, 23–30.

217. *backs a single-payer system*: American Medical Student Association, http://www.amsa.org/about/priorities.cfm.

217. *American Medical Association does not:* Associated Press, "Universal Health Care Push Being Revived," July 10, 2005.

217. *"The doctors interviewed":* David Snyder, "In U.S. Hospitals, Emergency Care in Critical Condition," May 1, 2006, http://www .foxnews.com/story/0,2933,193883,00.html.

218. *number-one risk factor:* Tamara Draut, *Strapped: Why American 20- and 30-Somethings Can't Get Ahead* (New York: Doubleday, 2006), 151.

218. *$2,750:* USDA, Center for Nutrition Policy and Promotion, "Expenditures on Children," 2004, http://www.usda.gov/cnpp/Crc/crc2004 .pdf.

218. *"Bank of Mom and Dad":* Anna Bahney, "The Bank of Mom and Dad," *New York Times,* April 20, 2006.

219. *one-third of American women:* Stephanie Mencimer, "The Baby Boycott," *Washington Monthly,* June 2001, 14–15.

219. *taking time off:* Lisa Belkin, "The Opt-Out Revolution," *The New York Times Magazine,* October 26, 2003.

219. *only 63 percent of college graduates:* Editorial, "Happy Labor Day?" *Philadelphia Inquirer,* September 4, 2006.

220. *People under thirty-five:* David Moberg, "Most Young Workers Have Missed Out on the Boom," *Boston Globe,* October 16, 1999; Draut, *Strapped,* 21.

220. *Mississippi was a blue state:* Music for America election map. http//www.musicforamerica.org/youthturnout.

222. *"To some generations":* Franklin Roosevelt, 1936 Democratic National Convention Nomination Acceptance Speech, online at http://millercenter.virginia.edu/scripps/diglibrary/prezspeeches/roosevelt/ fdr_1936_0627.html.

Conclusion

223. *"the seduction of money":* Po Bronson, *What Should I Do with My Life?* (New York: Random House, 2002), xiv.

223. *"screwing society":* Ibid., 107.

224. *"For all those":* Ibid., 112.

225. *"constantly talking of abolishing slavery":* Marquis de Chastellux, quoted in John Chester Miller, *The Wolf by the Ears: Thomas Jefferson and Slavery* (New York: Free Press, 1977), 30.

225. *a "blot" and "stain":* Thomas Jefferson, quoted in ibid., xi.

225. *dozen pieces of legislation:* Ken Burns, *Thomas Jefferson: A film by Ken Burns* (Walpole, N.H.: Florentine Films, 1997), disc 1.

225. *tried to block slavery's expansion:* Ibid., disc 2.

225. *owned over two hundred human beings:* Ibid., disc 1.

226. *giving them away as wedding presents:* Annette Gordon-Reed, *Thomas Jefferson and Sally Hemings: An American Controversy* (Charlottesville, Va.: University Press of Virginia, 1997), 108.

226. *Dying in debt:* Burns, *Thomas Jefferson,* disc 2.

226. *only slaves Jefferson freed:* Gordon-Reed, *Thomas Jefferson and Sally Hemings,* 2.

226. *neologism coined in 1965:* *Webster's 9th New Collegiate Dictionary* (Springfield, Mass.: Merriam-Webster, 1986).

226. *"If men were angels":* James Madison (attributed), in *The Federalist Papers,* ed. Clinton Rossiter (New York: Mentor, 1999), 290.

227. *"lazy dole-happy people":* Barry Goldwater, quoted in John Micklethwait and Adrian Wooldridge, *The Right Nation: Conservative Power in America* (New York: Penguin, 2004), 56.

227. *"democratic style":* Werner Sombart, quoted in *Failure of a Dream?: Essays in the History of American Socialism,* ed. John H. M. Lasett and Seymour Martin Lipset (Garden City, N.Y.: Anchor, 1994), 600–601.

227. *"I am an American":* Saul Bellow, *The Adventures of Augie March* (New York: Penguin, 1949), 3.

ACKNOWLEDGMENTS

Doing anything for the first time is daunting; writing a first book is an especially overwhelming task. I could not have done it without the help of my family, friends, mentors, and professional colleagues.

This project began in 2003 when I typed out some notes and bounced my ideas off two dear friends, both budding American historians—Daniel Amsterdam of the University of Pennsylvania and Michael Jo of Yale. With their encouragement, I pursued the possibility of writing a series of articles guided by mentors Lincoln Caplan, Ken Emerson, and Corey Robin. Sherle Schwenninger of the New America Foundation gave me the advice and confidence to pursue a book-length project.

Agent Larry Weissman's enthusiasm for the project was genuine and infectious. He and his wife and partner, Sascha, provided guidance as I refined my thinking and proposal. Most important, Larry reminded me that at its best, social criticism makes you laugh till you cry and wins over both the head and the heart.

Larry had the foresight to get my proposal in front of Vanessa Mobley at Henry Holt. Her simple title of "editor" does not do justice to her contribution. "Partner in crime" is more like it. In theory, writers write for a mass audience of anonymous readers; in truth, they write for their editors. "What would Vanessa think?" (WWVT?) was a near-constant refrain as I drafted the manuscript. Generous with her time, Vanessa gave me confidence in my authorial voice and expanded the book's scope and ambition. Robin Dennis picked up the project at a key moment. Her old-fashioned sense of headline and eagle eyes polished the manuscript. Thanks are also due to everyone at Holt who worked on the book, in particular editorial assistants Patrick Clark and Sadie Stein. (Even superheroes need sidekicks.)

I am blessed to have wonderful friends whose thoughtful comments helped me as I wrote. They include but are not limited to JPD, IB, PJ, PN, ABA, CE, MK, HB, SE, PMJ, MR, MM, NS, ND, FN, MW, KAF, AH, MS, JK, JI, SS, SA, SD, DJB, and GH.

Three particularly bright friends, editor John Swansburg, attorney David Tannenbaum, and Daniel Amsterdam were generous enough to read my manuscript and provide feedback. Their suggestions have made this a better book.

The Free Library of Philadelphia and its staff proved that one can still research a book with no loftier institutional affiliation than "citizen of the Commonwealth." Despite scandalous underfunding, the Free Library remains an institution worthy of the city that invented the public library.

Nam, Ryan, and the rest of the staff at my "corner office,"

The Last Drop, graciously gave me coffee, a quiet place to write, and the silly nickname "Danimal."

Family friend, attorney Don Florman, generously agreed to read over my literary contract and explain it to me. His pro bono work is greatly appreciated.

One cannot write about the world without seeing it. This project could not have been conceived without an extended trip to Europe or come to fruition without an extended stay in California. The support of the Forsberg Fellowship, named in honor of Ronald Reagan's ambassador to Sweden, allowed me to spend two months in Europe, based in Stockholm. For my two months in San Francisco, I was the beneficiary of the warm hospitality of Jackie and Ray, Claire and Bear.

The imprint of my family is so clearly on this book they need merely read it to understand. Josh, Jon, Amy, Jama, Micah, and Abel provided a mix of inspiration and advice. I am most grateful to my parents, Helman and Judy, whose devotion to family and public service constitutes a truly invaluable inheritance.

DANIEL BROOK is a journalist whose work has appeared in *Harper's*, the *Boston Globe*, the *San Francisco Chronicle*, and *Dissent*, among other publications. He was born in Brooklyn, raised on Long Island, and educated at Yale, where he won the 2000 Rolling Stone College Journalism Competition. He lives in Philadelphia. This is his first book.